Michael Blakemore arrived in the UK from Au[...] fifteen years in the theatre were spent as an actor. During this period he wrote his novel about an actor's life, *Next Season*. He began directing at the Glasgow Citizens Theatre and his first London success, *A Day in the Death of Joe Egg*, transferred from there. Laurence Olivier then asked him to become an Associate Director of the National Theatre, where he directed Olivier in *Long Day's Journey into Night*. Among his many other National Theatre productions are *The National Health*, *The Front Page*, *Macbeth* and *The Cherry Orchard*. His work has embraced new plays by dramatists as diverse as Arthur Miller, David Hare, Peter Shaffer, Don DeLillo, Woody Allen and David Mamet. He directed four of Peter Nichols's early successes, and many premieres of plays by Michael Frayn, including *Noises Off* and *Copenhagen*. Recent productions are *Democracy* at the National, *Three Sisters* in the West End and, on Broadway, *Blithe Spirit*. Extensive work on Broadway includes two original musicals, *City of Angels* and *The Life*. At the 2000 Tony Awards he won an unprecedented double as Best Director of both a play, *Copenhagen*, and a musical, *Kiss Me, Kate*. He has written and directed two films, *A Personal History of the Australian Surf* (Standard Film Award, 1982) and *Country Life*. His memoir *Arguments with England* is published by Faber.

Praise for *Stage Blood*

'This is a most unusual book. It is a theatrical memoir that is remorselessly honest: this in itself is enough to mark it out from pretty well every other such memoir in existence . . . The man in the dock is Peter Hall, whom Blakemore has had in his sights for a very long time: his 1969 novel *Next Season* features a barely veiled portrait of the young Hall as an empire-building director at Stratford-upon-Avon in the late 1950s; and his superb memoir *Arguments with England* (2005) covers – among many other things – the same ground in non-fictional form. *Stage Blood* tells the story of Hall's assumption of the directorship of the National Theatre prior to its move from the Old Vic to the South Bank. The man he succeeded, Laurence Olivier, is the book's hero, just as surely as Hall is its villain . . . As his previous books attest, Blakemore is a needle-sharp observer of the life of the theatre, both on and off stage, and his account of Olivier, as actor, company leader and potentate, during the extraordinary sunset of his career at the National, is masterly and moving, encompassing all that was magnificent about the man and a great deal of what was maddening about him, too . . . The book, contains, too, an excellent account of what a director – or, at any

rate, a director like Blakemore, of whom there are few – actually does. But right at the heart of it is the terrible but compelling spectacle of the enactment of righteous revenge. A most unusual book indeed; one whose scope goes far beyond the theatre, though it is a landmark in writing about the life of the stage.'
Simon Callow, *Guardian*

'What makes Blakemore's book valuable is the historical hindsight it brings to its recollections of that remote feud. Forty years on, the personal tiffs and whispered denunciations hardly matter; Blakemore is now able to see that the interregnum between Olivier and Hall marked a turning point for the nation as well as the National. His reading of events is almost an historical allegory. Olivier, who boosted morale by performing *Henry V* at the Old Vic during the blitz, is a Churchillian figure. Sacrificing his health and accepting a niggardly salary, he dwindled into an administrator because he believed he was performing a public service by founding a theatre that would be – and at its best still is – the envy of the world. Hall, a shrewd fixer and busy multi-tasker who absented himself from the National to direct operas or make television programmes, seems to worry most about maximising profits from his productions when they transferred to the West End or to Broadway. He belongs, in Blakemore's estimation, to the nastily rapacious Britain that Margaret Thatcher soon ushered in . . . A book that I feared (and half hoped) would be merely vituperative turns out to be warm, wise, and even sternly moralistic as it looks back, more in sorrow than anger, at a defunct England. For me, best of all, it vividly recalls the great performances I saw, by Olivier and others, in productions by Blakemore and his colleagues during the 1970s. Theatre is evanescent, yet it can provide us with experiences so intense that we gratefully retain them for the rest of our lives. Memory compulsively preserves ancient grudges; more importantly, as Blakemore demonstrates, it is the impregnable archive of our affections.'
Peter Conrad, *Observer*

'A wonderful and detailed account.'
Craig Raine, *New Statesman* Books of the Year

'In this sequel to *Arguments with England,* his superb first volume of memoirs, Michael Blakemore presents us with an enthralling account of his five embattled years as an associate director of the National Theatre.'
Selina Hastings, *Spectator*

by the same author
ARGUMENTS WITH ENGLAND
NEXT SEASON

STAGE BLOOD

Five Tempestuous Years
in the Early Life of the National Theatre

—————————

MICHAEL BLAKEMORE

FABER & FABER

First published in 2013
by Faber and Faber Limited
Bloomsbury House
74–77 Great Russell Street
London WC1B 3DA

This paperback edition published 2014

Typeset by Country Setting, Kingsdown, Kent CT14 8ES
Printed in the UK by CPI Group (UK) Ltd, Croydon CR0 4YY

A CIP record for this book
is available from the British Library

ISBN 978 0 571 24138 5

2–4–6–8–10–9–7–5–3–1

To the actors

AUTHOR'S NOTE

The idea for this book occurred to me not long after I had resigned from the National Theatre as an associate director in 1976. However, it was not until the publication of the Peter Hall *Diaries* in 1983, in which that resignation was, to my mind, misrepresented, that attempting it became a requirement.

I started making notes and had completed a few chapters when my agent, Mark Lucas, suggested we submit an outline of the book (then called *The National Interest*) to Clare Alexander, Managing Editor at Penguin Books. For the welcome she gave to the proposal, and indeed for Mark's initial belief in it, I remain grateful. Alas, progress on the book was extremely fitful. My career as a theatre director was at its busiest, and at such times as I was able to return to my manscript it kept mutating into a different sort of book altogether. It was as if before I could confront my time at the National (its highs and its dramatic lows), I had first to examine the twenty-odd years I'd spent in England leading up to it. In 1999, despairing of ever delivering the manuscript I'd promised, and with Clare having moved sideways to become a distinguished literary agent, I asked Mark if we could return the advance and void the contract. Penguin agreed to this with grace.

However, intermittently, I kept returning to my pages and little by little one chapter was added to another. Five years later the book became what apparently it had always wanted to be – a memoir about a young Australian arriving in London in 1950 and his early struggles to make a life for himself in the theatre. Called *Arguments with England* it was picked up by Dinah Wood, recently arrived at Faber and Faber, and it was to become the first book she edited for them. I was now free to come to grips with the biggest argument I had so far had with my adopted country, the one that took place within the walls of the new National Theatre.

I discussed it with Dinah, who was not only enthusiastic, but managed to convey her enthusiasm to her colleagues. Once again I was given an advance. Once again years passed with nothing much to show for it. But Dinah stood over me, sometimes frowning, mostly smiling, and now, some forty years after the events which it describes, the book is published. The fact that it has come out a month before the fiftieth anniversary of the National Theatre is wholly fortuitous, but if it can make a small contribution to discussions about the future of this great institution, relatively new to British life and at present being led with particular flair and resourcefulness by Nick Hytner, then it will have served some purpose.

There are other people I would like to thank: Gavin Clarke, the National Theatre Archivist, who guided me to relevant photographs and documents; Daniel Rosenthal, whose own elegant and comprehensive book *The National Theatre Story* is being published only weeks after mine, and so was ideally placed to straighten me out on some of my facts; Janet Macklam, who has typed and typed her way cheerfully through various drafts; Rhonda Barkow for her constant encouragement; and as always my children for their love and support. Finally, my particular thanks to everyone at Faber and Faber. If I single out Dinah – obviously – and her colleague Steve King, and my patient, judicious line editor, Simon Trussler, it's because they are the people with whom I have spent most time.

ONE

The pealing of a telephone waiting to be answered was the signature tune of the last century. Tidings of good fortune or ill, all came winging along the cable. I wasn't at home when Laurence Olivier rang, but my wife, Shirley, gave him a number where I could be reached.

'Hello, boysie! Where are you? What's going on?' The voice at the other end could be no other; likewise the curiosity. He came quickly to the point. Would I, he wanted to know, be interested in joining the National Theatre as an associate director? He was planning to bring in a pair of associates, and had thought of Ronald Eyre and myself. Perhaps it would be a good idea to ring dear Ronnie and arrange a meeting with him, just the two of us, to see if we were of a like mind? He gave me Ronnie's number and the conversation was over. It was just after ten thirty on an October night in 1970. At once I had a picture of him at home in Brighton fifteen minutes before, fretting about his candidates, wondering whether either of us was really right, then impulsively picking up the receiver and dialling. Then persisting on the telephone until he'd tracked me down.

The circumstances of his call had taken me by surprise, but not the call itself. It was one that I had been half expecting. Two years before he had invited me to the National on a freelance basis to direct Peter Nichols' *The National Health*, which had been a considerable success and was still in the repertoire. There are times, particularly in a career just taking off, when everything one attempts seems to succeed. As I have since seen it happen to others, this had now happened to me. However, it can never be an unalloyed pleasure because of the certainty that it cannot possibly last.

This is as true of institutions as it is of individuals, and few important theatre companies can escape from the cyclical nature of reputation. In the first three or four years after its launch in 1963 the brand new National Theatre, playing at its temporary home, the Old Vic, enjoyed a blaze of success with a string of hits ranging from *Uncle Vanya* to *The Recruiting Officer*, from *Hay Fever* to *The Royal Hunt of the Sun*. Encouraged by his new wife, Joan Plowright, Olivier pursued a policy of providing house room for a rising generation of talent whose members, had they been left outside, would have been the first to throw stones at the new institution. The two young directors whom he invited to help launch the theatre, John Dexter and Bill Gaskill, came from the Royal Court, and they brought with them some of the actors and designers they had fostered there. Though he engaged established stars such as Michael Redgrave and Edith Evans, the focus of Olivier's National was on the company work of his younger actors, and a remarkable number of them rapidly became stars themselves.

Olivier also employed as Literary Manager Kenneth Tynan, the most gifted critic of the day, but also the one with the sharpest opinions about the purposes of a National Theatre. All this meant largely abandoning the talent of his own generation in whose company Olivier had first staked his claim to be a great actor and among whom he probably felt most comfortable, so it was a courageous as well as a perceptive course to follow. But there was a cost. Old friends felt neglected, and Olivier, encircled now by young colleagues whose artistic and political assumptions he did not always understand or share, became increasingly wary and watchful.

Now the wheel had turned for the National Theatre and its luck seemed to be running out. Dexter and Gaskill had left and gone on to other things, and the associate director who replaced them, Frank Dunlop, was also eager to get away and run his own theatre (the Young Vic, under construction down the road). Even the man with whom he had worked most closely, if contentiously, Ken Tynan, had become a less effective ally. He'd had his wings clipped by the Theatre Board, who had been affronted by his promotion of two outside shows; one, Rolf Hochhuth's *Soldiers*, which dealt with the carpet bombing of German cities during the war, was considered by the Chairman, Lord Chandos, to be a slur on the memory of his friend Winston Churchill; the other *Oh! Calcutta!*, was an explicit sexual revue with abundant nudity and four-letter words. Ken had been demoted and obliged to share his responsibilities with a new member of staff, Derek Granger.

Against this background of uncertainty the greatest challenge the National had yet faced loomed in the immediate future – the opening of its huge new building on the South Bank. Despite delays and cost overruns, both unforeseen, its cast-concrete bulk was now imposing itself little by little beside the Thames. Would it vindicate the hopes of all those people who over so many years had pledged to bring a National Theatre into being, or would it become a great grey elephant tethered to the river, consuming money and talent on a scale impossible to sustain? It is hard to believe now, but at the time these were decidedly open questions. The new building would require an administrative staff at least three times as large as that needed to run the Old Vic, besides an army of technicians, maintenance staff and cleaners. It would need to produce two or three times as many shows in any one year as it had attempted so far, employing double the number of actors, and it would be dependent for its existence on a principle relatively new and as yet far from enshrined in British life – generous public subsidy for the arts.

This in turn would depend on something else new to British theatre – an extensive network of supporters in high places, whose efforts and commitment would be crucial to the launch of such an extravagant (and un-utilitarian) project. With their easy

3

access to business and the world of money, to government and the law, these were the sort of people theatre boards like to attract, and the few I had encountered during my two years at the Glasgow Citizens Theatre often surprised and rather exhilarated me with their conviviality and directness. Such figures often have an informed love of the thing they are supporting, and they expect little more in return for the hours they put in than the chance to add a cultural flourish to the sum total of their other achievements. If an honour comes along, a knighthood or a peer-age, so much the better. Well-run theatres have mostly benefited from the oversight of such public-spirited people, but the National would require an entire stratum of such supporters, picking up the telephone to each other every day, discussing funding and appoint-ments and lubricating the political process at Westminster. At dinner parties in the evening you can be sure that they would be arguing points of artistic merit because, where the arts are concerned, everyone is an expert, and such people feel that hav-ing confident opinions in these matters goes with the territory, which perhaps wouldn't be the case if the subject was molecular biology or engineering.

Beneath this confidence, however, there is always a certain nervousness, even fear – that of being associated with something either disreputable or with the whiff of failure about it. This is apparent in the private alliances, shared prejudices and waves of misgiving that criss-cross each other along the telephone lines every day. Little of this reaches the people who are actually run-ning the theatres or engaged in putting something on stage. They learn about it only when they run smack up against a glass door they hadn't realised was there. This heightened political dimen-sion attendant on the launching of something as costly as the National had not really been anticipated by theatre people, nor were they equipped to deal with it. It would take an artistic director who was himself a sharply political animal to turn the new climate to his own advantage.

Olivier was not such a man. When he had made his Shakespearean films and run his previous theatres it had been pretty much as an artistic autocrat, a role most people were happy to concede him because of the size of his talent and his charismatic leadership. However, the National Theatre was far too large an operation, even at the Old Vic, to be run the way actor-managers from Henry Irving onward had run their companies. For a start so many productions had to be mounted that it was impossible for any one person to leave an artistic mark on all but a handful. The contradiction in Olivier's case was that the shows in which he performed tended to be the box-office staples of any given season. This combination of personal responsibility on the one hand, and on the other a huge load of administration with none of the stimulus of direct artistic involvement, had taken its toll, and now there was another grey elephant in the auditorium – Laurence Olivier's health. He'd had two major illnesses: prostate cancer, followed a couple of years later (possibly as a result of the treatment he'd received for the first condition) by thrombosis in one of his legs. His well-being was a source of much speculation, within the building and without. From this, of course, he was excluded, but he was far too alert and driven not to guess the drift of the gossip or to know which group of important people was most exercised by it.

This, towards the end of 1970, was the National Theatre that Ronald Eyre and I were being invited to join. As requested, I rang Ronnie and we arranged to meet one lunchtime at an Indian restaurant in North Audley Street. He was a thoughtful, decent man, who had recently made a TV series for the BBC on comparative religion, and as we forked our way through the piles of spicy food, each cautiously assessing the other as a potential colleague, we both agreed that we were being offered a chalice which, if not poisoned, smelt distinctly brackish. A few days later I had a second call from Sir Laurence telling me that Ronnie had withdrawn and suggesting that I visit him at the Aquinas Street offices the following afternoon to discuss other candidates. This was a moment to consider carefully. One foot was through the door. Should the other follow?

Two and a half years earlier I had come down to London from the Glasgow Citizens Theatre with a startling new play, *A Day in the Death of Joe Egg*, and the morning after the first night its author Peter Nichols and I woke to find that, as the saying goes, we had arrived. Within a year *Joe Egg* was running on Broadway and I was soon back in London with another Glasgow production, *The Resistible Rise of Arturo Ui*, with a virtuoso performance by Leonard Rossiter in the Hitler role. Later that year I was invited to stage Peter's next play at the National, *The National Health*. And on top of all this in 1969 a novel, *Next Season*, on which I had been working on and off for about six years, was published to a gratifying reception. Was joining a large and apparently faltering institution the wisest next step?

More than any other I revered Olivier as the man whose work had drawn me to the theatre in the first place; I had watched him, thunderstruck, at the Sydney Tivoli, during the Old Vic tour of Australia just after the war. This was true of many young actors of my generation, and the talk in theatre dressing rooms during the fifties tended to circle obsessively around his great roles – Richard III, Oedipus Rex, Titus Andronicus, Archie Rice. There may have been others in the British theatre as gifted – there indeed were – but none who could get anywhere near him as a sheer performer, a kind of player-magician who dealt in the least expected, the astonishing, in moments that could unite an auditorium packed from stalls to gallery in a single suspended breath.

However, the great actor was only one of numerous Oliviers. There was also the lesser actor capable of giving overwrought indifferent performances in plays such as *Semi-Detached* and *Rhinoceros*, when the tectonic plates failed to shift or the earth to move and, watching, you began to wonder if they ever had. There was the effusive theatrical Larry, larding his conversation and his correspondence with flowery endearments, and there was the polar opposite of this creature, the man in the room doing the watching, alert to pretence and folly, missing nothing, and who in a treacherous profession had an aching need for real friendship, as well as the steel to forego it if it was a check on his ambition. It was the multiplicity of these and other personalities that made him sometimes difficult to deal with because, from one day to another, you were never quite sure which one of them you were addressing. You juggled with affection and impatience, admiration and rage.

The Aquinas Street offices to which I had been bidden after my abortive meeting with Ronald Eyre were the temporary administrative headquarters of the National Theatre while it waited on the completion of its many corridors of office space on the South Bank. Built on a neglected bomb site, this makeshift base consisted of a series of wartime Nissen huts arranged in a line like dominoes which branched out at both ends into larger spaces, providing at one extremity a rehearsal room and a canteen, at the other a boardroom. Connecting them was a long corridor, vaguely nautical in feel, off which, from side to side, were a number of tiny cabins large enough to accommodate a small desk, a filing cabinet and a few shelves. The Artistic Director was allowed the luxury of two of these spaces knocked into one. He had a more imposing desk and it faced a padded bench running round the walls on which six or seven people could perch during meetings. His office was next door to the entrance into the building, and so gave him a view of people coming and going across the slatted wooden ramp.

I had always found this improvised Lego-like structure a congenial environment. It was the kind of place in which something audacious might have been afoot in time of war, code-breaking perhaps, and its austerity underlined that the proper place for show and display was not here but on the stage of the Old Vic a few streets away. Aquinas Street was shipshape – and it needed to be, because the National was on a voyage into uncharted waters.

As I approached the car park I noticed first Olivier's famous London taxi, one of the few privately owned and painted his favourite colour, purple. In this vehicle, as recognisable to his public as a state coach, he would be driven back and forth to Victoria Station where, aboard the Brighton Belle, he would arrive in the morning and depart at night. Just beyond the taxi and observing me through his office window was the man himself in the company of Joan Plowright. They greeted me affably and came straight to the point. To replace Ronald Eyre they had two suggestions to make, and they would leave me to decide which of the two men I would feel most comfortable working with. One of them was a surprise: John Dexter, who had already had a long and successful association with the National, but who had departed angrily after he and Olivier clashed over Dexter's production of his all-male *As You Like It*. Now it seemed the quarrel had been patched over, and John had expressed a willingness to come back.

The other candidate was someone who had recently become a friend, and with whom I would have been delighted to work: Jonathan Miller. We had become directors at about the same time, and, both up-and-coming, had sought each other out. We met one lunchtime in the restaurant of the Mermaid Theatre, and immediately got on. I had expected him to be funny and from his television appearances was already impressed by his amazing cross-referential mind, which sucked up scraps of knowledge like an anteater and never seemed to forget them. In conversation he could discuss a subject juggling with two or three different disciplines at the same time. What I hadn't anticipated, however, was his gift of intimacy, chatting with unguarded candour about the ups and downs of both his professional and personal life. There are rules to friendship, and he seemed to take it for granted that I was the sort of person who would abide by them, which I found attractive and flattering.

However, with regard to the National the problem for both of us was our inexperience. We'd established that we could direct plays, but as far as helping to run a huge organisation we were relatively untried. Which John Dexter was not. He had been central to the National's early success, and for years had been exercised with the challenge of the move to the new building. I didn't know Dexter personally, but I'd much admired his productions, which ranged from the spectacular *Royal Hunt of the Sun* to the spare, graceful naturalism of the work he had done with the designer Jocelyn Herbert on Arnold Wesker's plays – in particular *Chips with Everything*, which seemed to me a fine play, flawlessly done. In the rehearsal room he had the reputation of being a martinet, sometimes even a bully, and his embrace of the severe Royal Court aesthetic, which consigned the work of most other theatres to outer darkness, smacked a little too much of a party line for my taste; but he was clearly equipped to play a role in the future of the National Theatre. I didn't give it any thought at the time, but John must also have been positioning himself for the succession in the event of Olivier's retirement. To this there was one formidable obstacle – his conviction some years before on a homosexual charge, for which, like Oscar Wilde, he had served time in prison. The law had now been altered and public attitudes were changing fast, but the stigma of a jail sentence still lingered in the minds of the sort of people with whom such an appointment would rest.

Almost against my better judgement, and struggling to put the National's interests ahead of my own, I told the Oliviers that John Dexter was perhaps the person I should meet first. They seemed pleased, particularly Joan Plowright, who at the Royal Court had done some of her best work with John and was a close friend, and they suggested another lunch. Joan Plowright now left the room so that Olivier and I could go on to discuss more general matters. There was one thing I knew I had to bring up if I was to accept this job. Throughout the organisation the Artistic Director was

9

almost always addressed as 'Sir Laurence', which is how I had addressed him as a young actor in the *Titus Andronicus* company, and continued to do as a freelance director on *The National Health*. There were certain people who were exceptions to this general rule. A comparable star or an old colleague would call him 'Larry', or a younger man like Dexter who had directed him in *Othello*. I didn't in the least begrudge him this deference – he was after all unique – but I knew that if I was to be of any use to the organisation I had to put myself among the exceptions. Already we'd had differences over *The National Health* and I suspected that there would be quite a few more. Without the equality of first names I could consider the argument, if such there was to be, already half lost. Somewhat clumsily, and perhaps at too great a length, I explained why I thought it sensible if I called him 'Larry'.

He listened, his expression amiable but totally mask-like. After I'd finished there was a beat before he purred, 'But I was hoping that you would.' Whether he meant it or not I hadn't the least idea. Fifteen years before, as 'Sir Laurence', he had offered a young actor his encouragement. However, it is one thing to show interest in a promising newcomer; quite another to have that person reappear some years later as a potential equal. I don't believe Olivier felt any resentment towards me; rather, it was simple incredulity that this young man from the past had now flown up from nowhere and landed beside him on the same branch.

As with many subsequent decisions, it was John Dexter who elected where we would lunch together – Burke's, a small modish club in Mayfair, opposite the fashionable tailor Dougy Hayward, that had mushroomed up in accord with the times and has since disappeared. John was a short, stocky, driven man with a darting mind, the workings of which he attempted to conceal behind a half smile and a neat, barbered moustache and beard. He was passionate about the theatre and ferocious in his loyalty to those such as the designer Jocelyn Herbert of whose work he approved. But, like the scorpion in the fable who begs the frog to give him a lift to the far bank of the river only to sting him half way across, John arrived too often at the position where he could only mutter to some aggrieved frog as they both went under, 'Sorry, but it's my nature.' Curiously, it was this lack of ease with himself, his inner conflict, that made him at times quite sympathetic. He was a man who frequently sweated. Over lunch he didn't seem inclined to spend time discussing an artistic credo, which was not what I expected given his Royal Court background; he knew my work and I knew his, and apparently that was enough. Instead he moved directly to the terms of our employment.

'What do you think we should be paid?' he asked. At Glasgow I'd received forty-five pounds a week, so off the top of my head suggested a figure of seventy-five. 'A hundred,' said John, and the more I thought about it the better it sounded. John had done many more shows in London and on Broadway than I had, and was on speaking terms with all the famous names on both sides of the Atlantic. I rather looked forward to being tutored in his worldliness. We concluded the meal agreeing that we must act as a team, that we must always be totally candid with each other and that trust between us was an absolute essential. These things are easier to say than to do. Then I rang my agent, Terry Owen, and asked him to take it from there.

So began my five years at the National Theatre. For people whose job it is to put work on stage – actors, designers, directors – the theatre promises a creative life without loneliness and it often delivers, but the price is accomplishments which, though preceded by a banging drum and not without their importance, are as ephemeral as the seasons. And such work, put in front of the public with a sort of blind faith, has to be achieved in the face of the thing which represents its opposite – the guile which comes into play when, in any group, there is an internal struggle for dominance. Because of the number of people involved and the scope of its ambitions, the National Theatre company would prove fertile ground for these strategies, alliances, secrets and betrayals, and my time there, though it would provide enormous rewards, ended by becoming the most distressing of my career.

*

The engagement did not get off to a good start, and nearly ended before it had begun. The first hurdle was my contract. Terry Owen told me the National was offering a non-negotiable £75 a week. Remembering my conversation with John, I asked Terry to persist. He came back saying they wouldn't budge. I couldn't believe that Dexter would accept such a figure, so I asked Terry if he could find out more. The next day he informed me with some embarrassment that John was being paid £125 a week. I was stunned, and not solely about the size of the differential; it would mean starting my new job not as the equal of a colleague I had chosen but as his junior partner, and my salary would make this evident throughout the organisation. It was not the engagement I had been offered. I asked Terry to fight and there was a stand-off of about a week. Then Olivier's secretary rang to tell me that Sir Laurence would like me to come and see him.

We met at four o'clock the following afternoon. He greeted me with ominous ease and I realised at once that the National's intractable position emanated from his office. What was the justification, I asked him, for paying such differing salaries? He cited the fact as if it was self-evident that John was much more experienced, had directed a film, and had had a production on Broadway. But then I'd had a production on Broadway, *Joe Egg*, and had received a Tony nomination to boot. Moreover I was two things John certainly wasn't, a published novelist and someone with fifteen years of honourable service in Olivier's own profession. Did this count for nothing? In a constrained manner we argued back and forth. I began to get a little angry.

'But, Larry, you asked me to choose someone with whom I felt I could work as an equal, and as soon as I do so you promote him over my head! You can't have it both ways!'

He was listening to me as still as a predatory animal and with a smile on his lips that was razor-blade thin.

'I can have it any way I like!' he crooned. Richard the Third had just addressed me.

The moment was so extraordinary that I felt myself almost standing apart from it. The threat was real enough, but what had so arrested me was this perfect expression of it, which without being in the least theatrical was as shaped and potent as a moment in a play. Like a member of an audience I almost wanted to grin at the audacity of its execution. Any true politician – his successor, Peter Hall, for instance – would have regarded such a naked assertion of power as a provocative and pointless indulgence. It was the language of the stage. A moment later Olivier seemed to realise this too and he abruptly resumed his previous manner, businesslike and now concerned with what was next on a busy agenda.

'Well, Michael, do let us know if you'd like to accept the offer,' he said squaring off some pages. I was by now pretty certain that he had another candidate waiting, literally, in the wings.

'I'd like a few days to think about it,' I said.

'Be as quick as you can, dear fellow, we've got to make a start.'

I'd already decided to accept the job, but I had no intention of making it easy for him.

'I'll let you know the beginning of next week,' I said. This irritated him but he seemed to accept it, and the meeting was over.

The following weekend I composed a careful letter of dignified capitulation and delivered it by hand. He read it as I stood there and acknowledged it with barely concealed satisfaction.

'Only Round One,' I reminded myself. His attitude had not really surprised me because there was a telltale history attached. From the beginning of his reign at the National he had been mistrustful of the new breed of directors because he saw them as usurping the centrality of the actor, the figure people come to see

13

and the one who has to go out there each night and deliver. Films are directed, he would say, but plays are *produced*, and he insisted on this old-fashioned usage on all National Theatre programmes and publicity. The indispensable components of an evening in the theatre were the play and the players who would bring it to life, and somewhere in the middle – sometimes useful, even brilliant, sometimes less so – there was this director/producer figure acting as a kind of mediator between the two indispensable components. Coming from an acting background, and having occasionally been at the wrong end of directorial incompetence myself, I was not unsympathetic to this point of view, or to Olivier's fierce sense of ownership of his own work. His extraordinary inventiveness and theatrical intelligence were his own, and he wanted everyone to know where the great moments of his performances came from – certainly not from an academic thesis imposed upon the text by some recently graduated upstart.

One of the ways he expressed his suspicion of directors at the National (a number of film directors he revered) was by paying them badly, and when as a freelance I had directed *The National Health*, a show which required a great deal of planning and the resourcefulness of a musical, I had been paid only £500. Averaged out over the fifteen weeks I'd worked on it, it made me the worst paid person in the rehearsal room. This state of affairs was not good for directors, nor indeed for the National Theatre if it was to attract the best of us, and I and two other freelance directors whom the National had employed on similar terms, Jonathan Miller and Clifford Williams, composed a joint letter to Olivier, moderately expressed, arguing the case for better fees. The letter was meant to be confidential but it was leaked to *The Times*, which reported it with direct quotes in a classy gossip column they had in their centre pages.

When I read it I was appalled. The leak could have come from any one of us, it could have come from someone within the organisation we were complaining about. I had never deliberately leaked anything to a journalist in my life, but how could I prove this? A leak, like a poison-pen letter, puts everyone under suspicion, and this general contamination fed in the short term Olivier's mistrust of his young colleagues, and in the long term was to have malign consequences for me.

I had become so preoccupied with Olivier's involvement in the curtailment of my salary that I failed to ask myself what role John Dexter had played in the matter. Perhaps because I didn't want to begin our relationship on a note of rancour, I put it down to the fact that his agent was evidently more aggressive and wily than mine and left it at that. However, John made it very difficult to take a charitable view of such things because of the frequency with which they continued occurring. There was usually a time lapse before you realised what he'd been up to. There was, for instance, the matter of secretarial assistance for the two of us. One morning the National Theatre's Administrative Director, Paddy Donnell, told me with rather too much enthusiasm that he had found the perfect secretary for John and me to share. She was John's nominee and had worked for him in New York and on his film *The Virgin Soldiers*. Her name was Caroline Coates, she was American and he suggested I meet her as soon as possible.

'You'll like her,' he said, and I did. She was young, attractive and seemed to be extremely bright and competent, if a little over-qualified for the job she was being offered. For the next month or two the arrangement was a honeymoon for three. Caroline worked all hours and had an American resourcefulness one couldn't help admiring. The word 'impossible' was not in her vocabulary. You could ask her about anything and if she didn't know about it, she would by lunchtime. However, as the months passed, Caroline seemed to be making fewer and fewer appearances at Aquinas Street and my pile of unanswered correspondence was growing. I managed to catch her in her office one morning transferring a pile of dirty clothes from a carrier bag into a carryall and I asked if she could find a moment to do a few letters.

'Not today, I'm doing John's laundry,' she replied. This didn't seem quite right so I said with a touch of insistence, 'When then?' Caroline gave me a look as if I'd been born yesterday. 'You must know!' 'What?' I replied. She sighed. 'John pays the other half of my salary. The National only picks up the first half.' This cosy arrangement by which the National got a secretary at a cut price and John got 75 per cent of her services was something of which I had never been informed.

The last shock John gave me I experienced after a delay of some thirty years and when John himself was dead. During the first few weeks of our association, when we were meant to be getting to know each other, John invited me to spend a few days with him and his partner, Riggs O'Hara, at the ancient mill house they had recently acquired in the Lot-et-Garonne. It was a beautiful building, its old machinery of waterwheels and mill-stones still intact and so dominating the interior spaces that one half expected them at any moment to creak and rumble back to life. Riggs, who oversaw all John's domestic arrangements, had undertaken the renovation with flair and discretion, and there were well-appointed outbuildings providing accommodation for guests. I was duly impressed and wondered as a practical possibility if one day I might be able to acquire something similarly fanciful. And indeed it was with John's example in mind that at the end of that same year I used an inheritance of some £10,000 to buy a dilapidated house in Biarritz on the top floor of which some forty years later I am writing this sentence. This debt I owe to John far outweighs the differences I had with him half a lifetime ago. Our acquaintances guide our behaviour without even knowing it and where their interests and initiatives are concerned we are all magpies.

John and Riggs were attentive hosts and they took me on drives up and down the lovely hills of their part of France and we ate in pretty restaurants. On my last morning we were sitting in the sun having a drink before lunch when John turned the conversation towards a discussion about our careers, and began quizzing me about my hopes and ambitions. Knowing that John had directed a film and a Broadway musical, both things I one day hoped to do, I assumed the role of novice and questioned him deferentially. His answers were informative but he was one of those people who tend to dwell on the daunting complexities of any given task whereas I was more inclined to warm to the approach exemplified by the great cinematographer Greg Toland who, when asked by the young Orson Welles for guidance, replied that he could teach Welles all he needed to know about movie-making in an afternoon. For the next hour our conversation meandered pleasantly enough along the byways of upmarket show business. In the unexpected warmth of a February sun, John had taken his shirt off and throughout I was distracted by his little white pot-belly, hirsute and as hard as a melon. It was like an insistent note of reality challenging the litany of legendary shows and deathless reputations.

Fast forward to the next century and I am reading Joan Plowright's memoir which deals extensively with the National Theatre. I turn the page and there reproduced in full is a letter from John addressed to both the Oliviers in which I am attacked. He deplores my attachment to the commercial theatre and questions my suitability to be an associate director of the National. The invitation to the mill house was not, then, intended as an exercise in professional bonding but as a form of entrapment. I can hardly believe this unexpected sting from beyond the grave. But what would once have been enraging now almost amused me because it was so quintessentially John. I could imagine the righteousness with which he had convinced himself that his letter served the greater good. Worse things have been done and heads have rolled in earnest when people have put pen to paper in the name of the future.

During our time together at the National I was continually outfoxed by John, by his virtues no less than his vices. He was extraordinarily energetic and could juggle efficiently with half a dozen concerns at once. There was an urgency about everything he attempted, and he had an appetite for detail – for schedules, lists and forward planning – all of which were important for a successful launch of the new building. He was also, alas, deviously competitive and in our relationship chose intrigue over co-operation. However, this struggle of his choosing was one which I would win and he would lose, and for reasons that had nothing to do with the merit of either of us. It was simply that I was heading randomly into a good patch with a coincidental string of hits, and he was heading randomly into a bad one when his next three shows wouldn't quite work. It hardly needs saying that a few years later the tables would be turned.

Before I could take up my post at the National Theatre full time I had an outside show to direct. This was Peter Nichols' *Forget-Me-Not Lane*, our third collaboration, which Peter had elected to have staged at the theatre in Greenwich, where he now lived. However, I was able to make time to attend planning meetings at Aquinas Street one afternoon a week. Extra chairs were brought into Sir Laurence's office and we all squeezed in, usually drawn to the same seats we had occupied a week before – Larry behind his desk, old hands like Ken Tynan and John Dexter under the window, Derek Granger, Ken's new colleague in the literary department and another new boy like myself, on a chair in the middle of the room. The most illustrious new recruit, slightly stranded among the associates, was Paul Scofield, who spoke little but always to the point. He was extremely courteous, if wary, and he seemed to exist a little apart from the rest of us as if he was the uneasy conscience of the group, attending with a mask-like face as the futures of playwrights, directors and his fellow actors were tossed around the room and sometimes dropped like so many beach balls. Also present were the administrators, Paddy Donnell and Anthony Easterbrook.

The problem with joining any large organisation is that to begin with you're required to implement policy you have had no part in initiating. The fashion in subsidised theatre at this time was towards size, and this was conspicuously dramatised in the new building then under construction on the South Bank. This fashion for size also expressed itself in a drive towards greater productivity, for more shows in many places, and all over the country subsidised theatres were expanding – into second 'studio' houses, into touring, into meeting the needs of specialist audiences – and in the process much increasing their administrative and backstage staff. I do not deny the value of theatre as an aspect of further education and the social services, but I was unimpressed by the virtue of scale for its own sake. Perhaps my own laziness and lack of public spirit contributed to this, but I had a clear and very simple view of what I thought theatre was for. It was to bring to the stage productions of such accomplishment and concentrated intent that anyone who saw them would remember them for the rest of their lives. It was their impact rather than the categories to which they happened to belong that mattered.

They could be anything – tragedies or comedies, musicals or one-man shows. Not surprisingly such occasions are a rarity. But they do happen and are perhaps the one good reason why people who should know better persist in such a clumsy, compromised and often disappointing medium. It's impossible to legislate for this kind of excellence; all you can do is get the work done as best you can, keep your fingers crossed and trust that once in a while in the life of an institution or an individual, against the odds, it happens. This hardly constitutes a policy and is certainly not a programme, nor is it much use in the daily and arduous demands of running a theatre, but as a thought on hold at the back of one's mind, a sleeping aspiration, it can warn against wrong turnings and highlight misjudgements.

The paradox, of course, is that the more arrows you shoot at the target the better chance there is of a bullseye, and the policy of the new National Theatre envisioned a full quiver. This was something John Dexter had been thinking about and planning for since its inception. Back at the National once again, he now had the chance to put the plans that he, Olivier and Tynan had been discussing for years into practice. The completion of the new building was about a year away. It would require a doubling in the size of the acting company and the attendant staff to service the two auditoria (the third, adaptable space followed later). The thinking was that the National should anticipate the challenges ahead by attempting a two-theatre policy in advance of its move to the new building. A West End theatre, the New (soon to become the Albery, and now the Noël Coward), had been rented, and the plan was to run it in tandem with the Old Vic. This policy was under way by the time I had staged *Forget-Me-Not Lane*, and was free to join the organisation full time.

Our first concern was firming up the repertoire in both theatres. At the Old Vic a programme of plays for 1971 was already in place; now, beginning in June, we had to decide on five productions to run at the New. Logistically it was a mammoth task, since at both theatres the shows would be in repertoire, each playing in cycles of a few days at a time, and all cast from the same pool of actors, who would be making their way back and forth across Waterloo Bridge according to what was playing that night. Fortunately in Michael Hallifax the National had someone on the staff with the patience and zeal to make all this work, and his charts and diagrams soon became indispensable aids.

Representing the literary department, Ken Tynan had strong views about the sort of repertoire we should be mounting in both houses. He had long felt that the British classical theatre was far too inward-looking and neglected a wealth of material from across the Channel. Chekhov was performed, occasionally an Ibsen or a Molière, and that was about it. He saw the new National as embracing not only drama from around the world but also its most gifted international interpreters.

The risks attached to this aspiration were soon to become all too evident. The first production that had been scheduled for the Old Vic in 1971 was a contemporary two-hander, *The Architect and the Emperor of Assyria*, by the French-domiciled Spanish dramatist Fernando Arrabal. The director was Victor Garcia, an Argentinian who spoke no English. He was a small man with an enormous head of curly black hair, who dressed exclusively in white, and he was to take an already perplexing work to a new realm of obscurity. He conducted rehearsals rather like someone in a circus cracking the whip at a pair of hapless circling horses, and during the first dress rehearsal had demanded that in mid-performance the two actors remove all their clothes. A much distressed Jim Dale refused, but Anthony Hopkins coolly obliged, and came out on top when not too long after he was languidly asked to put his clothes back on again.

At the final dress rehearsal the artistic directorate and the production team were scattered dejectedly about the auditorium staring at the stage and absolutely certain that trundling towards them was a catastrophic flop. The panicky listlessness that attends theatrical failure is an atmosphere that everyone within the walls of the theatre has no choice but to breathe, and worst affected, because most responsible, was Ken Tynan. At the post mortem afterwards his habitual stutter and the emphysema from which he suffered dramatised the situation in a most literal way as he struggled with gulps of air to argue his way out of the mess. But there was nothing to be done – no concrete play to elucidate, no proper parts to be better interpreted. I'd just joined the organisation (at what it was becoming increasingly clear was the wrong moment) and thought all we could do was grit our teeth until the first night had come and gone. I caught Olivier looking at me demanding some sign of optimism, but a closing of the ranks was all I could offer him.

The Architect and the Emperor of Assyria may have been a failure but it was an honourable one, because it sprang from

Ken's conviction that the National Theatre should be international in outlook and anything but safe. His passion for good theatre was transparently genuine, but he had never been able to promote the work he believed in other than at second hand, initially as a critic and now as a figure in the shadows whispering into Sir Laurence's ear. He longed for a show to direct himself, but Olivier wouldn't consider it, and Ken didn't have the stomach to go hunting for an opportunity in the provinces or on the fringe. I suspect he had a terror of failure, of losing his footing on that plateau of artistic celebrity that he had first secured at Oxford, and this may account for the erratic use he made of his gifts. As a prose sprinter turning out his pieces each week for the *Observer* he was incomparable, and his enthusiasms had been thrillingly infectious, but he baulked at the prospect of work that involved isolation and the long haul. He was one of those people every generation throws up, like Beau Brummell, who leave behind an indelible profile, but are remembered as much for who they were as for what they achieved. More than anyone I've ever encountered in the theatre, his life had the arc of tragedy, and ahead of him, though none of us guessed it, was a decline of cruel swiftness.

On my way to the theatre on the first night I ran into Ken and we walked into the foyer together where we at once collided with Olivier. There was a moment's pause while the two men mentally circled each other. Olivier got in the first thrust. 'Ken, baby, on behalf of the National Theatre and from the very bottom of my heart I really must thank you for bringing this brilliant, audacious play into the repertoire of the Old Vic.' He didn't get much further because Ken, shaking his head and grinning nervously as if he knew exactly what his boss was up to, swiftly parried 'Y-y-y-you know very well, Larry, that the decision to do this play was t-t-t-taken by the two of us! You read it and said you absolutely l-l-l-loved it!' The hot potato was passed back and forth between them, then we went our separate ways into the auditorium, leaving the blame for the evening we had yet to endure to settle where it would. It was one of those hilarious moments you pigeonhole for your memoirs and there, some forty years on, is where it has found a home.

TWO

Rescue of a temporary sort (in the theatre it is never anything else) was around the corner. The next production at the Old Vic, Carl Zuckmayer's *The Captain of Köpenick*, directed by Frank Dunlop, was an unqualified success, particularly for Paul Scofield in the name part, and rapidly sold out. This was followed by John Dexter's first production since his return to the National. He had chosen a minor Elizabethan tragedy, *A Woman Killed with Kindness*, and, working with his great collaborator from the Royal Court, the designer Jocelyn Herbert, was to give it an exemplary staging. Though the play was well acted by Joan Plowright and Anthony Hopkins and had its merits, it had not been neglected for centuries without reason. The critics accorded it the same fate as the woman of the title.

The repertoire playing at the Vic now consisted of two flops propped up by one success, so a great deal was riding on the fourth play of the season, *Coriolanus*. This was intended to welcome back to London the brilliant Canadian actor, Christopher Plummer. He had made his name in the classics, playing a number of the great parts for Tyrone Guthrie's Festival Theatre in Ontario, and there had been plans to bring his Hamlet to London some ten years previously, but the production was abandoned at the last minute when Guthrie fell ill. Since then he had rocketed to the higher reaches of showbiz fame, playing opposite Julie Andrews in one of the most successful films of all time, *The Sound of Music*. He had been on a percentage of the gross, so not only did worldwide celebrity follow but truckloads of money. Now the fuss had died down and he was looking for a place to come down to earth again where he could resume doing the sort of work that most interested him. Coriolanus was the perfect part to provide such an opportunity. He had bought a huge house in Kensington, the interior of which he had gutted and entirely remodelled, and he now looked set for a new life and a reinvigorated career in London.

Coriolanus, a play that over time has often been neglected, was very much in vogue in the seventies. Olivier himself had enjoyed an enormous success in the role at Stratford twelve years earlier and since then there had been numerous productions, of which perhaps the most admired was the East German production of Bertolt Brecht's version by the Berliner Ensemble, which played at the Old Vic when the Ensemble visited London in 1965. The staging, the design and the acting had an organic perfection which can only be achieved when a company is able to rehearse over months rather than weeks. Its meticulously directed battles and crowd scenes were so mesmerising that English audiences almost forgot that they were being spoken to in German. Had they understood the language they would have realised that this was not quite the play Shakespeare had in mind. It had been ruthlessly cut and reorganised by Brecht to bring it into line with Marxist doctrine.

The reputation of this production may have been one of the factors that made it difficult to find a director. Those we approached were either unavailable or uninterested. One day someone on our planning committee wondered out loud whether we should approach the two directors of the East German production, Manfred Wekworth and Joachim Tenschert. It was the most improbable long shot but it suddenly seemed to all of us worth a try. An offer was made and to our astonishment accepted. Too late we realised we had waded into deep water because any contract would involve not just two theatres but two governments, the East German and our own. More was at stake than simply the outcome of a first night.

The German directors duly arrived and we were aware that we had in our midst that familiar duo, the bad cop and the good cop. Wekworth was small, dark and scowling, and utterly uncompromising even in matters of common courtesy. He was the one with talent. His colleague Joachim Tenschert was geniality itself, the diplomat exuding good humour and fellow feeling. It was his job to ensure the space within which Wekworth could do his work. I watched them rehearse one morning. Tenschert sat comfortably to one side observing, but Wekworth was constantly leaping to his feet to interject a direction after almost every line. Restaging his production he was like some fierce territorial bird flying back and forth as he meticulously rebuilt his nest, twig by twig, peck by peck.

Alas, within days the production was in deep trouble. Christopher Plummer had arrived at rehearsal with his entire part learnt. It did not take him long to realise that he had wasted much of his time. With its many cuts and transpositions, Brecht's version was no longer the Shakespeare play specified in his contract and until his role bore a closer resemblance to the original text he refused to rehearse and left the building. Equally adamant were the directors. The National had seen their production when it had visited London and we knew what we were getting. There could be no question now of asking them to compromise its political content. The rehearsal room at Aquinas Street had become a hot spot of East–West confrontation, and neither side was blinking.

In Larry's office it would be fair to say that there was a degree of panic. Ken was particularly exercised because as a critic he had long been a champion of the Berliner Ensemble and in any scandal he was convinced the British press would hold him responsible. Larry, who inclined to a weary stoicism in such situations, seemed more concerned with Christopher Plummer's state of mind. Were we now to expect outraged statements to the press, appeals to Actors' Equity, possibly legal action? Even if the stalemate were broken, it was a crisis to which there could be no satisfactory outcome. The Olivier regime itself could be in jeopardy and we had every reason to be worried. Even so, observing the two men I was aware that both in their different ways derived, certainly not pleasure, but a kind of reassurance from being at the centre of this storm. Though fearful, Ken could not resist the drama of it, because drama of any sort released his energies and his sometimes misguided resourcefulness. In Larry's case he had lived a lifetime with these sorts of pressures, in the betrayals and conspiracies that went with both his elevated professional status and also his tempestuous private life. Escaping through a side entrance to avoid a mob of reporters gathered at the stage door, booking into a hotel room under an assumed name, these were tedious complications to an already fraught life, but what they whispered to you was that you were still holding your own in the public's imagination.

Desperate though the situation was, my own view as to how we should proceed was very clear. No organisation that receives public funding can justify creating a diplomatic incident for the government that supplies the cash. We had walked into this situation with our eyes open but without thinking the matter through. At the very least we should have warned Chris Plummer about what he was getting into. Both sides in the dispute had a case, but as an institution we had no choice but to come down on the side of the Germans.

'What are we to do then?' asked Larry.

By this time Christopher Plummer had holed himself up in his luxurious new house in Kensington, provoking a resolution.

'I think we should go and see him, apologise for the mess we've got him into but explain as clearly as we can the political ramifications of the situation,' I suggested. I had got to know Chris slightly and believed he would respond reasonably, but Ken and Larry were certain there would be major fireworks. However, since there was no other course open to us, the following afternoon a small party, in which Larry had delegated me to be spokesman, made our way to his house. The interior was lofty, beautifully appointed and strangely empty. We were expecting perhaps to be offered a cup of tea but Chris produced a bottle of Dom Perignon champagne and had it served in brand new flutes. I began to explain the situation as honestly as I could while Chris listened carefully. He nodded, thought for a while, then said he understood perfectly the wider ramifications and offered to withdraw. It was dignified and rather moving. I felt a wave of sympathy for this fine actor as I sometimes have for other men who become extremely rich without being particularly interested in money. They have found the pearl but have finished up inside the oyster. We emptied our glasses, thanked him and left.

Afterwards Larry commended me for the way I'd handled the matter. It was the first time, though not the last in his regime, when he'd allowed me to make a significant contribution. He had that indispensable attribute of the leader – the empathetic curiosity that allowed him to find out what you could do, then leave you alone to do it, and this more than made up for the sharp surprises of which he was also capable.

Anthony Hopkins, the most promising young actor in the company, took over the part and did so splendidly. We soon had a show. However, the National was a very different place from the bracingly disciplined and doctrinaire Berliner Ensemble, and the electricity which surrounded the production when the actors barked at each other in German and the stagehands were as well drilled as a team of acrobats was no longer there. *Forget-Me-Not Lane*, Peter Nichols' comedy which I had directed, was running at the Greenwich Theatre and I invited the German directors to a performance. Afterwards they were polite but reserved, I suspect because the audience had laughed so much.

'You like doing this sort of play?' a twinkling Tenschert asked me, while Wekworth stood beside him not uttering. They seemed uneasy with what I regarded as the English-speaking theatre's greatest strength – its refusal to draw a line between what was entertainment and what was art.

At the final dress rehearsal of *Coriolanus* I was sitting beside Olivier listening to Hopkins deliver one of the great speeches. Every word of it was of course instantly familiar to Olivier – and to me, since I had been in the company when he appeared in the role at Stratford.

'What a marvellous text,' he murmured. And I responded, 'Yes, it's a great play.' But he gently corrected me. 'No, not a great play. A great text.' It was a distinction so simple as to go unremarked but to a theatrical professional it was crucial. *Hamlet* and *Three Sisters* are great plays because they can survive not only the passing of time but the misjudgements of their many interpreters yet still speak to an audience. Most plays are less foolproof. I've remembered Olivier's words and the almost dreamy way he said them because they were so typically Larry – intuitive rather than intellectual, and right on the money.

A few days later, and five minutes walk away at Aquinas Street, another Olivier would be waiting for me. Performances of the play which I had previously directed at the National on a freelance basis, *The National Health*, were becoming infrequent and most of them were mid-week matinees. This was inexplicable because the poster for the production carried an unprecedented health warning: 'Not Recommended for Young Children'. As director I had not been consulted about this and knew it could only have come from the top. The play dealt graphically with illness and death, true, but I suspected there was another reason it was deemed unsuitable for tots: it was the first production in the history of the National in which a derivative of the word 'fuck' was spoken out loud on stage. This happened only once, in the last ten minutes when the alcoholic tramp, Loach, is being discharged from hospital and sent to another institution to dry out. 'Great barn of a place,' he complains. 'Miles from fucking civilisation.' At that time this could still make an audience wonder if it had heard right.

The National Health had its origins in a short play Peter Nichols had written for television, *The End Beds*, based on his experiences as a patient in a National Health ward during two long stays. He is not a character in the play but his listening ear, truthful observation and shaping comic intelligence are always on stage. The 'end beds' of the title are those nearest the door that the staff reserve for patients approaching death. As they start their decline their beds are shifted further and further down the ward towards the exit. The play is faultlessly observed, funny but also extremely bleak, which was possibly why it never found its way on to a television screen. To amplify it for the stage, Peter had invented a subplot about a Labour politician with a health problem who for career reasons is obliged to use the Health Service rather than go private. Though well enough done, this subplot served as a platform for Peter to air his opinions, and it contrasted uneasily with the rest of the play which left editorialising to the audience as they made their way home from the theatre.

This was the first appearance in Peter's work of a dichotomy between on the one hand a dramatist who breathes life into his characters then gets out of the way and allows them to live, and the pundit who can't resist using his characters to tell us what's what. It was as if Chekhov was guiding the pen in his right hand and Bernard Shaw the one in his left. He gave me the play to read and I was in no doubt which side of his talents I preferred. I told him so as tactfully as I could, and he nodded and heard me out. Some weeks later I received a new draft offering a brilliant alternative to the existing subplot. On television during the sixties there had been two extremely popular series romanticising the medical profession. From America came *Dr Kildare*, with the almost freakishly handsome Richard Chamberlain in the title part, and from Scotland the more homely *Dr Finlay's Casebook*, with Andrew Cruikshank as a snowy-haired general practitioner, irascible but saintly. Peter drew from both these sources to create his own soap opera, 'Nurse Norton's Affair', and the idea was to cross-cast it with the doctors and nurses who inhabited the unflinchingly real world of *The End Beds*.

Here Nurse Norton is a put-upon black nurse doing her best to cope, then, as the set changes and the music begins to swell, she walks into a parallel play where, in sexy white uniform and little red cape, she becomes a figure of glamour and poise. Peter's pastiche was broadly and extremely funny, and he introduced another element from recent newspaper headlines glamorising the medical profession – successful organ transplants. 'Nurse Norton's Affair' presented a world in which modern medicine was a miracle and doctors and nurses always rushed to the side of the sick with tough but unconditional love; and, as in the two series on which it was based, once you were watching it was impossible to remain entirely aloof from the absurdity of its dramatic propositions. At the climax of the story Nurse Norton has offered to save the life of the stricken young doctor with whom she is in love by offering him one of her kidneys. As later staged, twin gurneys rose up on a lift from the darkness below on their way to the operating theatre, and as the music soars we see in the space between them a black hand reaching for a white.

This combination of conflicting elements in the one evening enabled us to play tricks with an audience's susceptibility to drama and their expectations of the form. On one side of the stage, in a ridiculous but satisfying mix, challenges were bravely met and tragedy averted; on the other death made its random and mono-tonous progress through the ward, and left nothing behind but a question mark. Both Peter and I began to realise that we were on to something that maybe hadn't been done on stage before.

The work we did together over the next few weeks, tailoring the production to the play and occasionally the play to the produc-tion, was characterised by a sort of conspiratorial glee. Peter seemed to have no vanity about his work and was open to any suggestion. The text consisted of a succession of scenes spread between the two stories, so it was possible to shift them about in the interests of more telling juxtapositions. One morning I realised that with a few adjustments we could stage the two climactic incidents of both narratives simultaneously – on stage left the immaculate transplant of Nurse Norton's kidney into the body of her beloved, and on stage right the death from heart failure of one of the ward's younger patients because of human incompetence and defective machinery. Since one scene was in dumb show and the other interspersed with bursts of panic-stricken dialogue it was possible to shift the focus from one side of the stage to the other like back-and-forth cuts in a film.

Later on, with the show a success and our reputations secure, this period, which at the time was exhilarating and unshadowed, became a matter of contention between us. Peter began to resent sharing any credit for work which was, of course, basically his, and I sulked because I thought my contributions were being deliberately unacknowledged. This was foolish of us both. We failed to see what a rare and fortunate thing our collaboration was. We sparked ideas off each other because, artistically, we were coming from the same place. Though our formative years had been spent in different hemispheres, we had been conditioned by that same worldwide transatlantic popular culture that had reached out to us on movie screens, wirelesses and radiograms. To us Fred Astaire and Louis Armstrong seemed as remarkable in their way as, say, T. S. Eliot or Sir Thomas Beecham, and there were people of our generation all over the country who shared a similar scepticism about prim divisions affecting culture and class. We were being given a chance to speak on their behalf, and moreover, on the stage of an institution that was part of the British Establishment.

What I loved about our show and was determined to champion was precisely what Laurence Olivier didn't. He wasn't a snob and didn't pay much attention to class, but he did believe in hierarchy, beginning with the monarch then graduating downwards from there. As leader of the British theatre I imagine he would have placed himself about level with a distinguished general or a bishop, or, indeed, a leading consultant at the sort of hospital we would be showing on stage. Since he had recently been cured of cancer he was uncomfortable with the idea of the medical profession being mocked, particularly in the character of a senior specialist who visits the ward with his entourage and exercises authority in a way that Peter had skewered with unforgiving accuracy. He was also uneasy with the play's pessimism, which to his generation suggested defeatism and pointless complaint – after all, his film of *Henry V* had made a significant contribution to maintaining morale during the Second World War.

I, however, believed fervently in the play and was determined to fight for it. For all of us younger directors working at the National, Olivier was the artistic father figure against whom the exasperated sons muttered and sometimes rebelled. And yet with the passage of time I can see that there was a degree of wisdom attached to his reservations. The National Health Service in 1969 was certainly hierarchical, but then so is artistic talent, and the hospitals at that time were at least in the control of the doctors and staff who provided the care, just as the BBC was then more in the hands of the people making the programmes. No one anticipated that these and other British institutions, of which we were approving and critical in about equal measure, would one day be hijacked by tier after tier of management, whose targets and priorities would often conflict with those of the people doing the hands-on work. Hierarchy would go, but so would a sense of obligation and public service, attributes without which a National Theatre, and probably a health service, would never have come into being in the first place.

One morning in the long corridor that ran the length of the Aquinas Street offices I encountered a concerned Michael Hallifax.

Tall and correctly dressed, he wouldn't have looked out of place in the upper reaches of the Foreign Office, and like a good civil servant he was resolutely courteous, urbane and unopinionated. His primary responsibility was for the advance planning of the repertoire, taking his orders first from Larry who would explain his priorities so that Michael could implement them in his complicated series of charts and graphs.

'I'm afraid it looks as if *The National Health* may be coming to the end of its life,' he said.

'Why?!' I asked, astonished. I had attended an evening performance the previous week and it had been absolutely packed.

'The usual – box office. The matinees are doing particularly badly.'

'Hardly surprising when we suggest children and old ladies stay away.'

'Sir Laurence would like to drop it before the summer, when a lot of important Americans will be coming over. He'd prefer to see it replaced with something more representative of the National's work.'

I knew Larry disliked the play, but this was plain barmy. It had won the *Evening Standard* Award for Play of the Year, and particularly with younger audiences had been immensely popular. Moreover it had shown that the National Theatre was unafraid to take risks with provocative new material and that it had put out a welcome mat to new writing.

I felt my energies gather in rebellion, then falter, as I realised I had no choice but to confront my boss. But how should I proceed? A couple of days later a chance meeting provided me with a strategy.

I was coming out of the Piccadilly underground when I ran into Irving Wardle, drama critic of *The Times*. He had championed a number of my productions, particularly the work I had done with Peter Nichols, and a year or two before when he had interviewed me for his paper we had become friendly. It so happened that some new actors had recently taken over leading roles in *The National Health*, and I asked Irving if his paper would consider this recasting as sufficient pretext for reviewing the production anew – and I confided that the show could do with a boost. This was the only occasion in my career when I have ever lobbied a critic. He said he'd do his best.

There was a performance of the play the following Monday which I had decided to attend and I was surprised and pleased to see Irving among the audience. I was in my preferred seat in Row F on a side aisle, and he was further to the front on the other side of the auditorium, so he didn't see me and we didn't speak. The next morning in *The Times* there was a second rave for the play, in which questions were raised about the reasons for taking it off. The cat was not only among the pigeons but eating them alive, and I went to work with considerable trepidation.

Michael Hallifax had been instructed to keep a lookout for my arrival. 'Michael, Sir Laurence would like to see you in his office as soon as you've got a minute.'

'The *Times* notice?'

He responded with a significant nod.

'I'll be there in five minutes.'

I needed a moment alone to steel myself for the confrontation and think what I was going to say. There was a small washroom intended solely for the use of the Artistic Director at the far end of the corridor, and presuming this was now unoccupied, I locked myself in for a bit, took some deep breaths and tried to summon up a few sparks of righteous indignation. Then I set off.

'*COME IN!!*' As soon as I was through the door he launched in. '*What's this about you and Irving Wardle?!*' He was clearly very angry.

'You mean that excellent notice in *The Times*?'

'Tom Pate says that Wardle came to the performance last night.' Tom Pate was the Front of House Manager.

35

'That's correct, I was there myself.'

'And that the two of you watched the show sitting *side by side*!'

'That's not correct, we were on opposite sides of the theatre.'

With the deliberation of someone reaching for a weapon Larry suddenly stretched across the desk for the in-house telephone. He didn't pick it up but left his hand resting ominously on the receiver. For a couple of seconds we stared at each other in a frozen tableau. It was like the moment before a shoot-out.

'Go ahead. Ring Tom up. Ask him!'

His hand relaxed his grasp on the phone. 'But you did get him to come to the performance last night? You don't deny that?'

In as moderate a tone as I could muster I explained exactly the circumstances of running into the critic at the Piccadilly underground.

'But Michael, the show is *failing at the box office*!'

'I'm not sure that need be the case.'

With great impatience he reached for the telephone again, this time picked it up and dialled Michael Hallifax's extension, then asked him to join us. We waited in silence. Michael's arrival some minutes later with copies of the box-office returns was like the relief of a siege. He took us meticulously through the figures. In the past month there had been one evening performance which, like all evening performances, had been packed. The problem had been the sparsely attended matinees of which there had been an incredible four. Tactfully I suggested that it was not really a play for a matinee audience, and that surely we'd made this clear on our posters. However, I think it was less my argument than Michael Hallifax's eloquent neutrality that carried the day.

'Apparently since the notice this morning, the box office has been quite busy,' he remarked mildly. I saw that Larry was conceding. *The National Health* would not be dropped from the repertoire.

In a sense I'd won, but it was a source of regret to me that I'd had to engineer this confrontation, because I was not Olivier's enemy and never would be. And who knows what other pressures had been brought to bear on him, by some pompous member of the Board, or individuals in the audience with influence writing indignant letters? What was vastly in his favour was the fact that he'd allowed the play to be staged in the first place.

Increasingly at our planning meetings the focus was on the approaching season in the West End. We were not halfway through the year and all the new work which was meant to sustain the repertoire of the Old Vic until December was up and running. However, of these four productions only one could be counted a success. In the British subsidised theatre grants from the government are predicated on taking a healthy sum of additional revenue at the box office. If attendances fall below say 80 per cent, and stay that way, the organisation will soon plunge into debt. At the Vic we were playing to under 50 per cent with little possibility of improvement, so a great deal was riding on the productions to be launched at the New Theatre in St Martin's Lane. First up was Pirandello's *The Rules of the Game*, which with Scofield and Plowright in the leads and Anthony Page directing looked a good bet. This was to be followed by Giraudoux's *Amphitryon 38*, which in S. N. Behrman's Broadway adaptation had been a huge success for the Lunts in the thirties. This was to be directed by Olivier and provide Christopher Plummer with what would now be his first role. Yet to be cast was the Lynn Fontanne part, and this was at the top of the agenda at our next planning meeting.

Geraldine McEwan was Larry's first choice, which we all endorsed, and John Dexter suggested he leave the meeting and ring her right away with a firm offer. He returned, the offer made, and we went on to discuss other matters. Suddenly the telephone rang on Larry's desk and his secretary told him that Geraldine McEwan was on the line again requesting a further word with John. But in private. With a certain self-important gravity John got up to leave, our eyes following him to the door. It seemed a very long time before he bustled back into the room and resumed his seat. We all looked at him eager to know what was going on. John gave a sigh, then sat up straight and assumed a decisive expression. He began to talk about himself in the third person. 'John's going to be a good boy from now on,' he said. 'Now he's back at the National he's decided to turn over a new leaf and always tell the truth.' He then turned towards Olivier, behind his desk. 'Larry, Gerry is prepared to play the part but only if you don't direct.'

Uneasily and one by one we turned towards the artistic director. He had a look on his face like a wounded animal and what made it worse was his effort to disguise it from those of us who were observing him. What was John playing at? Surely Geraldine McEwan's intention was that this information be delivered in private at the end of the meeting. Watching Larry, I realised I had seen that same pain being put to use in his acting. If one could trace it back to its source where would it lead – to the loss of a mother in childhood, to an overbearing father or a stern school? However, of all the screwed-up children in the world artists are the lucky ones. I had forgotten that Larry had a skin as tough as an alligator, that not only would he recover but probably get his own way into the bargain, and sure enough a week or two later Geraldine McEwan had signed up to the part, happy to accept Olivier as her director.

Every day now Larry was putting aside his morning to prepare for the new production. In his office he had set up the model of the set with little cut-out cardboard figures to stand in for the cast. On hand he had an array of coloured pencils with which he would inscribe his working script with every move of every actor, every lighting and sound cue. His method was to work out the whole show in advance, then go into the rehearsal room and ask the actors for their patience and obedience while he gave them moment by moment his complete production. This, he explained, would take about ten days. After that the cast were free to question any move or challenge any point of interpretation. His job was now to give the show over to the people to whom he believed it rightly belonged, the actors.

This was the procedure he had absorbed before the war when directors had been 'producers' and were more hard-working but perhaps less regarded. They were disciplinarians often responsible for lighting, sound effects and duties now associated with stage management, and they occupied an uncomfortable terrain, being authoritarian on the one hand and, at least where star actors were concerned, obsequious on the other. This was a model my generation of directors had rejected. Moving cardboard figures around a model box often bears little relation to real actors spaced out in a rehearsal room. With my own shows I always had a rough blocking worked out in my head, particularly for busy moments, but I tried to prevent it interfering with the director's most important obligation once he's done his thinking about the play – to give his passionate attention to what is happening right in front of him. This is where his dialogue with the actors begins and where, in collaboration with them, many of his best ideas will come from. The previous generation of directors spent a week and a half with their faces buried in their scripts wondering why ideas that seemed to work to perfection in the model box were getting such a frosty reception from their leading actors. They then proceeded to take out their frustration by bullying the less important members of the cast.

Word was now coming out of the *Amphitryon 38* rehearsal room that Christopher Plummer was not altogether happy. He revered Larry and would not have dreamt of defying him, but he was being asked to rehearse in a way that put a brake on the initiative and playfulness that go into the making of comedy. Perhaps this had been at the heart of Geraldine's earlier reservations. But as the work proceeded a more insoluble problem began to make itself apparent: the play was an absolute dud. What had once seemed smart and audacious was now tame and dated. Fashions had changed and it was like something inert, left behind by the tide. Larry knew this better than anyone, and in the mornings I would see him setting off along the corridor deliberately straightening his spine and lightening his step so that he could walk into the rehearsal room with apparent confidence. But his body knew what he needed to deny. In the last week of rehearsals something in his neck gave way, a muscle or a ligament, and he worked in agony.

One of those important Americans Olivier had been trying to protect from *The National Health* was in town, the New York producer Morton Gottlieb. I had known Morty for over twenty years, ever since as young men we had both worked for Robert Morley on the Australian tour of *Edward, My Son* and he had become a good friend. He had just had an enormous success on Broadway with Anthony Shaffer's thriller *Sleuth* and had now acquired the film rights. He telephoned me and asked if we could meet because there was an important matter he wanted to discuss that had to be in the utmost confidence – Laurence Olivier's health. He was thinking of pairing him in his film with Michael Caine, but show business was awash with rumours and he had decided I was in a better position than most to give an honest assessment as to whether Olivier was up to playing a long and demanding film role. It had been two years since his last major illness – thrombosis in one of his legs, which had almost killed him. He'd made a good recovery, but had done no acting of any consequence in the interim. Certainly he had become a little more fretful (with good reason given our current predicament), but I was pretty certain that his skills and energy as an actor were undiminished, and I said as much to Morty. To reassure him I suggested we travel to Oxford where Larry was dress-rehearsing *Amphitryon 38* for a week's try-out prior to the West End opening. That way he could see for himself.

In a break from the technical rehearsal we managed to catch Larry backstage. He looked utterly exhausted, but this was to be expected at this stage in a production. What we hadn't anticipated was that he would be clamped inside a huge neck-brace out of which his head emerged as rigid as the end of a bolt. Whether he was well or on the point of death it was impossible to say. Afterwards I told Morty that I thought he would be his old self once the show had opened but wasn't at all sure if either of us was convinced. However, the following year Laurence Olivier did indeed play in the film of *Sleuth*, the first in a whole string of movies that restored him to film stardom. Refusing to play safe, Morty had stuck by his hunch, and in a producer this ability to intuit a decision, sometimes in the face of conflicting evidence, is often the thing that tilts the balance towards elusive success.

On his return from Oxford, Larry's anxiety about *Amphitryon 38* was compounded by a bitter disappointment. For years one of his ambitions had been to mount a National production of the Broadway musical *Guys and Dolls*, with himself in the role of Nathan Detroit and Geraldine McEwan as Adelaide. He saw the current expansion of the repertoire as the opportunity to find a slot for it and he and Geraldine had already begun taking singing lessons. However, Paddy Donnell, the National's Administrative Director, was against the idea on the grounds of cost. During Olivier's week away in Oxford he had called a secret meeting of the Board to lobby against the project. Without consulting Olivier the Board closed the show down. It was not the first time in his career that he had been betrayed in this fashion, nor, alas, would it be the last. There was something about him that his critics found hard to deal with face to face, something intimidating and perhaps a little frightening. In 1948 he had been sacked from the directorship of the Old Vic from a distance of 12,000 miles when he was touring Australasia with the company's work. Rather than face that dead-eyed stare it was easier to go behind his back.

Had *Amphitryon 38* been a commercial production it would have been on and off within a week, but as part of the National's repertoire the show was locked into a schedule of performances over a given number of weeks. The season at the New had only just begun and as yet we had had no big success. We were now losing money at both theatres on a dramatic scale. The fifth and final slot of the West End season was as yet unfilled, and it was becoming clear that there was only one tried and true way of ensuring box office success: putting Laurence Olivier back on stage. Approaching sixty-five and the survivor of two major illnesses, it was probably the last place on earth he wanted to be, particularly in a role substantial enough to draw the public. On the other hand the reputation of his regime, of himself as the first artistic director of the National Theatre, was at stake. He was still ambitious enough to know he had no choice.

There was a play that Ken Tynan had long championed as a vehicle for Larry, Eugene O'Neill's *Long Day's Journey into Night*, but the actor had always resisted it because he thought that the evening belonged to whoever played Mary Tyrone, the wife in this semi-autobiographical drama of a single 'long day' in a dysfunctional household. Ken brought it to the table again. Most of the big classic roles Olivier had already played; and this would be a new direction for him, one of the great parts from the American canon. Besides, the show would be inexpensive: with a cast of five and one set, and coming at the end of the season, it would be possible to arrange a straight run of two or three months. With luck we could clean up at the box office and balance our books.

These were compelling arguments, except perhaps for the man who had to learn one of the longest parts in world drama, then spend four or five hours, six nights a week, performing it. Ken and I were sitting with him in his office when he agreed to take the part. It was a sober moment because we were aware of what we were asking of him. Then he turned to me and without much enthusiasm said, 'And would you like to direct it?' I knew he preferred the old-fashioned word 'producer', which he still insisted be used on all publicity material and posters, and the word 'direct' came out with a certain distaste. But I understood. As one of the most inventive and resourceful actors alive he was simply protecting his own turf, his copyright.

'I love the play and would love to do it,' I replied carefully. 'But would you like to sleep on it? Maybe you'd prefer to work with someone you already know?' I was thinking of Dexter, who'd directed him in *Othello*. I was also protecting myself. I believed in him, but did he believe in me?

'No, I'd like you to do it,' he said decisively. Ken and I looked at each other. It was going to happen.

The following day I ran into Larry in the corridor looking glum. I tried to reassure him. 'It's a wonderful part,' I said, but he shrugged. 'With some lovely comedy,' I added. 'The meanness, turning off the lights to save money and so on.' At the mention of the word 'comedy' he gave me a sharp, interested look.

However, I had another obstacle to clear first, which in the event was to prove less of a hurdle and more of a high jump. This was a co-production with John Dexter of the next show into the West End, *Tyger*, a new work by the poet Adrian Mitchell. This had come to the National Theatre through Ken's friendship with the author, and it was an extraordinary melange of poetry, music, broad comedy and political theatre. Its premise was that the nineteenth-century artist and sage, William Blake, was alive and well in contemporary London, and struggling to do his work in the present-day arts world, where patronage was no longer dependent on the whim of an aristocrat but on some moribund committee at an arts-funding body. The National Theatre itself was likewise dependent, so Adrian's musical was not the most diplomatic inclusion in our repertoire. However it was a work of such exuberance and originality that I agreed with Ken that it deserved a place among our other more familiar and less disruptive plays. When I first read it I thought it was just the kind of show through which I could make the sort of contribution I had with *The National Health*, but I soon learnt that John Dexter had already been assigned to direct.

In the tiny room in Aquinas Street that housed the literary department there was a special cupboard where new scripts, arriving by post or delivered by hand, were stored until a time could be found to read them. John knew about this cupboard but I didn't, and being by temperament and application very much the early bird he soon caught a number of choice worms. One of these was *Equus*, a play which deserved to fall into his lap anyway because of the spectacular work he had done on Peter Shaffer's earlier success, *The Royal Hunt of the Sun*. *Tyger*, I felt, was another matter. Surely the decision about the choice of director should wait until the rest of us had had a chance to read it?

I brought this up at the next planning meeting, and John surprised us all by immediately suggesting that we direct it together. I was taken aback. Co-directing was something I had never attempted, but this seemed a generous proposal that it would have been boorish not to consider. I knew the show would involve taking on more actors to meet the requirements of a musical and I realised that it could be an opportunity for both of us to familiarise ourselves with this enlarged company and bond with them. And hopefully bond with each other. I thanked him and said yes. It was no fault of John's that I hadn't really thought the thing through, because among the most important decisions a director makes is the choice of his collaborators, the people who will provide the scenic design, the lights, the sound and so on, and John, who'd already been working on the show for a month, had them securely in place. I would perforce be joining him once again as a junior partner.

It wasn't that I didn't admire the people he'd chosen. As set designer he had chosen Jocelyn Herbert, whom I considered the most brilliant designer in Britain and, had she been available, would have been my first choice for *The National Health*. Her work, though less inclined to draw attention to itself, was in tune with the selective realism of the Berliner Ensemble; everything you saw on stage was there for a purpose, either to help tell the story or to facilitate the action, and a set by Jocelyn became an aesthetic distillation of her thinking about the play. *Tyger*, however, was unusual in that it was one of the very few scripts for which I would have considered her seriously miscast. For much of the time the show needed to be as highly coloured, as deliberately two-dimensional and robustly comic as a Regency cartoon, something rude and disrespectful by Gillray or Rowlandson. It needed a designer who knew the uses of vulgarity. The narrative co-existed in two centuries at once – Blake's own and the present day – and its characters included a version of King William IV who walked around always wearing his crown, a murderous soldier in khaki representing the mercenary throughout the ages, and in a pinstriped suit the Chairman of the Arts Council. One half of the evening was as shameless and vivid as a comic strip. Then every so often the stage was, as it were, cleared of the bustle of the world and Blake's own work – his words, his paintings and his fervent radicalism – were allowed to address us.

John took me one afternoon to confer with Jocelyn in her studio situated in a street on the less grand side of Holland Park Avenue. Both designer and director were in each other's debt, Jocelyn because John had given her her first play to design when he found her painting scenery backstage at the Royal Court, and John because she had been so central to his early successes and had helped to educate his eye. Her upper-middle-class breeding and apparent lack of the coarse ambition of most theatre people had a subduing effect on John, and in her presence he became almost gentle. What may also have united them was an appetite for fairly merciless gossip.

Once we started talking about the show it became apparent that what most interested them was the purer, Blakean side of the evening. However, I felt the dark satanic mills needed to be put firmly in place before we could attempt to build Jerusalem. Besides, as a theatrical exercise the dark satanic mills promised to be fun. There was one element in the show about which we were all agreed, and this was Mike Westbrook's brilliant score. Adrian had brought him along already attached to the project and he and his band would be in the pit performing throughout the run.

In the meantime we had to find actors to meet the needs of a musical. John and I held auditions and it was an opportunity to induct into the company talent that I'd had my eye on ever since I'd started directing. In a Howard Barker play upstairs at the Royal Court, I'd seen a brilliant young unknown, Maureen Lipman, playing not a comic role but an emotional one with real tears streaming down her young cheeks. Similarly, years before when I was a performer myself, I'd worked with Denis Quilley, already a star of the musical theatre but grossly overlooked as a straight actor. I was able to recruit them both and, together with the existing company members with whom I'd already established a strong bond in *The National Health*, they became the core of a troupe who the following year, when the National had retrenched to a single-theatre operation at the Vic, would give the organisation the most successful season in its ten-year history.

The way such companies come into being is as elusive as a precise explanation of why at any one moment we have the friends we do. Chance and sheer availability play their part, but so does temperamental affinity, and anyone who runs a theatre will be looking for actors who share a similar view about what constitutes good acting. In my case the things I was looking out for were behavioural accuracy, feeling uncorrupted by theatrical shaping and a nose for the comic possibilities that to a greater or lesser extent are always to be found in a well-written part just as they are in a real person. These attributes of observation, openness and humour would in a non-theatrical context have drawn me anyway towards one person rather than another, and a well-constituted company of actors is likely to be one where many things are held in common. The work of such companies can be as different as the individuals who lead them but, like a good football team, they all bring with them a working intimacy which is immediately recognisable and which provides a thread of continuity between one production and another. For audiences it provides the basis of a following. The British theatre in the aftermath of the fifties and sixties was rich in company work – at Joan Littlewood's Stratford East; with the pool of actors who worked at the Royal Court; at the RSC, particularly the group which was to reach its apotheosis in Trevor Nunn's brilliant production of *Nicholas Nickleby* in 1980 – and of course Olivier's own company during the National's early years. Now Larry's ideal of a true company had somehow got lost in the sheer scale of the operation, running two theatres on opposite sides of the river. One of my hopes was to help restore it.

Tyger got off to an inauspicious start. Because actors rarely left the theatre much before eleven o'clock at night it was customary at the National never to rehearse the following day before eleven in the morning. However, the first day's rehearsal of *Tyger* was on a Monday after a day off, so John decided to begin half an hour earlier, at ten-thirty. He informed the stage management, who duly informed the company but neglected to tell me. I turned up to work mid-morning and opened the door on a rehearsal that had already begun. Fifty-odd people were sitting in a rough semi-circle while John stood in front of them, holding forth. All faces in the room turned to me. Various explanations, apologies and awkward jokes followed, and eventually the room recovered its sense of purpose. I don't think for a moment that John had arranged this deliberately, but it was symptomatic of the way I was to find myself wrong-footed throughout the weeks of rehearsal.

My co-director had already done a musical, on Broadway no less, a Richard Rodgers show which opened and closed within days (not unsurprisingly given that the subject was suicide). However, it represented experience which I hadn't yet had, and we therefore agreed that John and our choreographer should start on the big musical numbers in the main rehearsal room while I went to a church hall five minutes' walk away and rehearsed the book scenes. This seemed a sensible division of labour and, with the author present and beaming his enthusiasm, we soon settled down and began to enjoy ourselves. I was particularly pleased with a scene in which Adrian had attacked consumerism. It was set in one of the new supermarkets which were just beginning to take hold all over the country, and the customers, having ransacked the shelves, were queuing up at the checkout pushing and shoving to make off with their booty. I'd staged it in such a way that they seemed to be humping their laden trolleys, and though gross, this was funny and emphatically made the point. Adrian loved it.

Midway through the second week John decided to call a run-through of the first half. I am of the view that a run-through serves no purpose unless the actors can emerge from the experience with their confidence in the show and in themselves enhanced. In this instance the book scenes, far less time-consuming to rehearse than the sections that involved dance and music, were in good shape, so I made no objections, but it made for an uncomfortable afternoon. The scenes worked, the numbers were extremely ragged. Afterwards John complimented me on the work I'd done and we continued to rehearse as before. However, a bridge was being built from both sides of a river in the hope that the two structures would meet in the middle but the silhouette remained obstinately lopsided.

John soon came up with another suggestion. The two halves of the show needed a unifying overview, so he proposed that he absent himself from rehearsals for an entire week to leave me free to impose my own shape on the material, then the following week it would be my turn to go away, leaving him in overall charge.

The idea had an immediate appeal to me because of the work waiting to be done in casting and preparing *Long Day's Journey*, and I could make good use of this extra time. Once again I said yes, but without really thinking it through. I hadn't seen that the end of my week's absence would coincide with the beginning of dress rehearsals, and artistically the production would belong to the director who had last got his hands on it. This proved to be exactly the case. I rejoined the project to find the musical numbers in much better shape but not so the book. John had done some editorial work on it, moving scenes around, to my mind pointlessly, and radically redirecting most of them. I was particularly dismayed by what had happened to the supermarket scene. Its whole tone had changed, but I couldn't recall with any precision what we had done that had made it so different. The comedy had gone out of it and taken with it the belief of the actors.

The interpretation even of the most brilliant director can never represent the only possible way a play can be staged, except of course to the director himself, who has no choice but to work within the limitations of his own strengths and weaknesses. Like a piano tuner, he is listening constantly for what he subjectively considers to be a right or a wrong note, and any other sound, even a melodious one, is likely to feel discordant. So the distress I felt one afternoon watching *Tyger* at a dress rehearsal is probably not an accurate reflection of John's work, for this is what the production had largely become; but all I could see on stage were elements that no longer worked.

Not all of these miscalculations were John's. A scene I'd directed which remained largely unchanged took place at the Arts Council (or an organisation it closely resembled) with three dignitaries awaiting the arrival of William Blake, come to petition for a grant. One of them bore a suspicious resemblance to the Chairman of the Arts Council, Lord Goodman, and when the lights came up on the scene all three of them were asleep behind their desks and snoring, doubtless after a good lunch at the club. It was common knowledge that Arnold Goodman, one of the most brilliant fixers in the British establishment, a man who seemed to have influence in every aspect of the national life, was *never asleep at his desk*, and it was juvenile to suggest otherwise. Indeed, his alertness, both for good and ill, would play an important part in my own fortunes over the next year, and even as we were poking fun at him on stage at the New he was secretly laying plans which would dictate the destiny of the National Theatre.

That afternoon for technical reasons we broke early, intending to resume after dinner at seven and work through till eleven or twelve. With three hours on my hands and utterly drained, I wondered where I could find somewhere to snatch half an hour's sleep before the evening session. The only safe place I could think of was ten minutes' walk away, backstage at the Apollo Theatre where *Forget-Me-Not Lane* was still running. The stage doorman gave me a key to a dressing room with a couch in it and I had just stretched out when I remembered that we were expecting to hear back from an actor about a role in *Long Day's Journey*. The dressing room had a telephone in it and I stared at it for a long time before reluctantly picking it up. On the other end of the line Larry sounded edgy and suspicious. No, he told me, they hadn't heard anything yet. 'But where are you, boysie? Shouldn't you be dress-rehearsing?' I explained we'd had to break early but didn't inform him where I was or what I was intending to do. Somehow I was convinced that he'd guessed, and not only that, didn't much like it. 'If you're free at the moment would you mind coming back to the office? There are so many things to discuss.' 'Right now?' I asked, regretting I'd ever picked up the telephone. 'Yes, right now! There are a million things that need attention!'

I dragged myself back to Aquinas Street. He was leaning out of the window of his office, apparently waiting for me. At my approach his features assumed an expression of contentment, like one of the big cats just after it's dispatched some leaping creature and eaten it. We chatted about this and that, him inside the building, me outside, and he couldn't have been more pleasant. I waited for him to explain the urgent matters that had necessitated my trip across the river. However, it soon became clear that there was nothing whatever to talk about. This was Larry at his most exasperating. He ruled over his domain with the unpredictability of a monarch. Most of the time he gave his ministers their heads, but every so often, and usually when you least expected it, he demanded the bent knee. This I had just given him and I was now at liberty to return to my dress rehearsal.

Tyger went uneasily into previews. Some people liked it, most were less sure. An important member of the Board, the West End impresario Binkie Beaumont, was at an early performance and was particularly affronted by Adrian Mitchell's politics. He complained to Larry, who called an urgent meeting with me and John the following morning at the theatre. 'Binkie says the show is positively seditious,' he said, and I was so tired and exasperated that I immediately leapt to an aggressive defence of a political position that I wasn't sure I shared.

'You're treating us like children, Larry,' I said. 'But we're older than you were when you made your *Henry V* film. Would you have tolerated interference from J. Arthur Rank? We all read *Tyger*. We all liked it. Let's stick to our guns!' He looked back at me, wounded and angry, and I wondered why on earth I was yelling. John Dexter had remained very subdued throughout.

That night outside the theatre John took me to one side and started referring to himself in the third person so I knew something unpleasant was on the way. 'John's got something very difficult to say and it may mean the end of our working relationship. But John's got to say it. The supermarket scene – it's just not working. I think we should cut it.' My protective instincts alerted, on this occasion I remained super cool. 'I've got a few ideas. Give me some rehearsal time tomorrow afternoon, then we'll see how it goes tomorrow night. We can make a decision after the show.'

I spent much of the night wide awake trying to locate the ideas I'd laid claim to, and finally arrived at what I thought might be a better conclusion to the scene. The following afternoon I gathered with the cast and we managed to restore some of the lost laughs, as well as adding the new ending. The greedy customers now turned on William Blake, shoved him into a shopping trolley and put a price tag round his neck. John conceded the scene improved and it stayed in. I was gratified later when one of our more favourable reviews singled it out for praise.

However, there was still much that was not quite right about the show, including an invention of John and Jocelyn's which I much admired and had great hopes for. They had imagined an ending in which the entire cast, singing Blake's words in one of Mike Westbrook's uplifting settings, quietly brought on stage all the physical components of the set – the chairs, the tables, the desks and so on – and began constructing a mountain centre stage. Behind them on giant screens Blake's paintings came and went, evoking the building of Jerusalem. Finally, the mountain now in place, a small child was lifted to its apex and stood there with arms raised towards the images.

Had this finale been staged at the Roundhouse or the Young Vic it might have been spectacular and moving. Within the formal confines of a West End theatre it looked indulgently poetic. Adrian's freewheeling radical show deserved something better than we had been able to give it. We should have seen that it could never have survived the contradictions of its staging, an attack on the existing state propped up by a huge state subsidy. I regretted that we had disappointed Adrian and made Ken's position as the play's champion more precarious than it already was.

At the National we had another flop on our hands and our losing streak was not over. The next show into the New was Büchner's *Danton's Death*, another of those vigorous texts to which theatre people are habitually drawn but which in performance never quite becomes a play. It was given an interesting production by Jonathan Miller, and the part of Danton, the last role specified in his contract, was played splendidly by Christopher Plummer. However, audiences stayed away and our deficit continued to soar. Christopher called it quits and returned to North America where he resumed the successful career we had so conspicuously been unable to foster.

THREE

Tyger had opened in July and I wouldn't be rehearsing the Eugene O'Neill play until October. There was time for a holiday, which I had never needed more. Peter and Thelma Nichols had offered us a week staying with them at their newly acquired house in south-west France, and my wife Shirley had had the bright idea of extending our own holiday by going on to nearby Biarritz on the Bay of Biscay. At the last minute she had located an up-market package deal based at the Plaza, an imposing hotel overlooking the main beach. Because the exchange rate then favoured the pound, it would be luxury at a bargain price. Biarritz was a town I had visited as a hitch-hiking student twenty years before, and it had made such an impression on me that I had determined, one day, to return. Now I would be able to introduce our ten-year-old son Conrad to what had most coloured my own childhood and I had never stopped missing in London – living beside an ocean. Putting the tumult at the National behind us, we set off.

The Nichols' farmhouse was an old single-storey building situated in extensive grounds, with to one side a large barn ripe for conversion into further living quarters. To the rear was a field with a pond. The English invasion of the Dordogne had just begun and the Nichols had acquired their house for a good price, though what may have been a factor was something undisclosed until after the purchase had been completed: during the war this had been the Gestapo headquarters for the region. However, the sounds of exuberant children will soon write a fresh chapter in the history of any house, and on the day of our arrival we shared in the pleasure of the Nichols' three and our one in having the two families reunited on another holiday.

Peter had now written three hit stage plays in succession, two of which he had sold to the movies. His work was being performed all over the world and was collecting awards on such a regular basis that when one was passed over he reacted with piqued surprise. Two critics in their reviews of *The National Health* had compared him to Chekhov. The problem with believing your good reviews is that when the wind changes, as it must, you're obliged to take with equal seriousness your bad ones. I didn't begrudge Peter his success because he'd worked hard for it, and in any case as the director of his three plays I shared in it. In the newspapers our names were frequently twinned, something I accepted with a degree of complacency, but which I was beginning to realise he didn't. His labours over many years had taken him to the front rank of British dramatists and now he was determined to consolidate that position, but preferably unencumbered with indebtedness. Our professional relationship was now showing some of the tensions that, in a long affair, prefigure the beginning of the end.

The holiday began well. It was good to be once again in the company of the most amusing man I knew. Like his plays, Peter was *seriously* funny – that is to say the laughter he generated was always rooted in something he had observed or experienced and therefore seemed to have a purpose to it. Shirley and Thelma got along splendidly, and in the lush French summer had the leisure to enjoy the routines of the house and its kitchen. We would have long lunches outdoors, then take turns swinging in the hammock, while the kids in the care of an au pair gave exultant yelps somewhere off in the distance. Peter would soon be back at his desk to continue working on the play which became *Chez Nous*. Set in a French barn exactly like his own, it apparently described the sort of life we were presently living. I had always admired and rather envied the working habits of this dedicated writer, but now they carried a hint of self-importance and admonishment to those of us left idling beside the pond.

One sunny afternoon Thelma, Shirley and I decided to go for a long walk through the wooded country. We followed a leafy trail for an hour or so until suddenly it opened out to reveal a large pond of clear, sunlit water. The day was extremely hot and the pond offered a cool and delicious invitation. Shirley was the first to start taking off her clothes and was soon splashing about in the water. Thelma and I were not far behind. There was an undoubted charge of libidinous curiosity in stripping naked together, then wading cautiously into the transparent water not quite sure what it had in store for us – a leech or a slimy eel underfoot? There were no such surprises, and the event was as proper as Manet's famous painting of the naked picnickers. We returned home like children, exhilarated by an adventure but a little unsure to what extent it was transgressive. Should we come clean to Peter who had been labouring all afternoon on his play? Thelma confessed all before they went to bed that night. As his published diaries record, he was furious, less about what we'd actually done than that he'd been left out of it. He was particularly angry with me and for the next few days was barely civil. It would have been easier to sympathise with him if it had not been so funny – Peter obsessing like Othello over a swim. We all knew that had it not been him but someone else in a fierce and similar sulk, what merciless entertainment he would have made of it.

To change the subject, our host involved us in the evenings in solemn games of Scrabble. I've never much enjoyed games because they seem to imply that the company have run out of things to say to each other, and I further irritated Peter by not taking the Scrabble seriously enough, pretending I'd found words that clearly didn't exist. Shirley and I started going to bed a little earlier than usual; and, waiting to go to sleep in our as yet undecorated room, it was hard not to wonder what had once taken place within these bare, stained walls. When we set off for Biarritz it was not too soon. As Peter wrote in his diary about us and other guests that summer, 'It was good to have them here and good when they left.'

The Nichols had a hunger for the company of other people and a talent for attracting them because they could often be such wonderful company themselves. But their need to find things they liked about the people that gathered around them was soon followed by a matching need to identify things they didn't. Perhaps that's true of everyone, though in the interests of harmony most of us endeavour to put on hold the second of these requirements. Yet it had been a holiday with many good moments, a number of which Peter recorded with his cine-camera. Seeing these old films years later I was astonished not only by how we looked, but by how fast we moved, leaping in and out of chairs, moving back and forth in front of the house, with smiles breaking out and disappearing from our faces in seconds. We didn't think so at the time, but of course we were still quite young.

The Plaza hotel lived up to our expectations. It was a stylish art deco building with architectural details inside and out as intact as the day it was built. We had a room on the side with a view of the sea – provided you leant out of the window. This didn't matter because all we had to do was cross the road, go down some steps, and there was the ocean. Having arrived, this was the first thing we did, and I saw what I was hoping for – huge waves in long lines rolling towards the shore, then splitting open in a noisy avalanche of white. Out to sea the heads of body-surfers bobbed about waiting to catch a precipitous ride, while closer to shore where most of the bathers were gathered you could hear the fairground shrieks of terror and joy as a wave reared up and crashed on the sand.

Since my last visit twenty years earlier there was a new presence in the water: a select group of French board-riders sliding across the sides of the waves as if the ocean was their natural habitat. My Australian past rushed back to join hands with my European present, and I walked along the promenade with Shirley and Conrad, staring out to sea and recording everything I saw like a movie camera in one long all-seeing tracking shot. Shirley watched me watching with delighted amusement. I couldn't believe my luck. We had arrived at what was for me a perfect place and on a perfect day.

In 1971 Biarritz was no longer the fashionable resort it had been between the wars. Still popular with the French, it had lost the British to the Mediterranean, where two weeks at St Tropez would guarantee you constant sunshine and the certainty of a tan. In Biarritz if you are unlucky you can spend fourteen days with your umbrella up. Its best weather is incomparable, sunlight filtered by a haze from the ocean and the mountains, but heavy rain is not unusual and sometimes huge storms come in from the Atlantic or roll down from the Pyrenees bringing with them a fireworks display which sends domestic animals scurrying terrified under the bed. The thunder seems close enough to break the window panes and the lightning will illuminate an entire room. Before the skin-cancer scare such erratic weather patterns were not good for tourism but they were to bring long-term advantages to Biarritz, since it was not subject to the large-scale new developments that blighted so much of the Mediterranean during the sixties. Even today its intricate seafront of sweeping beaches, small coves and rocky promontories is one that Edward VII would recognise were he to set out on one of his bracing constitutionals of over a century ago.

I bought some swimming fins and every morning studied the surf to see what it offered. Just gazing at it was halfway to feeling fit. We swam every day, ate a prodigious lunch, and in the afternoon explored the town, by no means the prettiest in France but packed with architectural surprises and sudden vistas. The sea held the town tight in its grip, and down a steep street you would suddenly catch sight of the blue Atlantic looking so close that its waves might as well have been breaking in the town centre.

Like most tourists we dawdled outside the windows of the estate agents and this soon became an obsessive interest. Everything in France was so cheap! If John Dexter and Peter Nichols could risk it, why not me? I had a small inheritance in Australia of £10,000, at present in conventional investments that did no more than hold their value. Five years ago, when I'd been an actor never too sure of the next job, it would never have occurred to me to use this money to acquire something as risky, as superfluous, as a house in France. Now with a thriving new career it was something I could realistically consider. Almost uncannily things happened that seemed to be guiding us towards a purchase. Cashing travellers' cheques in Barclays Bank we met the English bank manager who explained how easily it could be done. He introduced us to the town's most reliable estate agent, whose wife was a dealer in English antique furniture, frequently visited London and spoke the language. The trail continued to an architect who had practised in South Africa and was a fluent English speaker.

One afternoon, through the window of a bus taking us to nearby St-Jean-de-Luz, Shirley spotted a wreck of a house with a sign outside bearing our estate agent's name. The following day we went to his office to make enquiries. He seemed vastly amused. The sheet of paper he handed us giving the house's specifications was a catalogue of warnings: the roof had to be replaced, the balconies were falling away from the house because they had been built without foundations, and the house itself was infested with termites and woodworm. However, what our eye had moved to was the figure at the bottom of the page, an asking price of 65,000 francs. We quickly did the maths. At fifteen francs to the pound this was under £5,000! Even in those days this was an astonishing figure – less than the Nichols had paid for their farmhouse, less than half the cost of Dexter's mill.

We asked if we could take a look. The house was on a street of shops and belonged to a clockmaker who had died some years before and whose now deserted shop had been built over half the front garden. On the masonry above the dusty plate-glass window, from which the paint had flaked and faded, you could just make out the words HORLOGERIE. His widow, now in her nineties, was failing in a nursing home in Bayonne, and their children, equal heirs under French law, wanted to make a quick sale so that after her death they'd have a sum of money to divide rather than a house to argue about. We entered the premises through the empty shop, now stripped of all signs of the clock-maker's trade except for a beautiful glass lampshade, green outside, white within, on an extendable brass arm which was clamped to his empty workbench. Such is the lunacy of coveting property that for a moment I wondered whether I wanted to buy the house to acquire the lamp. Beyond the shop were the two large ground-floor rooms in which the old couple had lived. The rest of the house – the two upper floors, all the rooms of which were shuttered – had earned the couple a little extra money as a primitive lodging house catering to the town's less affluent holiday-makers. You looked up at an ancient circular staircase which curved beneath a low ceiling to disappear into darkness, and ascending it was as disconcerting as climbing into a cave inhabited by bats. You reached an old wooden floor laid out in the antique manner – short lengths of wide boards meeting a narrow crosspiece. The planks, though worn into ridges and shallow declivities like a relief map and frequently wormy, were a match to the staircase and both were rather beautiful.

They were the only things that were. I had never been in such a weird interior. The stale air in the various rooms hung there in blocks as if undisturbed for a lifetime. Underneath the scattered fragments of furniture were little pyramids of woodworm dust and in the corner of one room some filthy pillows and bedding were curtained off behind material as flimsy and still as a spider's web. At the top of the next flight of stairs, and surrealistically exposed, was a porcelain lavatory in the bowl of which lay what can only be described as a period turd, circa 1936, crescent-shaped and mummified. We ventured towards the balconies which hung away from the wall of the building by a good six inches, and stepping on to them was like cautiously boarding a small boat. They were constructed entirely of timber in an elaborate *art moderne* design and someone had once been extremely proud of them. Now there was not a square inch of wood that was not worm-eaten and rotten.

A potential French purchaser with his wits about him would have taken one look at the house and run a mile. I was enthralled. The building had the mesmerising squalor of a novel by Emile Zola. It had many rooms and the price was ridiculous. With Conrad in tow, Shirley and I left the premises in a state of surreptitious excitement. Our new friend the architect went over the building and provided us for free with what amounted to a survey and a prospectus. The house could be restored for about £2,500. There was an additional expense. In Britain strict exchange controls still applied, and the Bank of England, whose permission had to be given before you could acquire property abroad, imposed a tax of 25 per cent on the purchase price. There wouldn't be much change left out of £10,000 but it was actually possible.

Our holiday was coming to an end. We asked the estate agent to give us a week to think about it. The moment we were back in England we realised there was nothing about which to think: we wanted the house! In those days it was much harder making and receiving calls to France, and I spent two anxious mornings hovering over the telephone. Eventually our offer was accepted with the proviso that we despatch the deposit at once. But this was impossible; getting permission from the Bank of England would take months. Criminal action was required. Shirley had an old money belt, and a day or two later I flew to Paris with wads of banknotes concealed under my shirt, located a branch of the right French bank, despatched the deposit to Biarritz and flew immediately back to London.

*

The casting of *Long Day's Journey* was falling into place. My hope was to find our actors from within the existing company, but Ken pressed for an all-star cast. For the mother, I'd had my way over the choice of Constance Cummings, who had joined the National for *Amphitryon 38* and had been appearing above the title for years in the West End, though mainly in sophisticated comedies. Married to the playwright and politician Benn Levy, Connie was an American who had lived in Britain for four decades. She was in her early sixties, still immensely attractive, and like the character she would be playing had been raised in very respectable circumstances in the Middle West. On the face of it she was perfect casting, but did she have the acting depths? I thought so because I had seen her years before, on tour in a play called *The Shrike*, playing the role of a woman bent on totally destroying her husband. We had also agreed that in the company there was an excellent candidate to play O'Neill's self-portrait, the younger son Edmund. This was Ronald Pickup who had already distinguished himself in leading roles. He was married to an American and had a comfortable grasp of the idiom.

This left the Irish maid, for whom there was already a candidate in the company, Jo Maxwell Muller, and the elder, wayward brother, Jamie – perhaps the most interesting part of all, at least in his extraordinary final scene. I was absolutely convinced that Denis Quilley could play it, but Ken and Larry, wary perhaps of Denis' associations with musical theatre, thought we could do better. A couple of young stars were approached, but swiftly turned us down. It seemed that the National was becoming a place that successful talent regarded with caution. Time was running out. Denis got the part, and *Long Day's Journey into Night* became a company show. This was good for morale and, if we could pull it off, even better for the integrity of the institution.

Before our first night the National had two other openings: *Danton's Death* at the New, and at the Old Vic *The Good-Natured Man*, a neglected comedy by Oliver Goldsmith which tended to be rediscovered and revived every thirty or forty years in the belief that it would prove to be another *She Stoops to Conquer*. However, it was a further example of Olivier's pertinent distinction between a good text and a good play. In this instance it was John Dexter's rediscovery, and in both the choice of play and his production he stumbled badly. This would be his last show at the National for over a year because he would soon be leaving us to take up a key position in New York with the Metropolitan Opera. He left behind a theatre sliding further into the red with a deficit now in excess of £100,000 and growing, at the time a serious amount of money. And there was further bad news. Once again the completion date of the new building was being delayed. Obviously a drastic change of direction was required. We would have to abandon our two-theatre policy and retrench back to the Old Vic, reducing the acting company by half. *Long Day's Journey* would be our last production at the New Theatre.

My energies were now focused on preparing for the production. As designer Olivier had proposed Michael Annals, someone I knew and liked and with whom I'd wanted to work ever since I'd seen his spectacular design for *The Royal Hunt of the Sun*. As with all Larry's suggestions, you were expected to take them seriously, though acting on them was never obligatory. In this case I was only too pleased to be able to do so. It would begin my collaboration with Olivier on a note of agreement. So one afternoon I visited Michael in his small flat, which also served as his studio, situated in a modern block at the top end of St Martin's Lane. In his sitting room two tilted drawing boards fought for space with a coffee table and a sofa. In these same confines we were to have innumerable meetings over the course of eleven years and nine productions, and this first encounter set the pattern for the rest. It began with a cup of strong black coffee and some tentative chat, then after our work was done ended with two stiff whiskies and some reckless gossip.

At our next meeting Michael presented me with a model that was a sort of visual equivalent of what he felt was the mood of the play: a sombre turn-of-the-century interior with a high ceiling and tall windows. However, I had envisaged something more neutral. In ordinary life there is more often a disconnect between our miseries or joys and the spaces within which we experience them. I remembered the old beach houses of my childhood, scattered along the east coast of Australia, timber structures on sandstone foundations, surrounded on three sides by shady verandas. They had happy associations for us children, mysterious and possibly darker ones for the adults whose eyes met a few feet above us. Occupied mainly in the summer, they had the same temporary feel and random furnishings about which Mary Tyrone complains in her Connecticut seaside home. Michael's next model incorporated these thoughts as well as some detailed touches of his own. It was now a space which looked pleasant enough when morning sunshine poured through the windows, but as light drained away over the passage of a single day could become the site of a tormented reckoning.

There had been an earlier production in London of *Long Day's Journey into Night* at the Globe Theatre in the fifties. The play had bowled me over but not particularly the performances, with, however, one extraordinary exception. This was Gwen Ffrangcon Davies as the mother. The actress had come to prominence in the thirties as one of the leading talents associated with John Gielgud's circle, and what distinguished her work was an exquisitely modulated voice – mellow vowel sounds with just a hint of a tremolo – something which you heard often in the precincts of a London theatre if nowhere else in the rest of Britain. It was the sort of acting to which my generation had developed some resistance. I was astonished, therefore, when she came on stage at the beginning of the play and within seconds made clear that she owned the part and would guide the audience through the four hours ahead without a single misjudgement. It was as if for the first time in her career she had been allowed to dip into her South African past. Her fellow actors, though celebrated and gifted, made implausible Americans – which in those days was true of most English actors. But Gwen Ffrangcon-Davies brought the New World on with her. And what exactly was this dimension that she had and her colleagues didn't? Was it perhaps no more than an awareness, a source of both hope and crippling disappointment, that outside every front door the land went on for ever. Her genteel accent and even the way she moved had a particularity that reminded me of my American grandmother. It was a faultless performance and probably the reason why Olivier had for so long resisted appearing in the play.

Yet now that I was studying the text closely I began to realise that the very excellence of her performance had skewed the production off course. At the final curtain Mary Tyrone stood there as the play's tragic heroine, the victim of her own doomed family. But I was beginning to realise that O'Neill had constructed a more deeply considered human equation, in which the interlocking weaknesses, betrayals and anguished attempts to love of the four members of the family were so scrupulously balanced that all were equally guilty and deserved equally of our pity. The length of the play, its apparent repetitions and often prosaic diction distracted attention from the extraordinary pains that had gone into its design. For *Long Day's Journey into Night*, though undoubtedly a great play, is also one written out of the modesty of old age. O'Neill here eschews the lofty ambition of his earlier work – to create new forms and to aspire to be a modern Euripides – and instead goes back to the idiom native to his own country's drama, an almost pedestrian realism. As Edmund, the aspiring writer in the family, confesses to his father: 'I couldn't touch what I tried to tell you just now. I just stammered. That's the best I'll ever do . . . Well, it will be faithful realism at least.' So unsure is O'Neill of his own eloquence that he has the two sons explain their feelings by quoting reams of lines from the pens of other men – poets like Dowson and Baudelaire who influenced O'Neill as a young man.

And yet in performance the play never seems verbose or rambling or remotely derivative. From the outset it seizes our attention and commands our respect because what lies under every scene and every line of dialogue is a stubborn, racked determination to tell the truth. The playwright certainly requires from his audience close attention and all the empathy they can muster, but otherwise no special attributes of education or intelligence are expected. To respond to *Long Day's Journey into Night* all anyone needs is the experience of being a member of a family, and it is this democracy of spirit, this accessibility, which marks it out as not only a great play but a great American one.

While I was doing my thinking, Larry was engaged in a far more onerous task, probably the most challenging of his career: getting his huge part off by heart. He was now sixty-four, a few months away from the exact the age of the character he was playing, and learning lines and retaining them often becomes a problem for older actors. In his case this was complicated by a crisis of confidence that had come out of nowhere during the run of *Othello*. He was now the most famous stage actor in the world and he suddenly buckled under the weight of expectation that this reputation had placed on him. The line of people who queued up all night with their sleeping bags outside the Old Vic in the hope of picking up a ticket in the morning, and whose presence would once have been a source of imperious satisfaction, now became a demand he wondered if he could meet. Some years later, playing Shylock in Jonathan Miller's production of *The Merchant of Venice*, he recovered his nerve, but having had the bad dream of standing on stage and being unable to speak he could never quite forget it. However, what had never deserted him were his habits of work and application, and when he took on a task he pursued it with obsessional determination. In the case of *Long Day's*

Journey one of his strategies to help him learn the lines ahead of rehearsals was to gather his fellow actors together for a series of readings of the entire play. Since the idea was that these readings should be uninterrupted I was a fairly redundant presence, but they proved useful in identifying and agreeing on certain cuts.

The first of these readings was decidedly uneasy. We were all nervous and Olivier, like the rest of the cast, was a long way from the performance he would eventually give. However, since everything he did had size, so did his present awkwardness. I was reminded of those occasions in his office at the end of a working day when he would produce a bottle of non-vintage champagne (his preferred tipple) from the fridge beside his desk and invite those present to join him. After a glass or two he would sometimes embark on some anecdote replete with impersonations and funny voices but with such excessive energy that you wanted to open a window. Those qualities of sinew and muscle that can kick a performance right to the back of a large auditorium so that everyone experiences much the same thing and which are essential to great stage acting can seem inappropriate and even embarrassing in more intimate spaces, where nuance and suggestion carry greater force. After the reading Denis Quilley said to me, with concern rather than criticism, 'Sir's American accent is a bit all-over-the-place, isn't it?' I think we were all a little taken aback by the clumsiness of his reading. He was like a man in a straitjacket vigorously trying to punch his way free. This was unusual. His reputation was for coming to rehearsals knowing exactly what he wanted to do. On the first day of *Othello* he had electrified the room by giving a reading as full-throttled as a finished performance.

Since there was nothing I could or was allowed to do during the four hours it took to read the play I was relieved when Olivier suggested I skip the last few readings. He was extremely sensitive to anyone he felt to be an audience, and I dreaded that I might betray my concern or indeed my restlessness with an accidental sigh or a tapping foot. I left them to it, drawing some comfort from the fact that rehearsals were still four or five weeks away.

However, as in one's schooldays when the approach of a new term, once remote, is suddenly upon you, so in no time we were days away from the first rehearsal. Within the organisation the necessity for a success had mounted in accord with what seemed the odds against it. My own principal anxiety was not only how to deal with Olivier, but how to make myself useful to him. I didn't sense any hostility from him but I knew in his eyes I had yet to prove myself fully, and what I suppose I feared most was a failure of my own self-confidence. Not only was he an actor who had achieved historical renown, he was also my employer, and any artistic authority I could lay claim to could come only with his permission. I wondered if attempting to direct him (or in the usage he preferred, 'produce him') would feel like a hollow impertinence. Moreover he would have certain expectations of me that I wouldn't be able to fulfil. He would expect me to arrive at rehearsals with my copy of the play inscribed with all the moves of the actors and probably the lighting cues as well. I'd thought about attempting this but had soon abandoned the idea. There were so many spatial possibilities that could only be tested when I was working with the actors and when, in Tyrone Guthrie's phrase, as 'the audience's representative', I could see them there in front of me.

A day or two before we were due to start, Peggy Gilson, Larry's secretary and a sweet woman devoted to her boss, who had a good supply of oil in her office to pour on troubled waters, apprehended me in the Aquinas Street corridor. 'Sir Laurence is very apologetic,' she said. 'But he can't be with you on the first day of rehearsals. There's an important meeting he has to attend.' This made for an untidy beginning. The play is one in which each scene develops out of the one before, and to pick it up in the middle without a chance to digest what has already happened would be pretty much a waste of time. I saw my concern mirrored in Peggy's sympathetic expression. 'It's okay,' I said. 'There's some stuff with the two brothers I can do.' I duly prepared a scene later in the play which until then I hadn't anticipated getting round to for some weeks.

We were due to start rehearsing at two o'clock in the afternoon. That morning I saw that Larry was in his office and decided to pay my respects before he went off to his appointment. He was affable but edgy. 'We're not going to read, are we, Michael? Just start at the top and get the bugger on its feet.'

'But I thought you weren't going to be with us this afternoon?'

'What! Who told you that?!'

'Peggy said you had an appointment.'

He scowled at me, then bellowed through the closed door. 'PEGGY!' Peggy's office was on the other side of the corridor and she appeared at once. 'What's this about me not being free to rehearse?'

'You remember, Sir Laurence, you had an appointment this afternoon.'

'Yes, but I cancelled it! *We changed it!*'

'I know, I'm very sorry.' She turned to me. 'I'm sorry, Michael, I forgot to tell you. I'm very sorry.' Then she slipped back to her office, leaving the two of us looking at each other.

'It doesn't matter,' I said. 'I was going to do a scene with the boys but over the lunch hour I can have a look at the beginning.'

'You mean you haven't *prepared* it?'

'Of course I've prepared it! But it's a long play. I just need an hour to remind myself.'

He stared at me as if he was surrounded on all sides by incompetence, and there was nothing for it but to follow Peggy out of the door.

For the director the first day of rehearsals is his first night, his moment of truth, and the audience he has to win over consists of all the people he finds waiting for him in the rehearsal room, each of whom will make their particular contribution to bringing the show to the public – not only actors, but designers and a variety of technicians. He needs their trust and co-operation but he cannot take it for granted because there may be some present, particularly among the cast, who, when push comes to shove, have greater clout than he does. In the commercial theatre the prospects for a show are usually more dependent on the casting of its star than the appointment of its director. His authority is by consent, and earning it will require not only his guile and determination but more interesting qualities of empathy, focus and impartiality. Of all the people in the room he must be the one least concerned about himself and most absorbed in abetting the work of others. On the first day it will be his initial push that will get the caravan rolling, and it will be the director who suggests the rules of conduct that are to apply in the rehearsal room so that it becomes a place of trust and good humour to which actors go willingly in the morning and where they will feel free to drop their defences and take risks.

Most first days begin with a reading and frequently a long-winded address by a director as edgy as everyone else. However, in the case of *Long Day's Journey* we'd had our reading, in fact a number of them, and given the make-up of our cast I didn't feel inclined to expatiate on what the play meant. That hopefully would emerge in the course of rehearsing it. We gathered after lunch and I noticed at once that Larry's mood had improved. I guessed he must have had further words with Peggy and now accepted that the misunderstanding had been genuine. Denis Quilley and Ronnie Pickup were both rather sweetly deferential in the presence of Olivier, which I knew needed to change if they were truly to take charge of their parts.

Connie Cummings was the person in the room who had known Olivier longest, was herself a star, and consequently the least intimidated. While I was trying to explain the set to the cast she persisted in asking me the location of the staircase up which the mother so often makes the journey to assuage her morphine addiction. It was a reasonable question, though a theoretical one since the staircase was out of sight of the audience and was not part of the set. Had the model been in the room I would have been able to answer her question, but it had gone to the workshop and the set was indicated only by a ground-plan, marked out on the floor by stretches of coloured tape. Connie repeated her question, and staring at the criss-crossed lines beneath my feet I realised I was unable to answer her. I saw her seeing my embarrassment and I also saw the moment in which she gracefully let me off the hook and changed the subject. It was a double relief because it told me she had a good heart and would be pleasant to work with.

The play begins when James Tyrone and his wife Mary come into their living room after breakfast. They have an affectionate moment together in which we are allowed to glimpse the loving young couple they once were. Then both sit at the oval table that dominates the room, waiting for their two sons to join them from the dining room.

A few days prior to rehearsals John Dexter had given me a useful tip about how to handle Olivier. 'When he makes his first entrance,' he explained, 'he's a bit like an animal released into a new cage. He wants to sniff out the available space. Let him go for a bit of a roam. He likes to show the audience both sides of his face.' I thanked John for this interesting tip and didn't disbelieve him, but when the moment came to put it into practice my nerve failed. Larry and Connie had exchanged their first few speeches in a loose embrace; now they were to sit down. The father's rocker was barely a yard away from where Larry stood. It seemed absurd to suggest to him that he go wandering around the room for no reason. I asked him to sit down and he did so. However, some days later when we returned to the scene, he asked politely whether there could be a copy of the daily paper resting on the desk on the opposite side of the room. The stage management scuttled around to find the appropriate prop. During the next page of dialogue he crossed to the desk, picked up the paper, came downstage facing the audience, thumbed his way absently through its pages looking to left and right, crossed downstage the way he'd just come, deposited the paper on the window seat on the opposite side of the stage, then came to the table and sat in the rocker. I cursed myself for my earlier timidity, but I was also reassured that he had set about getting his way over this small matter with the utmost courtesy.

Neither then nor at any time during the rehearsal period did he ever make me feel challenged, because notwithstanding his unpredictability, his eccentric misjudgements, his occasional spitefulness, in important matters he had a grounded sense of the common good. In his eyes I was the producer and should be treated as such. This capacity to keep in his mind the larger picture would become most evident in the way he responded to the shabby manoeuvres surrounding his departure from the National, and which even as we were busy rehearsing, were already advanced. He was to feel monstrously betrayed, was to lose his health and almost his life, but nevertheless desisted from ever going public with his side of the story. The future of the National Theatre was more important that the mistreatment of any one individual. It was enough that he had been the key figure in bringing the National into being. Now it was the turn of others to take on what had become for him an almost impossible job. Let them get on with it.

In the rehearsal room the first long day became the second and then the third, and before long we were at the end of our first week. Something had happened that began as a stroke of luck but soon became a strategy. Whenever Olivier wasn't rehearsing he returned to his office down the corridor to attend to his workload as artistic director. The first time he left us the rehearsal room became a little like a class where the children have been temporarily left to their own devices. The atmosphere lightened.

It was not Larry's fault that he was an intimidating presence, but for the moment that's what he was, and work on the play became easier without him in rhe room. The other three principals knew the strength of their roles, had come well prepared and were hungry for further input. My job was suddenly less stressful. With Larry present I was monitoring my words too carefully so that some chance to intervene usefully would come and go before I had been able to act upon it. Now, like the cast, I could take risks, say whatever came into my head and not worry too much if later I had to qualify it.

A way forward became clear: I would work as closely as I could with Connie, Denis and Ronnie until their scenes were crackling with life, leave Larry pretty much alone, and hope that little by little he would join us of his own accord. This was soon happening. He would return from his office to find us absorbed in a scene, or perhaps discussing with conspiratorial relish some new possibility we had unearthed in the text. Out of the corner of my eye I would see him standing at one side, head raised, his curiosity ignited. He was extraordinarily sensitive to atmosphere, and could take the temperature of a rehearsal room the moment he entered it. He began to sniff that something was happening of which he was not yet part. I was still none too comfortable directing him in a two-handed scene because he seemed to have such a clear, and to my mind correct, idea of what he wanted to do that I felt almost redundant. But in scenes involving all four principals I was growing in confidence. Larry himself was well aware that such scenes can't be rehearsed around the impulses of just one of the participants and he now joined us as a team player. Moreover I knew that, having won the trust of his colleagues, anything I now said would have the support of three silent votes.

Because of the length of the play I had been given an extended rehearsal period, and this allowed us to concentrate for the first two weeks on the first of its four acts, in which the audience observe the family as their pasts begin to be disinterred in fragments from their present dialogue. From the start the play is never less than interesting, but towards the end of the first act there is a scene between the mother and the younger son when you feel a gear change to something more unsettling and profound. The play has cast its spell. Later, when the production was on its feet, it would be precisely at this same place that during every run-through and every performance I would feel the clamp of the story close around its audience. The only other time I've experienced something similar was in another great play, Ibsen's *The Wild Duck*, where, again after an expository beginning, there comes a moment in which the drama leaves the page entirely and is suddenly there as a presence occupying every corner of the space in which it is being performed. Perhaps it was at this point in the writing of both plays that the full shape of the projected work coalesced in the author's mind, but the experience is like watching some hibernating creature of alarming strength awaken from its sleep, open one slow eye and begin to stretch.

Before long the cast were rehearsing Act One without their scripts. In the way they spoke and listened, in the way the actors moved towards and around each other the rehearsals were beginning to achieve a rhythm absolutely specific to the awesome drama with which we'd been entrusted. One of the notices later described the production as 'steadily unfurling and furling again across the wide deep stage' and this is how it began to feel, as driven from within as the unfolding of some sombre bloom.

One day Larry proposed (though instructed might be a better word) that we invite his old Hollywood friend, the screenwriter and playwright Donald Ogden Stewart, to view what we'd achieved so far. An American, he suggested, could tell us whether our accents passed muster and whether we were on the right track. I suspected he also had a need to test himself early on against an audience. Donald Ogden Stewart was a member of that distinguished colony of US citizens who had taken up residence in London in flight from the witch-hunting of Senator McCarthy. He was now a man in his eighties, gentle and quite frail, but with eyes that had not lost their look of acute intelligence. We sat him down in one of those spindly chairs you find in rehearsal rooms, and suddenly we were off and running. The cast were very nervous, but clear and confident about what they were doing. Within a minute or two the play had come alive and by the end of the act was mesmeric. With no more words to say, the actors became silent and could now look shyly at the man towards whom their performances had been directed. He sat there quite still and then began nodding his head in vigorous appreciation. He praised each of the cast, then took me aside and told me at some length how well he thought the act had been orchestrated and moved. What gave us heart was not just being lauded but hearing the enthusiasm expressed in such an American way, without guile or ambiguity. Having our work endorsed by him was like a stamp of authenticity, and from then on rehearsals started to dance.

Up till now the reader may occasionally have wondered why anyone would want to spend their life in such a feverish and booby-trapped environment as the theatre. Here lies the answer. When a rehearsal period really begins to take off, when the work you are engaged on seems to have not only substance but a good chance of gaining wide public acceptance, there is no more enthralling activity. You set out for work in the morning high on anticipation (and always a little nervous because things can go wrong as well as right), wondering what the new day will bring. The director is like the leader of a benign conspiracy, undertaken behind closed doors, that the actors will soon be springing on an unsuspecting public, a Gunpowder Plot in which the instruments of change are not explosives but truthful utterance and passion. And there is often something less elevated about the exercise: the sheer mischief of wanting to poleaxe an audience

75

with emotion or render them helpless with laughter, having beforehand taken good money from their pockets. There is a sense of play, a disregard of everything except the work in hand that defines a good rehearsal, and something like glee when it yields results.

Not many rehearsal periods come into this category but for all of us *Long Day's Journey into Night* was undoubtedly one of them. More general concerns about the reputation of the National Theatre and our threatening deficit took second place to what was happening in the rehearsal room. This was where our world now was, and it would remain there until we brought our work out of hiding.

FOUR

It is often assumed that the subject matter of tragedy will cast a gloom over the process of rehearsing it, but the opposite is more often the case. Tragedy, which is essentially telling the truth, can be exhilarating. It is comedy that is more likely to induce anxiety and depression, because the attempt to be funny always awaits and depends on the verdict of an audience. Laughter was not our object in rehearsing *Long Day's Journey into Night* and so we were free to find things in it to laugh about, and surely this is no surprise given our ambivalence to the misfortunes of others. Sympathy and mockery sleep on opposite sides of the same bed, and especially for a director humour can be very useful in suggesting ways of playing a scene, the eventual performance of which will be anything but funny.

In any case there are few great tragedies, certainly in the English language, that do not have comedy built into them, and there was no actor better at sussing it out than Laurence Olivier. Every day he was coming to rehearsal with something new with which to embellish his performance. His accent was now splendidly judged, a resonant American but still Irish around the edges. One morning he turned up with a period haircut, short back and sides with a slightly off-centre parting. 'H. L Mencken?' I asked, recalling an old photograph, and he smiled enigmatically. He was also trying to incorporate the Barrymore walk into his performance, and when he was not rehearsing I would notice him practising it at the far end of the room. He told us he had sent to New York for a little medallion to attach to his watch chain. 'From the Lambs Club,' he explained. 'James Tyrone would have been a member'. The medallion never arrived so instead he asked for something else to attach to his watch chain, the key to the cellar door where Tyrone kept his whiskey – a detail that no member of the audience would even notice. But dangling across his waistcoat was another small thing to tell him who he was. However, all this was secondary to his work on the text, the marvel of which was waiting for me when we started work on the fourth act.

The other members of the cast were keeping level with him. To begin with Denis Quilley, possibly out of deference to his boss, had played the part of Jamie in accord with his father's description of him as a 'sneering wastrel'. Denis himself was a man of great geniality and I encouraged him to look for such qualities in the role, since sneers were unlikely to be the currency of the bars and whorehouses he was accused of frequenting. The poisoned cheerfulness he was soon bringing to his work carried him inexorably to the great scene with Edmund in which, drunk and grinning, he tells his younger brother that the love he keeps proclaiming for him has always come with an inner core of murderous hatred. It is perhaps the key scene in the play, and the most shocking, because O'Neill is here putting no single member of the family in the dock but instead life itself.

As the son who will one day write the play we are now watching, Ronnie Pickup would never have a better part. The American idiom seemed to centre him and as an actor give him new freedom. Even the long, somewhat overwritten speeches of alienation when Edmund tells his father about his days at sea became wry and true in his mouth: 'It was a great mistake my being born a man, I would have been much more successful being a seagull or a fish.' Watching his family constantly and seeing more than he wants to, longing to be elsewhere, his health under threat, Ronnie's Edmund was like a creature between skins, as exposed and without guile as the play itself.

And as for Constance Cummings as Mary Tyrone, no actress could have come to the part better equipped, a match to O'Neill's physical description of her: 'She still has a young, graceful figure, her face must once have been extremely pretty and it is still striking . . . Her most appealing quality is the simple, unaffected charm of a shy convent girl youthfulness – and innate unworldly innocence.' Constance's Mary was a conventional woman caught up in the worst possible nightmare for someone of her polite, mid-Western background – drug addiction. She still hungers desperately for the trappings and respectability of the life she has left behind her, to which her actor husband is indifferent, and she was quite unable to reconcile her own needs with those of her driven, talented family. Her suffering was not passive but to those around her dangerously active.

Connie was well regarded as an actress, but no one had dared believe that she had the emotional resources she was to demonstrate in this part, possibly because her own offstage personality was so sensible and good-humoured. These are qualities which any director will welcome in the rehearsal room and we soon developed a brisk, pleasurable shorthand with which to explore the part. She knew what a wonderful and surprising opportunity it was for her and worked ferociously. We would rehearse a scene, have a break while we exchanged some words about it, then once again I would see her own personality slide away as she returned to the torments of the very different sort of woman she was playing. It was acting at its best – immediate, unmannered and transparent.

One week slid into another and increasingly something very real, as silent as the approach of an iceberg, hove into view – the exposure of our work in front of hundreds of judging eyes. Whereas early in rehearsals Larry could ask for a prompt and not worry too much about it, now every stumble and hesitation carried an intimation of failure. He had become certain he could play the part, but could he remember it? The morning we arrived at Act Four he sat at the oval table opposite Ronnie Pickup with his script still in his hand. I'd already done some work alone with Ronnie on his big speeches and I knew he was 'off book', but

I noticed he still kept his script to hand, perhaps in solidarity with his fellow actor.

In the play it is now close to midnight. Edmund has returned home after a solitary walk through the fog which has drifted up from the harbour, and he and his father, their tongues loosened by alcohol and desperation, sit arguing over a bottle of whiskey and a desultory card game. The beginning of the scene resembles the preceding three acts, a circularity of regret and guilt in which the audience learn things which are already bitterly familiar to the characters on stage. Defending himself against Edmund's charge 'you stinking old miser', Tyrone launches into a vivid description of the wretched poverty of his childhood and then, encouraged by Edmund's sympathetic attention, he takes an unexpected turn to tell his son, and of course the audience, something which is new to both of them: how his great success in money-making (which in the case of Eugene O'Neill's actor father had been *The Count of Monte Cristo*) turned out to be the graveyard of his talent and his hopes of high achievement.

The scene is fairly static, the two men sitting at the oval table, and we decided to begin the rehearsal with a straight read-through. In the first production on Broadway the part of Tyrone had been played by Fredric March, a fine actor with whose work I was familiar from innumerable films, and I thought I had a pretty good idea of how he must have been in the role. Olivier's work I knew even better, but there is no way I could have anticipated how he was going to play the scene that morning. It was the most perfectly realised thirty minutes I have ever spent in a rehearsal room. He understood in his bones Tyrone's great speech about his high ambition as a young Shakespearean actor, and even with the book in his hand there was not a feeling, a moment unaccounted for, in the torrent of emotion he brought to it. All the gestures he would later use, the touches of invention, were in place. When Tyrone describes the occasion when the great star Edwin Booth praised his performance – 'That young man is playing Othello better than I ever did' – Larry particularised it by becoming momentarily Edwin Booth himself as he points significantly somewhere offstage where *Othello* is being performed and throws the remark back over his shoulder to the stage manager. It made the moment touching, a little absurd and vividly specific.

Yet all this was in miniature, an organised expression of teeming thoughts and impulses with his voice barely raised and his eyes still on the script. Even as I watched I said to myself that if we succeeded, if one day the production was filmed, this was how I would try to persuade Larry to play it. I knew where he would shortly take the performance. Once an audience was present he would add to it the thrilling power of his voice ringing around the auditorium, and a thousand people would hold their breath. It would be amazing. But an equal wonder was what was in front of me now – the genesis of that public event. I was watching the culmination of a lifetime of work and aspiration to which that everyday definition of genius applied, 'the infinite capacity to take pains', as well as definitions more unfathomable. And it seemed brutally cruel that such a gift enriched over a lifetime should now be threatened by something as mundane as a little trouble remembering.

In the first three acts Olivier had been giving an excellent performance, though perhaps not a perfect one. There was a scene with his wife when he seemed to be striving for a sympathy which I wasn't sure was there in the text. His fourth act however was on a plane that made direction or comment an irrelevance. It was a plane only he could reach and reach unaided. And from role to role it was touch and go if a part would allow him to make that ascent, but the attempt was what drove him. I began to understand his suspicion of directors, who could muddle and confuse the instinct which was his true guide. In moments of great acting it is not only the part that is being played but something that runs parallel to it. The mist clears and for a moment a second mountain range is perceived behind the first. The

81

audience sees the play and just beyond it the human essence of the person who is performing. When Olivier in one of his great roles reached such a moment it was like watching something in nature about which nothing more important can be said than that it is happening: a huge tree falls in a forest or an eagle rises up with its prey in its talons. You watch and are simply glad that you are there. This can occur only in moments, and it is always the text itself which prepares for them, but when it happens there is no doubting it. Coleridge described Edmund Kean's acting as like 'reading Shakespeare by flashes of lightning'. Not many actors in my lifetime have given me this glimpse into the depths of their personalities, but onstage Laurence Olivier was certainly one, and in movies a couple of times Marlon Brando.

There were of course less elevated components in an Olivier performance – strategic cunning and an appetite for conquest – and like any seducer he had his techniques and tricks. However he usually became weary of them well in advance of the audience he so assiduously wooed. Always on the lookout for a fresh way to go, he had made a spectacular break with his own illustrious past as a classical actor when he joined the Royal Court to appear as a faded music-hall artist in *The Entertainer*. Now attempting one of the great roles in American drama he would experience a similar freedom, and was able to put on hold the trade-mark delivery and rhetorical devices with which he was usually associated. In the last years of his career he would mine this new seam of American parts in any number of films and television plays.

So for an actor in his mid-sixties *Long Day's Journey* was yet another new beginning, another grenade to lob into the midst of those people in the audience (and indeed on the Board of the National Theatre) who thought they had his measure. This capacity for self-renewal, to turn adversity on its head, was one of the most extraordinary things about him, and added to the growing excitement and anticipation within the rehearsal room which we hardly dared express, so superstitious did we feel about it.

82

Something important, for all of us, for the National Theatre, was at stake but we couldn't take it for granted. Perhaps this was why at the end of that morning's rehearsal when I rose to express my admiration for what I had just seen, I hesitated to say what was at the forefront of my mind: that if we were ever given the chance to film our work he should play the scene just as he did that morning – forget projection and stage size and go back to the thoughts. Instead so hesitant was I about anticipating success that I kept this advice to myself, and have regretted it ever since, because the television special of the following year in which I was only peripherally involved, though an adequate record of stage acting, is a huge departure from the production on stage in detail and spirit.

And so we arrived at the last week of rehearsals. The performances were in place and only waited on the presence of an audience. Larry now had a grip on his lines, but still obsessively ran those parts of the play about which he felt unsure, particularly in that mammoth fourth act. Watching him, I had to remain completely still, since if I made the slightest movement – shifted in my seat or crossed my legs – it would deflect his attention, the lines would go and he would shout for a prompt. The fact that he had now achieved his performance, that rehearsals had gone supremely well, that the word was already out that the National was about to return to form, didn't seem to comfort him at all. There were whispers in the Press Office that people were coming over from New York for the first night. At the centre of this gathering whirlwind of anticipation, not all of it benign, was a man who increasingly was wondering who he actually was. His reputation and his past successes as the most famous stage actor in the world were real to others but no longer to him. How could he possibly match up to what was expected of him?

He was no longer travelling up and down to Brighton each day, but was staying by himself in the London flat while Joan remained behind with the children. A couple of times that last week, sensing that he didn't want to be left on his own at the end of the day's work, I kept him company in the evenings. One night we went to the Aldwych to see the new Pinter play, *Old Times*, and afterwards visited Colin Blakely in his dressing room. The work of others now intimidated him and he sat there meekly, nursing a glass of champagne and not saying much, as if he and Colin had somehow changed places. Afterwards I had supper with him at his flat, and he talked about the Old Vic before the war. There had been a famous production by Tyrone Guthrie of *A Midsummer Night's Dream*, in which Vivien Leigh had played Titania opposite Robert Helpmann's Oberon.

'When Bobbie pointed to Vivien on the line "Tarry, rash wanton. Am not I thy lord?" he managed to bend his index figure back in a great curve,' he said pushing his own index finger upward to demonstrate. Then he lapsed into a moment of gloomy silence. 'I could never do that,' he murmured.

At the end of the last day of rehearsals I took the company to the Donmar Warehouse where the Production Office had assembled Michael Annals' set so that the cast would have the opportunity of familiarising themselves with it before they were actually onstage. The Donmar had not yet been converted into a theatre but was simply a large, bare rehearsal room. We approached it up a long flight of concrete stairs, entered through a small door and were suddenly in this enormous, unadorned space in which the set had been assembled at the far end. At first sight it had the misplaced reality of something left behind in the corner of a movie studio. After the imagined walls and insubstantial rooms in which we had been rehearsing, the set had a sobering actuality – as real, in fact, as the audience we would be confronting the following week. I encouraged the cast to walk around and explore their new (and for the moment somewhat chilly) home, and they concealed their unease by opening and closing the folding doors, raising the sash windows and trying out the various chairs. Since we had half an hour at our disposal I suggested we run the first few minutes of the play.

The production opened on an empty set with, offstage, the distant voices of the family as they conclude breakfast in the dining room. The cast took up their places just out of sight. 'Curtain up,' I said in the tactful and encouraging tone employed by movie directors when they say 'Action'. Larry and Constance made their entrance from the dining room and launched into their first scene of marital affection. It swung nicely through two or three exchanges and then abruptly stopped. Larry had dried. 'What's the line?!' he asked, with subdued but unmistakeable agitation. I quickly intervened – 'No, let's go back to the top and make a fresh start.' This time my 'Curtain up' was so tactful as to be barely audible. The scene began with fresh vigour and then at exactly the same spot came to a halt. I asked the stage manager, Jason Barnes, who was on the book, to show Sir Laurence exactly where on the page he had tripped up. We started again, and again the play dropped into a pit of silence.

We were forty-five seconds into a four-hour evening. By this time there wasn't a face in the room that wasn't frozen with concern; an unthinkable possibility had reared up in all our minds. Larry made two more attempts and failed at both. After the last one he looked at me with a weak, grey smile and said, 'That's funny, I've got stage fright.' I hastened to reassure him. 'We're here to see the set, not rehearse. It's been a long day, so let's break now and when we next meet it'll be onstage at the New Theatre – our proper home.' The rest of the cast nodded briskly as if this was an extremely good idea and clearly the way forward. Being careful to include Larry, they chatted cheerfully among themselves as they collected their belongings. Then the company dispersed and the room emptied, leaving all of us to spend the evening with our own particular demons.

Technical dress rehearsals are usually tedious, but a little tedium was exactly what the company now required. It looked as if Larry had recovered his nerve, and he got through his first scene with little help from the prompter. I hoped the moment of nightmare was behind us. Nevertheless I felt I had to have a private word with the other three principals before the day was over. I managed to catch each of them separately with the proposal that we meet during the dinner break at a pub round the corner when Larry would probably be resting. At the appointed time the actors came into the bar, somewhat wide-eyed with curiosity but with a pretty good idea what it was I wanted to discuss. We settled into a quiet corner, ordered our drinks, and I said something very like this: 'I know you're all very concerned about Larry. So am I. That incident at the Donmar was very alarming for all of us and I know you want to offer him all the support you can. But the truth of the matter is the only person who can help Larry is Larry himself. He knows it, and so should you. You can't remember his lines for him or take on any of his fears. So what I strongly advise is this. Attend to your own performances. Protect your own territory. Because my hunch is that he's going to be all right. More than all right. His anxieties at the moment are absolutely genuine but what he's doing, even if he's not aware of it, is digging himself into a hole out of which on the first night he'll rise up like a rocket. And if you're not careful you'll be left behind on the sidelines with your mouths open. So first and foremost attend to your own work.'

This appeal to their enlightened self-interest was the best possible note I could have given them, because, of course, on the first night that's exactly what happened. However, what made the evening particularly thrilling was that between the four actors the ball was passed back and forth with hardly a fumble, and when each had their chance to run with it, they took it.

At the last dress rehearsal, a straight run prior to the first preview, I noticed a figure sitting to the rear of the stalls with a notepad. It was Ken Tynan. Afterwards I went up to greet him and found him mopping his eyes with a handkerchief. He couldn't have paid me a more sincere compliment because what made Ken cry in the theatre was not the sadness of the subject matter but the skill with which it was realised. Provided it matched his standard of a 'High Definition Performance', he could be brought to tears not only by a tragedy but by a farce, by a solo comedian, by a team of acrobats. They were not easy tears to induce, but it was this genuineness of emotion that had made him such an exceptional critic, and as I was beginning to learn (and rather to my surprise) such a loyal friend. He went on to say that he had some notes for me, and I was at first uneasy because I assumed they would deal with points of interpretation or tone, things which it would be difficult, even if I agreed with them, to implement at this stage. When I studied the list, however, the notes were all extremely practical and stage-savvy, and I was happy to act on almost all of them. They suggested what a director Ken might have become if he'd been allowed to.

The following night I went backstage with my fingers crossed to offer my best wishes for the first preview. When I knocked on Larry's door his 'Come in!' was so strident that I knew something was seriously wrong. As I entered he was waving a letter over his head as distressed and angry as I had ever seen him. 'How can the man call himself an artist and send me this?!' he protested. 'Tonight of all nights just before I have to go on!' The letter was from Ken and, given the contents, the timing was indeed in-explicable. For weeks now Olivier had been preparing for the most nerve-racking appearance of his career and of necessity had put his administrative responsibilities to one side. Now someone had just dumped all his worries about the institution back in his lap. Ken's letter began by pedantically reassigning the blame for the recent string of flops away from himself and in Larry's direction; then went on to complain about the quality of the acting company. Larry was furious, and distressed energy was pouring out of him like a hot tap which someone has wilfully left running. Would there be anything left for the performance? I calmed him down as best I could, then set out for the front of house with dread. What lay ahead of us?

I remember exactly where my seat was that night – on the aisle, auditorium right in Row J. At Larry's request we'd had a complete run of the play in the afternoon and it had gone smoothly, but now we weren't in an empty theatre but one rapidly filling with hundreds of people – chattering, locating their seats, undoing their coats and wholly preoccupied with their own concerns. Would they be prepared to put their lives on hold and give themselves over to our play for the next four hours? The curtain rose and to begin with it seemed unlikely. They were a restless house, and judging by the winter coughing, a diseased one. It didn't help that the cast were over-energising their performances, particularly Larry, who began by throwing himself physically into the role as if this was the only way he could maintain his grasp on the text. Then, unexpectedly, the house became quiet and attentive. We had arrived at the scene between Edmund and his mother and beneath the dialogue the play began to uncoil. The actors were now in charge and like horses on the homeward journey they knew it. The evening moved inexorably to a superbly played fourth act and to applause like a dam breaking. We were going to be all right.

After the show I found Ken in the auditorium as the audience were filing out. 'Larry get my letter?' he enquired in a surreptitious aside, and I asked him why he had chosen that particular moment to send it. 'He was upset?'

'Very.'

Ken looked downcast. 'It was just that I knew he'd be totally vulnerable at that moment and I thought my letter would have a better chance of making an impression.'

This was Ken at his silliest and most self-destructive. He was a romantic who longed to show those who opposed him that he could also be as much the worldly and effective schemer as they were. But his strategies always backfired and at the end of his life were to leave him deserted and broke. Olivier, whom Ken loved and revered, would never forgive him for this and other mis-judgements, and by the end had rejected him entirely.

Theatre is something which happens right in front of you and in real time, and it is perhaps irrelevant to try and pin it down on the page afterwards. Even a filmed record will over time lose any connection to what an audience had once experienced in a theatre. Just before the start of rehearsals I'd been tipped off that a print existed of the silent movie version of *The Count of Monte Cristo* – the production that Eugene O'Neill's actor father had toured for many years, and that in *Long Day's Journey into Night* becomes both the source of the family's prosperity and the blight that puts an end to the father's artistic ambitions. A special screening was arranged for the company at the National Film Theatre. Up there in that flickering rectangle of light was the great star, James O'Neill himself, now well into middle age, and in a supporting role, his elder son, the man on whom Denis Quilley's part was based. As we watched it was almost impossible to believe that this coarsely acted and crudely staged production could ever have been the long-lasting success it apparently was. We left the cinema glad to have seen it but in sober mood. Did all theatre work follow a similar trajectory?

Nevertheless, simply as a way of showing how a production evolves, let me describe in some detail the work we did on two scenes, one at the very beginning of the play and the other at the very end. When the curtain rises I had asked the lighting designer, Robert Bryan, to flood the set with fresh morning sunshine, so that the rather bare room in which the action is to take place had a comfortable, even attractive look. Offstage we hear the good-natured murmur of the family rising from the breakfast table, then James and Mary make their entrance. Both are affectionate and attentive to each other and project a mood of optimism.

There are punctuations of unease in the scene but for the moment they are the sort of thing which would not be unusual in any long-standing marriage, and their significance will not become clear until later in the play. In the dining room we hear the boys laughing loudly as their mother calls them in to join their parents in the living room.

There follows a scene of good-natured mockery typical of most families when parents and children are together. Jamie teases his father about his snoring, and there are fragments of a recurrent squabble between Edmund and his father about his socialist opinions. Again there are moments of an unease which we are not yet in a position to interpret. The mother asks the boys what had so amused them when they were in the dining room, and Edmund embarks on a long story about a recent dispute between a cunning Irish farmer of their acquaintance and his neighbour, an oil tycoon, whose estate abuts the farm. The story is not important to the play, indeed it is never mentioned again, but as local gossip it is of absorbing interest and amusement to those onstage, especially since the tycoon and the farmer are at opposite ends of a rigid social spectrum in which this theatrical family has never managed to establish a secure place.

The scene between the quartet was diligently rehearsed, indeed drilled, so that the actors could communicate with each other in the shorthand of family life. I encouraged them to look for the things that amused them, both as individuals and as a group, and to respond to what was being said not at the end of a sentence, but the moment they had grasped its meaning. This genial battle for conversational space, with its overlaps and sudden bursts of laughter, presented the audience with a family much like any other, one they could readily identify with. It also gave them a scene early on of unexpected energy and humour, which put to rest at once any idea they were in for a turgid evening. It would still be a long day's journey, but at least it was beginning in the fresh light of morning.

When the play ends it is well past midnight. The three men, exhausted by drink and confession, are spaced about the living room in the semi-darkness like gutted animals. Over their heads the addicted mother moves around the upstairs rooms rummaging among her belongings for trophies of her lost youth. She has been offstage for the entire fourth act. The men are suddenly alerted by her footsteps as she starts to come downstairs. O'Neill has meticulously prepared for this moment, drip-feeding the audience little by little with the information that will give it power. It is one of the most extraordinary moments of theatre in twentieth-century drama, and the most honestly earned, and it is achieved simply by someone turning on an electric light.

I need to digress for a moment to describe our set in a little more detail. It consisted of a living room beyond which, through folding doors, was a more formal space with a suite of furniture and a piano. The position of the four folding doors was slightly different for each scene. In the last act only one of the panels was open and the piano was out of sight. Michael Annals had supplied a wonderful detail to his design. Above the folding doors was a fanlight of fretworked wood. When the light was turned on by someone whom we cannot yet see but can only be the mother, the pattern of the fanlight reared up out of the darkness and a column of light spilled into the room through the one open panel. In performance, both onstage and in the auditorium, there was a silence so dense with anticipation that you felt you could slice it.

Then suddenly, out of sight, we hear the piano being played, a clumsy, childish attempt at a Chopin waltz. I'd insisted on live music, preferably played on a piano that needed tuning, and we'd engaged the vocal coach, Chuck Mallett, to supply it, which he did with great skill, mimicking the arthritic fingers which were meant to be doing the playing. The music abruptly stops and the audience's anticipation is now informed by misgiving. The mother, holding her wedding dress over one arm, steps into the open panel of light. Connie looked exactly as O'Neill describes her: 'The uncanny thing is that her face appears so youthful. It is a marble mask of girlish innocence.' Lost in the past and oblivious of her family she begins to recount her life as a young girl in the care of the nuns at her convent. She drifts across the room not addressing but by turns in the proximity of each member of her family. Finally I had her arrive stage right beside the rocking chair, which in the previous scene had been displaced from its usual position close by the oval table and now stood isolated some yards away. As Mary recalls her girlish vocation to be a nun she sinks into the rocker, facing the audience.

The last words of the play are: 'That was in the winter of senior year. Then in the spring something happened to me. Yes, I remember. I fell in love with James Tyrone and was so happy for a time.' I had suggested to Connie that after the line, 'Then in the spring something happened to me,' she begin rocking back and forth as she tries to puzzle her way back to what that something was. Then on the line, 'Yes, I remember,' she stops rocking and, in a desolate stillness, as if it were simply a matter of fact, says her last sentence. In the rehearsal room we worked with an improvised rocker knocked up by the props department out of an old wooden armchair. This was replaced in the final week with the actual piece of furniture we would be using onstage. We ran the scene with the new rocker and unaccountably it seemed to have less power.

For a while I had no idea why. Connie's performance had not altered by a jot. Then suddenly it occurred to me. The improvised rocking chair we had been using for six weeks had creaked and in that little pocket of silence in which Mary had rocked back and forth trying to remember, the creak was a distinct presence. It was not a calculated effect like a ticking clock but a detail which had come out of the ordinary reality of the rehearsal room and then insinuated itself into the fiction we were trying to create. It existed in two worlds at once, at that interface where theatre comes into existence. It was a tiny thing and the reasons why it was so potent are really beyond explanation because it was something of which a member of the audience would hardly have been aware, just as in the rehearsal room we had not noticed it for all of six weeks. But its potency was undeniable.

Thereafter, once we were in the theatre I asked one of our stage management to sit in the rehearsal rocker a few yards away from Connie but out of sight in the wings, and synchronise her swings back and forth with the rocker onstage. So quiet and attentive was our audience that the creak, though almost subliminal, reached every corner of the auditorium. As Mary abruptly stopped rocking the last line of the play was spoken into an absolute silence. Immediately the curtain fell out of the flies – a cut not a fade. I wanted it to descend with an almost shocking abruptness to suggest that the story had not ended, simply that this was the moment at which the audience was obliged to take their leave of it, and that it would carry on beyond the curtain until the lives of each member of the family they have been watching for over four hours has gone the way of the play.

Reading a great play it sometimes seems as if all it requires in performance is to be spoken out loud. However, five minutes in a rehearsal room will soon convince you otherwise. Every word that is uttered, every action the play requires, has to be particu-larised through the personality of the individual performing it. It has to be translated into a second language, the language of acting, and this is something that has to be found; it is not self-evident. In Act Two of *Long Day's Journey* there is a moment before lunch when the two brothers find an unguarded bottle of whiskey which their miserly father would normally have left under lock and key in the cellar. While he chats to a neighbour in the garden they surreptitiously pour themselves a drink, then top up the bottle with water to conceal the theft. It is a brief scene but given the overall context an amusing one, and therefore impor-tant to get right. On the page it seems simple enough, but it requires meticulous rehearsal, timing the dialogue to the business of pouring the drink, then measuring the exact amount of water required to top up the bottle, while all the time keeping an eye out for the father who is expected for lunch at any moment. We rehearsed it over many repetitions, accumulating detail until all the behaviour in the scene was true and rhythmic, and had, as good acting always does, a kind of inevitability. Repetition during rehearsals is very important for the performer, because it will eventually give him the confidence to reside entirely in the present moment and avoid any anxious peering ahead to lines that he may not be sure of or moments incompletely understood.

At our very first reading I had encouraged the cast not to regard the play as some great tragic Everest waiting to be climbed. It was a play in the same realist tradition of many others in which they had already appeared; what distinguished it was the nobility of its ambition, but this would look after itself if it was properly prepared. Because of its length I had proposed breaking it down into its component parts. We would rehearse Act One and stay with it until we had solved its problems and could run it with confidence. We would then move to Act Two, do the same with that, and then, but only then, when we were sure of ourselves, would we run the two acts together. Similarly with Act Three and Act Four. In this way we patiently assembled the show with the result that by the first night there was not a moment in the evening about which the actors felt insecure. The play was no longer daunting. It didn't even seem long. The company went on stage knowing what they had to do and they did it with a freshness and passion beyond my best expectations.

Before we faced the press we had a week or so of previews to ready ourselves. Much encouraged by our first encounter with the public, I didn't rehearse the following day but let the actors rest, suggesting that we meet in Connie's dressing room before the performance. I knew exactly what notes I wanted to give to three of the principals, but finding something genuinely useful to say to Olivier required thought and tact. He both resisted and expected direction while remaining unnervingly on guard against directors' blather. However, discussing their performances with his colleagues was as usual stimulating and productive, and by the time I came to Larry my confidence was up.

'I know in the past you've resisted playing James Tyrone because you thought the play belonged to the wife,' I began. 'But I think perhaps that was before you realised the extraordinary opportunity for you in the fourth act. So when you're working your way through the first three hours always remember that a great Act Four is waiting for you. Don't push the early scenes or try to make them yield more than is there. You've already found rewarding things to play – the comedy in the man's meanness, the squabbles with his sons and so forth. Enjoy the journey and play a waiting game.'

What I was really asking him to do was to forget his responsibilities to his reputation and become an ensemble actor. In the preview performances that followed this began to happen, as all the cast responded to and learned from their audiences. The show was settling into its true shape, and night by night the audiences with whom they were interacting were changing too, as the word spread that here was an evening that must on no account be missed.

Before the curtain rose on the first night the expectation and the goodwill in the auditorium were palpable. Would there be two things to celebrate that night – a return to form for the National Theatre, and, back on stage in a major role, notwithstanding severe illness and advancing years, the most remarkable English actor of the age, successor to Garrick, Kean and Irving? Everyone present knew that this promised to be a true occasion and they felt lucky to be there.

As soon as I heard the first words of the play spoken I was sure that we were safe and that the cast were in command of the evening. There was no coughing and the audience was following the play with rapt attention. At the first interval I'd been bidden to go to a small room off the dress circle where drinks were being served for members of the Theatre Board. The atmosphere in the room was excited yet subdued. Such a spectacular recovery on the part of the National Theatre under its present artistic director seemed to have thrown the Board members off balance. The new chairman was there, the property tycoon Sir Max Rayne, and I was also introduced to Lord Goodman, the great mover and shaker of London's cultural scene. He offered me a murmur of praise that was more like an apology. What I didn't know then was that these two men, without any discussion with Olivier, had already put in place his successor, Peter Hall.

It was a curious echo of the way Olivier had been treated when he was running the Old Vic in the forties and was peremptorily fired by letter while touring the company's work in Australia. Why were people so often reluctant to confront him face to face, this unsettling figure who could attend a Board meeting in a grey suit in the afternoon, and then in the evening paint his face and cast spells over a thousand people? Now Rayne and Goodman had betrayed him again. But in the theatre the sun shines and the rain falls in such unpredictable ways that there would come a time when I would be indebted to both men.

Onstage the performances simply got better and better. Larry rose to the fourth act like a great wave gathering and for everyone present there was no place on earth we would have preferred to be than in this theatre on this particular night. Then suddenly the two actors on whom we were transfixed had stopped speaking. They sat in their chairs, mouths slightly ajar, staring at each other as in a photograph. Three and a half hours into the play Larry had caught sight of one of his small children watching him from a box, and his concentration had wavered. The audience realised at once what had happened: that the great actor had forgotten a line. But they were so grateful for what they had already been given that instead of an embarrassed silence there arose from the house a rumble of understanding in which there was both goodwill and amusement. It was the most generous sound I have ever heard an audience make. Eventually Ronnie Pickup found something to say to put the play back on track, and the rest of the show moved with the purpose of an arrow to its conclusion. In that hard-won beat of silence that separated the descent of the curtain from the avalanche of applause that followed, I knew we had scored an absolute bullseye.

The notices the following day, all eight of them, were a clean sweep. I had had a good press before but always there had been at least one dissenting voice. Not now! Peter Lewis in the *Daily Mail* began his review with exclamations, 'Magnificent! Terrific! One of the Himalayas of our century's drama scaled in triumph!' All celebrated the National's return to form, but what particularly pleased me was the praise given to the actors as a superb ensemble, and one recruited from within the company. Some notices even led with an accolade for Constance Cummings, though the uniqueness of Olivier's performance was widely acknowledged. I floated through the rest of the day in a state of dreamy elation, even if there were moments when I wondered whether, from now on, my career would be all downhill.

At six o'clock that evening I went backstage to greet the cast. In this same building almost thirty years before Olivier had given his Richard III and his Oedipus Rex. Now he was back at the same address with a matching triumph. Forty years on the building was to change its name twice, first to the Albery Theatre then to the Noël Coward, with all its bygone successes folded away in the past. But on that day, 22 December 1971, nothing seemed more real, more ineradicable, than being part of this absolute, copper-bottomed London hit.

The star dressing rooms were on stage level and to reach them I had to descend a steep flight of concrete steps at the bottom of which there were two doors, one to the left and one to the right.

I had just arrived at the last step when, as in a farce, Larry and Connie emerged simultaneously from their dressing rooms. We stared at each other, grinning and surprised, but no one spoke. Instead, like children who have just got away with a hoard of stolen fruit, we all began to giggle.

'Can you smell it!?' said Larry, rubbing the tips of his fingers together.

'What?' we asked.

'Success!!' he whispered.

And he was right, it flooded the building.

Thus began the upswing in the fortunes of the National Theatre. *Long Day's Journey into Night* had a straight run of some months at the New Theatre and brought our tenancy of the building to a close. With the cast on National Theatre salaries, and royalties paid only to the author's estate, the National made buckets of money and seats became impossible to get. Even when the industrial disputes of that winter resulted in power cuts we still sold out and performed the show under two work lights powered by a generator in the alley. James Tyrone's lines about the need to economise on electricity were greeted with rounds of applause and much hilarity. It was like giving a performance in wartime.

Back at the Old Vic a new play, *Jumpers*, by a young dramatist Ken Tynan had championed, Tom Stoppard, gave us another hit, and success built on success with Jonathan Miller's production of *School for Scandal*, which he had set most effectively in the world of Hogarth's London rather than the usual chocolate-box version of the eighteenth century. By the middle of 1972 when my production of *The Front Page* was up, running and selling out, the National had paid back its deficit (around £1 million in today's terms) and was doing the best business in its history.

It was just after Christmas, and with nothing immediate to keep me in London, that my thoughts turned to distant Biarritz, where building works had just begun on the house. I'd been ruminating about the future of the National Theatre and had some thoughts which I wanted to get on paper. This I could do as easily in France as in England. I had been thinking that the National, as its name implied, should be a theatre for the whole of Britain, not just the metropolis, and I'd envisioned two companies, one based in London, the other in a big city to the north. Newcastle, for instance, had a magnificent theatre, the Theatre Royal, and was well placed to attract determined theatregoers from both Glasgow and Edinburgh as well as towns in the North of England. These two companies would, from one season to the next, change places bringing with them their established successes. Whether the plan was feasible I had no way of knowing, though some years later the Royal Shakespeare Company would set up a Newcastle operation very like the one I've described.

Shirley, Conrad and I found a family hotel just round the corner from the Biarritz house, so we were able to visit the building works two or three times a day. Once on site there was nothing we could do beyond get in the way of the builders, but we needed to reassure ourselves on a twice-daily basis that the house actually existed. In its present state, particularly in mid-winter, it made a dismal impression, like someone ill revealing their nakedness in a struggle to get out of bed. The front of the balcony had been ripped away and the interior rooms gaped at the street below. Roof tiles were missing and a collapsed interior wall revealed the truth of its composition – random stones and dusty rubble. On the ground floor one day a giant rat emerged from the open plumbing and made its way sluggishly into the garden, where a builder dispatched it with a hammer. But I still loved the house and realised that a key element of architecture, and the last to be put in place, is the mask it presents to the world. That would be something to look forward to in the summer.

In the meantime there was the town to explore. It was extremely cold that winter and when I wasn't working on my

National Theatre paper we went for long shivering walks. All over town were restaurants offering three- and four-course meals for less than a pound, and they were places where we could find warmth as well as massive amounts of food. Towards the end of our week all three of us went down with an identical illness and a French doctor had to be called. We listed our symptoms and described our days and he listened to us with amused gravity, then in perfect English he gave us his diagnosis: 'You have all been grossly over-eating. Stop and you'll feel better.'

It was no hardship returning to London and the protective embrace of a huge hit. Some successes are so hard-won that afterwards, as in a hot bath, you feel entitled to wallow a little longer than you should. I hung about the theatre most nights enjoying the buzz front of house and going to various parts of the auditorium to see moments in the performance I particularly liked. But the show had passed to the actors; it was theirs now and beyond giving an occasional note my work was over. One night I climbed the three flights of stairs to the gallery to catch Larry's fourth act. In the gods the sound resonated around the dome, and the acoustics were as good as anywhere in the house. It was in a seat way up in the gallery that as a drama student I'd twice watched Olivier's Antony at the St James's Theatre. Now I was marvelling again at the way every syllable and every nuance of his performance was reaching that remotest part of the auditorium. We were as spellbound up there as they were in the front row of the stalls. Olivier held the entire house in the palm of his raised hand.

After the show that night Larry had invited me to have supper with him before he caught the train back to Brighton. His mood was mellow and extraordinarily winning. As we left the stage door and walked towards his waiting purple taxi, he put his arm around my shoulders and said, 'You've done a beautiful production, Michael, and I'm very grateful.' I was ridiculously pleased and wondered, a shade prematurely as it turned out, if at last I had won his trust. He went on to say that he was looking for a follow-up part for Connie and she had expressed an interest in *The Cherry Orchard*. Would I consider directing it? The two previous Chekhov successes at the National he had directed himself, and he had a jealous devotion to the playwright, so this offer too was magnanimous. Of course I said yes. It would be my first Chekhov.

He took me to Overtons, a long-established fish restaurant with a view overlooking Victoria Station, and as we ate our Dover sole he told me that as a boy during the First World War he had stood in the street below and watched the troops, battalion after battalion, marching up and into the station where rows of trains were waiting to transport the new recruits on the first leg of their journey to the trenches. For hours on end the air was heavy with the approaching sound of marching feet as what seemed an inexhaustible supply of young men appeared from around the corner then vanished into the maw of the station.

FIVE

Good reviews continued to come in, and now we were being noticed in the foreign press. *Time* magazine described the production as the 'best ever', and other pleasant surprises were to follow. Without having to ask, my salary was improved to the same level as John Dexter's, and I was now getting some lovely correspondence – a postcard after an early preview from Alan Bennett who wrote that he wanted to get his superlatives in ahead of the critics, and later a letter from Oona Chaplin saying that it was the best production of her father's play she had seen.

I learnt that I was to be given an entry in *Who's Who*, and my first thought was the vindication this would represent in Australia, the country from which with so much confused feeling I had fled twenty years before. Convincing a sceptical father and the friends with whom I'd grown up was still a need for me, and at last I was beginning to wonder why. At every performance there were celebrities in the audience, and after one Saturday matinee I went to see Larry in his dressing room and was introduced to Shirley MacLaine. She was astonished how relevant the play was to modern American life. 'But there's no director mentioned in the programme,' she said to Larry. 'Did you direct it yourself?' He gave a somewhat preemptory nod in my direction. 'Oh, but you're billed as the producer,' she said to me, and I in turn nodded towards Sir Laurence, who was better equipped to explain his attachment to this abandoned usage.

Once a show survives a first night it goes on to have a life of its own and can often evolve in surprising ways. Some in the cast get better and better in their roles (as Denis Quilley invariably did), some get mechanical or mannered. Either way the show changes.

Occasionally it is a random shift in public perception that can alter the balance, and this was to be the case with *Long Day's Journey into Night*. It began with a single notice we received in the *Sunday Times* from its illustrious drama critic Harold Hobson, whose misjudgements were so frequent and peculiar that a fellow critic, Penelope Gilliatt, once described the characteristic sound of a Sunday morning as 'Harold Hobson barking up the wrong tree'. His review had the headline 'Olivier's Triumph' and he gave over the entire space to a eulogy of the great actor. The rest of the cast were praised in a few words and then forgotten. It was an ecstatic notice and very good for business, but was an inadequate description of the evening. Thereafter, little by little, in the press and in the currents of gossip and speculation that gather around a hit, Larry moved centre stage.

He did not encourage or collude in this, and his relations with his fellow actors continued to be generous and affectionate, but there is no doubt that he licked his lips over this development. Who would not? The show was another kill to add to his list, and like a dominant animal he was once again able to mark out his territory and protect it with a low growl; and, as always, with ferociously hard work. The performance in the evening after a day attending to administration often left him exhausted. I would go into his dressing room while he was making up and find him stripped down to his trousers with the skin across his broad back and bony shoulders slack with fatigue. Just raising an eyebrow pencil seemed to require effort. Then he would go out onstage and, as it were, mount his part and gallop off with it. The actor we had caught a glimpse of in the rehearsal room, naked and full of dread, was nowhere to be seen. King Richard was himself again.

We concluded our run at the New in the spring, having sold out at every performance. Let us fast-forward now to the following August. The production had been absorbed into the repertoire at the Old Vic and was playing a few times a week. This was less exhausting for Larry, though as usual he drove himself to make his performance as good as it could be. On the day we opened at the Vic he insisted that we run the entire play twice, which meant four hours onstage in the morning, four in the afternoon, and then, in front of an audience, four hours in the evening. He was determined to hammer every syllable of his part firmly into place, and the show that night was as good as it had ever been. Seeing the production for the second time, Michael Billington concluded his *Guardian* review with: 'Such is the quality of the acting and direction, we seem to be not merely watching great drama but to be eavesdropping on life itself.'

Afterwards celebrities came pushing through the stage door to pay their tribute. By the end of the year when the awards were given out (rather less than there are today) Larry picked them all up. At the most prestigious ceremony, the *Evening Standard* luncheon, Connie was passed over, unfairly I thought, because one of the judges, Bernard Levin, couldn't get Gwen Ffrangcon-Davies' performance in the earlier production out of his head. Larry was the clear winner and in accepting the award he gave one of his weird convoluted speeches, in which he paid tribute to his fellow actors, then thanked me for my 'inspired assistance' – a compliment in which the generosity of the adjective was some-what nullified by the dullness of the noun.

Another luncheon at which he picked up an award was that given by the Variety Club of Great Britain. I encountered him at close quarters emerging from his private washroom on his return to Aquinas Street mid-afternoon, rather too well wined and dined. He seemed startled to see me and his demeanour was distinctly shifty. If caught off balance he could be as transparent as a guilty child and I knew at once that he had been bitching about me to someone or other at the lunch. We stared at each other for a moment before he regained his self-possession.

'Hello, boysie,' he said. 'I've just been telling people about your wonderful production.'

'*Long Day's Journey*?' I asked.

'No, no, no, no! *The Front Page*! I've been telling everyone about it!' This was a show that had opened successfully in the summer, and of which more later.

In the confined space in which we stood the smell of digesting alcohol was pervasive. He was looking at me and swayed slightly as if pondering whether to speak. 'Have you got a minute?' he said. I nodded and he beckoned me with a finger.

In silence and with him leading we walked down the length of the corridor to his office. Once inside he closed the door significantly, found a blank sheet of paper and a pencil, and began a drawing. It was obviously a ground plan of some sort and when he added an oval table stage centre I knew it must be the set of *Long Day's Journey*. For rehearsals I had placed the table at a slight diagonal and in Act Four had sat Larry at the upstage end, so that he played down the table, and Ronnie Pickup on one side, so that he played across the table.

Larry now added two circles to his drawing to represent the heads of the two actors as seen from above. He then added two lines proceeding from each circle like the beams of two torches shining into the auditorium. Although James Tyrone was upstage of his son, his torchbeam was directed more to one side of the theatre, whereas Jamie's shone directly into the house. It meant that of the two actors Ronnie Pickup had marginally the better position, which was perhaps as it should be since his long speeches were the most demanding text in the play and benefited from stillness and a tight focus.

'See the problem?' Larry asked me like a sorely tried teacher, and I played the pupil. 'Yes, I *do* see.' Inwardly it was impossible not to be amused that he should find something to fret about in a scene in which he had scored an absolute triumph. But I was also astonished that for over a year he had kept this small niggle to himself, because, as he knew perfectly well, a single word from him would have been enough to put in place some sort of adjustment. However, out of respect for the authority vested in me as director, and perhaps concerned that he might have been perceived as taking something from a fellow actor, he had through all the weeks of rehearsal and over a year of performances kept his mouth shut. That is until he'd had a glass of wine too many at a Variety Club luncheon.

When *Long Day's Journey* first opened in the West End, our next production scheduled for the Old Vic was already in rehearsal. This was Tom Stoppard's *Jumpers*, and it coincided with the disagreeable task of reducing the size of the acting company by half. With a large debt to pay back, and now reduced to a one-theatre operation, we had no choice in the matter. Having been an actor myself I knew how painful it was not to have your contract renewed, and how impossible to regard this as anything but a vote of no confidence. (In passing it's interesting to note that this insecurity of employment, with which the theatrical profession has always had to live – and which was once the thing our mortified parents warned us against – is now a general condition of the workplace.) Few of our actors deserved to lose their jobs but some had been with us too long and were either exhausted or impatient for advancement to leading roles we were unable to offer them.

I was now Olivier's sole full-time associate director, and for a couple of weeks had to preside over a very unhappy company as the culling proceeded. I was however abetted by a new recruit, a young apprentice director, Roland Joffé, who would one day make that remarkable movie *The Killling Fields*. Roland had a steady gaze and an original mind. He was also familiar with the actors of his own generation in a way I was not, and he saw this reduction of the company as an opportunity to introduce fresh talent. We held auditions and recruited rising actors like David Bradley, Gawn Grainger and John Shrapnel. And with a core of regulars going back to *The National Health* – Anna Carteret,

David Ryall, Mary Griffiths, Gillian Barge, Harry Lomax, Maggie Riley and Ben Whitrow among them – we soon had a trim company of forty.

Jumpers was very much Ken Tynan's baby. He had first spotted Tom Stoppard's work when *Rosencrantz and Guildenstern Are Dead* was staged at the Edinburgh Festival. The National procured the rights and it became one of the company's big successes. Now Tom's second play had come into Ken's hands and he was determined to do his best by it. On the page, though much less in performance, the text had a daunting complexity, and Ken decided that the best way to introduce this new work to his colleagues was to stage a solo reading by the person he could say with certainty understood it, its author. I have always thought that the best way to assess a script is the simplest – to sit down and read it – but it is surprising how few people in the theatre think likewise. Producers, particularly in America, are always proposing readings and workshops as a way of discovering potential. What they're actually doing is postponing the moment when they have to make up their minds and start writing cheques.

Ken's reading had taken place when the National was at its lowest ebb. He had invited a small group of us to his house in Thurloe Square – Olivier, Dexter, Derek Granger and myself, all of us exhausted by the succession of failures with which we had been coping. At one end of his elegant drawing room Ken had rearranged the sofa and chairs to face a lectern on which lay a copy of the script. At the foot of the lectern, upside down on the floor, were what looked like a number of small placards. We each chose a seat and Ken stammered through a brief speech of introduction before a very nervous playwright took his place behind the lectern. Tom apologised in advance for his inadequacies as an actor and explained that to avoid confusion he had the names of all the characters in his play inscribed on the placards at his feet. His intention was to hold each aloft in accord with whichever character was speaking.

The reading began, but was inevitably halting as Tom bent down continually to replace one placard with another. Sometimes he would get them confused and seconds would tick by in silence. During the very long speeches he stood for minutes at a time with one placard raised above his head like a forlorn Statue of Liberty whose torch has gone out. I found it impossible to attend to what was being said because I was so concerned for Tom, caught up in the nightmare into which he had been inveigled by Ken. With a sinking heart I realised that Act One would take twice as long to perform as it would to read and that we would be here for quite some time. I glanced over at Larry on the sofa and saw that he was nodding off. The elements that would make the play so effective in performance – the use of television, the antics of the Jumpers themselves, the topless Young Woman on the trapeze, and the brilliantly prepared-for double death of the rabbit and the tortoise came and went unnoticed in a mutter of description. I left the house no better informed about the play than when I arrived.

Not so Olivier. When we met the following day he was overflowing with enthusiasm for it and insisted that if he hadn't already been committed to *Long Day's Journey* he would have grabbed the leading role for himself. I was bemused. Had he returned to the text overnight? Had he already read it before Tom's reading? It was a good thing that at that particular moment he and not I was running the National Theatre, because I'm ashamed to admit that I might easily have proposed dropping the play. As it was, Larry and Ken's ringing endorsements persuaded me, and *Jumpers* was scheduled for production.

A brilliant cast was soon assembled, led by Michael Hordern and Diana Rigg, and Peter Wood was approached to direct. One morning before I went to work I was rung by an old friend, the literary agent Robin Dalton, who represented Peter Wood. His career had run into one of those inevitable quiet patches so both agent and client were delighted by this offer from the National.

The problem was he had only the foggiest idea what the play was about. I was secretly relieved to hear this since it made me feel less stupid, but I assured Robin how excited the National was about the play's potential and strongly advised Peter to accept the offer, which he did.

The play sailed into rehearsals and seemed to be splendidly on course until the dress rehearsal when technical problems reduced progress to a snail's pace. In some ways the show was as complex as a musical and getting all the elements in place required more time than we had at our disposal. At one point Tarzan in leopard-skin briefs was meant to swing across the stage on a vine emitting his familiar yodel. These few seconds of stage time took hours to get right. The result was that at the first preview the cast were literally thrown on stage in a state of terrified uncertainty and were soon running a gauntlet of technical mishaps. Michael Hordern frequently lost his way in his enormously long philo-sophic speeches and a second prompter had to be dispatched to the opposite side of the stage. It was an evening of extreme con-fusion for the company, for the crew – and for the audience, who filed out of the theatre looking as bewildered as I'd been after the reading.

Only one of us remained on his toes and thinking hard: Ken Tynan. The curtain had barely descended before Ken had rounded up a small group of us and spirited us back to Thurloe Square to brainstorm, until dawn if necessary, about how to make the evening work. We had less than a week of previews before we had to confront the press. Larry usually avoided first previews, so gathered around Ken's table were the author, the director, Ken and me. In a situation which would have left other playwrights either hysterical or suicidal Tom remained his courteous and attentive self, but he was too inexperienced in the practicalities of theatre to have much idea where we should go next. For the moment Peter Wood was mute with exhaustion, and I was no use. We all looked to Ken, who for the first and only time in his career at the National had the opportunity to exercise not just influence, which could bring out the worst in him, but power.

On this occasion power was to bring out the best. He knew exactly how we should proceed and had a list of specific cuts and modifications (Tarzan was the first to go) that tightened and improved the evening, as well as a schedule to make it all happen. The following day he, Peter and Tom called a rehearsal and the spirits of the company rose when they perceived the intelligence and specificity of the proposed changes. Someone, it seemed, believed in the play and was determined to make it work. The press night I attended a few days later might have been a different show altogether. It was the most dramatic turnaround I have ever seen achieved in so short a time. The two leads were magnificent and the production lucid and elegant. The play had been given its due, and for the National and for everyone involved it was a major hit. Without Ken this might not have happened, and Tom said as much in the lovely tribute he paid at Ken's memorial service, when, addressing the two small Tynan children in the front pew, he described their father as 'part of the luck we had'.

With *Jumpers* now playing to standing room only I could no longer avoid confronting the question: with what production could I possibly follow *Long Day's Journey into Night*? It was a show that would be very difficult to top. However, there was one possibility I had not yet pursued.

Ken had long championed another American play, a master-piece of a very different sort, but he had never found a director at the National Theatre willing to take it on. 'Impossible to cast,' John Dexter had declared, and this seemed to have been the British view ever since the play's opening on Broadway in 1928; in the intervening years it had had only one short-lived London production, back in 1931. The play was Ben Hecht and Charles MacArthur's newspaper comedy *The Front Page*, and I knew of it by way of its influence on any number of black-and-white films

I had seen growing up in Australia. However, I had neither read nor seen the play performed so I asked the Literary Department if they could unearth a copy. The opening stage directions alone were enough to convince me that I had stumbled on pure gold. Here is the authors' description of the Press Room in the Chicago Criminal Courts building: 'It is a bare, disordered room, peopled by newspaper men in need of shaves, pants pressing and small change. Hither reporters are drawn by an irresistible lure – the privilege of telephoning free . . . Here is the rendezvous of some of the most able and amiable bums in the newspaper business; here they meet to gossip, play cards, sleep off jags and date up waitresses, between such murders, fires, riots and other public events as concern them.'

When the play begins it is eight thirty in the evening and the reporters are wearily filling in time during the long wait for the hanging the following morning of an anarchist who has been found guilty of murdering a black policeman. During the course of the first act the Press Room has a number of familiar visitors: a slow-witted German policeman doing his rounds, a Scandinavian cleaning lady, an Italian hoodlum currently in the pay of one of the newspapers, a forlorn Irish tart with a crush on the condemned man and the city's Sheriff, who comes to distribute tickets for the hanging. When the play was first performed it was barely a generation away from Ellis Island, and here the melting pot was brought onstage. We see a new idea of America coming into being, or at any rate a new idea of American comedy – on the one hand hard-boiled and clear-eyed, on the other exuberantly and joyously inventive.

The marvel of *The Front Page* is its first act, the least showy of the three, in which under cover of some sharp comedy the time bombs of farce are carefully wired and put in place. In this it resembles that other great farce of the twentieth century which one day I would also direct, Michael Frayn's *Noises Off*, where the laughs in the first act spring from the accurate portrayal of a company of actors as they make their way through a nerve-racking dress rehearsal. In both plays we are presented with believable people, albeit working in rather specialised professions. This is not the case with more traditional farce, where the characters are types who exist principally to be manipulated by the mechanics of the plot. However, the reporters assembled in *The Front Page* are portraits of the men Hecht and MacArthur mixed with during their own days in the Chicago Press Room. Each is delineated in a few bold strokes and given his own voice. In the case of the leading character, the ace reporter Hildy Johnson, they didn't even bother to change his name. There was a real Hildy Johnson who, like his stage counterpart, left Chicago for New York and actually came to the first night to see himself portrayed, and who some months later was killed by a motor car as he crossed the street one afternoon after a long lunch. I learned this from an elderly ex-reporter who wrote to me from Chicago after the National's staging of the play had been reported in the local press. He had known and worked alongside the real Hildy, and he supplied me with a story about the Press Room which was like a validation of the play. On arrival every novice reporter was urged to acquire a stethoscope because there was a radiator in the hall the pipes of which connected directly to the central heating in the jury room a floor below. By applying the stethoscope to the radiator it was sometimes possible to hear the deliberations of the jury, and learn the verdict ahead of the judge.

What generates the laughter in Act One is not a succession of carefully honed one-liners such as have come to characterise more recent American comedy but truthfully observed speech, such as you might hear among any group of men obliged to work in close proximity to one another. The reporters play cards, argue, send out for food, fight over space or complain about their lives at work and at home, and it is no surprise that between these tin-pot scribes the preferred mode of communication is the genial insult and the sardonic wisecrack. Essential plot is smuggled into the play without the audience noticing, and by the end of Act One the engine of *The Front Page* is fully assembled and ready to go. The prison break just before the interval is like a starting pistol, and from then on the play hurtles forward, topping itself with one surprise after another until it arrives at perhaps the best curtain line for a comedy ever written: 'The son of a bitch stole my watch.' And tops itself again.

I read *The Front Page* at a sitting, and as I closed the script I couldn't believe my luck. Here was a play that I not only longed to do but had a clear idea of exactly how I wanted to do it. The comedy of the piece was so brilliantly structured that if properly paced and timed it could look after itself. The priority I thought was to bring the world of the play to the stage with as much realism and persuasive detail as we could muster, starting with a set so authentic you could almost smell the stale tobacco smoke, a place where men's hats rarely left their hair-oiled heads.

Hecht and MacArthur were nothing if not good journalists and the play is a compendium of fragments of the social history of the America they knew. Chicago politics come onstage in the person of a corrupt Mayor who tries to have a reprieve for the condemned man suppressed because a hanging will improve his electoral chances. The 'nigger vote' swings on it. His cohort, the Sheriff, drums up the Red Menace (some twenty-five years before Senator McCarthy) with his slogan 'Reform the Reds with a Rope' in full knowledge that the man they are trying to hang is not a communist but an anarchist, indignant to be dubbed a Red. For a comedy the play is utterly reckless in its choice of subject matter. For the first fifteen minutes the action is interrupted by the loud thump of the gallows being tested in the yard below in preparation for the hanging in the morning, and in the second act there is an attempted suicide when a prostitute leaps from the Press Room window.

But surrounding the incidents in *The Front Page* there is a smell of authenticity that encouraged me to believe that we needed to stage it with robust verisimilitude. Life, as represented in the play, is a frequently grim and mostly grubby affair, but it has one redeeming feature: it is hilarious. And one way of coping with it is to mock it without respite. For the authors, writing in the twenties, political correctness was a concept as unimaginable as a landing on the moon, and anything and everything becomes their target – race, disability, chronic illness, paedophilia, women, women's mothers, duty and loyalty. Absolutely nothing is off limits. I asked Larry if it could be my next production and he didn't hesitate in giving it the green light.

Meanwhile the Easter holiday was almost upon us and I saw the chance of slipping over to France and checking on the building works. Our architect had told us that the top floor of the house would be just about habitable and, in advance of our arrival and on his own initiative, he had furnished it with three collapsible cots and three sleeping bags. Not knowing quite what to expect we caught a plane to Bordeaux, a train to Biarritz, and a taxi to the house, where a pleasant surprise awaited us. The rotting timber balconies had been replaced by concrete facsimiles and we now owned something that looked like a proper house. For the first time I realised how much it resembled the Victorian terraces of Sydney with their rows of balconies providing a shield from the sun. All this house lacked was their proliferation of decorative cast iron and this I would later correct on various trips back and forth to Australia when I would return with lengths and cornerpieces of this ironwork to adorn the facade of a house in France.

When I entered the building the surprises were less agreeable. Workmen were all over the place, carefully avoiding my eye as they scrambled to meet a promised deadline. The ground and first floors were chaotic with chasms where previously there had at least been wormy wooden planks and where dust from a collapsed chimney covered every surface. The top floor, though dilapidated, was clean and bare but was without running water. At the last moment this was supplied via a huge length of hose attached to a tap in the garden which then proceeded up the front of the building and through the top window before snaking its way through the house to what would eventually be the bathroom. We now had a working lavatory, but cooking or having a bath were out of the question. Nevertheless the following morning there was a primitive excitement about opening our eyes in these unfamiliar spaces, unlatching a window to the smell of the sea, then peering out from this new place of shelter which, like cats in a cupboard, we had now claimed as our own.

The weather was overcast, it was still too cold to swim and we were living in a dump but, notwithstanding, Biarritz was rapidly becoming a place without imperfections. It is the most shopworn of clichés where property is concerned for someone to say that they've 'fallen in love with a house', but over the next few years my absorption in my French dwelling had all the signs of a grand and loopy passion. I simply couldn't imagine anywhere else in the world that was better, and friends invited to share its primitive amenities knew better than to question my judgement. If my beloved had crossed eyes and a wart on the end of her nose I had no interest in anyone pointing it out.

To begin with I adored Biarritz itself, in parts elegant and quite grand but compared to other French towns hardly beautiful. At this time of year, out of season, it was relatively deserted, but the place had a lively local population and they enjoyed having their town handed back to them for the quiet eight months of the year. That stubborn reluctance of the French not to let go of their past in the face of the imperatives of the present meant that in the early seventies the nineteenth century was a far more distinct presence in Biarritz that it would have been in a comparable English town. Within a hundred yards of the house there were three small bakeries, each conducted as an independent business. Four doors down there was a blacksmith's run by two burly young brothers in leather aprons, open-faced and handsome, who might have stepped out of a Victorian painting glorifying manual labour. Then there were the small hardware shops to which I was constantly going back and forth to buy ornamental brass fittings to beautify the house, or sandpaper, wire wool and beeswax to stroke and caress it.

But most enticing were the 'brocantes', those shops stocked from floor to ceiling with an indeterminate mixture of antiques and junk. Here the history of nineteenth-century France was up for sale and going for a song. We acquired a gilded Louis Philippe looking glass for a fiver, a huge country cupboard with scalloped panelled doors for £40, a large Louis Napoleon oval table, which had lost its side flaps and now worked as an approximately rect-angular eating surface, for eight. There were curvy rush-seated upright chairs so cheap (and so rickety) it was worth buying a few extra ones as replacements. All these random purchases were stylistically bound together by a common feature – they were riddled with woodworm. The house soon reeked of insecticide and would do so for years to come. It didn't matter; the smell was balm to me.

For less than a pound there was another level of treasure wait-ing to be unearthed. In battered frames with broken glass I found bleached sepia photographs of the Russian nobility, who had once flocked to Biarritz for the winter season, and tarnished but brightly coloured pictures of Queen Victoria and Edward VII. There were lacy parasols and carved wooden boxes. The house would soon become almost as cluttered as the shops from which these things were purchased.

However, the town offered less material pleasures, not least the habitual and well-drilled courtesy of practically everyone you encountered. In the food shops a 'Bonjour Monsieur' or a 'Bonjour Madame', then at the end of the transaction a 'Bon journée', would ring out like a musical doorbell for every cus-tomer who stepped up to be served. There were wonderful smells, as defined as a patch of sunlight, that you encountered as you passed a cake shop or wandered from one stall to another in the market. It was too late in the day for me ever to be assimilated into this world, but it was marvellous to take pleasure in it and observe these people organising their needs and their relations to one another so as to make the transactions of their daily lives as pleasant as possible.

But the great wonder for me in Biarritz could not be described as French; it was something I had known all my life – the worldwide sovereign territory of the ocean. Just a street away from the house was the top of the clay cliffs from which one had a commanding view of the long stretch of beach known as the Côte des Basques. On a map the Atlantic coast of France proceeds downward in a rough vertical until it reaches the Basque country, whereupon it executes a right angle and becomes Spain. Biarritz is located just at the point where this change of direction takes place, and I could now stand at the top of the cliffs and gaze out over the Bay of Biscay, held in the giant embrace of two countries. To my right the view was limited by one of the rocky promontories around which the original fishing village of 'Biaris' had been built, but to my left was the unending arc of coastline along which you see France melting into Spain as you identify one town after another – Guéthary, St-Jean-de-Luz, San Sebastián, on and on until the visible world becomes lost in the mist over the sea.

Above this arc reared the distant Pyrenees, one range of mountains behind another, until they too faded into mist. Cradled within this vast stasis was the ocean, across the surface of which something was always on the move. That morning there was a surf running and huge waves glided round the point as intent and silent as an advancing army. They marshalled themselves into lines, then, with a roar, launched their assault towards the cliffs, only to come to nothing in a drawn-out submissive murmur and a wash of foam. These were the same waves that had thrilled and terrified me as a child, which as a young man with a surf-board I had attempted to tame. In London it had been an aspect of my abandoned Australian life for which nothing could compensate, and now I had recovered it. I had never felt so fortunate.

And yet as long as I could remember the spectacle I was now watching, of that restlessness coming out of the horizon, was a pleasure crossed with perplexity. The waves had been there, and would continue to be there, whether I watched or not. The sight of them against the static mountains, line after line, put you firmly in your place, and there was no talking back.

One evening a couple of years later with the house dressed up under a new coat of paint and everything in order, I had opened a bottle of wine with some friends on the top floor when unexpectedly the downstairs doorbell rang. We had all been feeling pretty pleased with ourselves, so I was a little irritated to have to descend two flights of stairs to see who was there. I opened the door to a stranger. He was a small bald-headed man of about sixty with the pasty face of a city dweller. He carried a cheap suitcase reinforced with rope and he was sweating. We stared at each other, then he gabbled something at me in a strange aggressive French. He gabbled it again, and then again, and at last I grasped what he was saying. He was one of the previous owner's summer lodgers and he wanted to know if his old room was vacant. I returned to my friends on the top floor with a good story to tell but a little uneasy. Most of us are inclined to think that the true history of the place we live in begins with our own occupancy of it. I had just been reminded that this house, which I loosely called mine, already had a past that didn't concern me, and by implication would one day have another. And another. It was as if when I opened the front door a wave had swept silently through the building – in and out again.

Like any resort the town of Biarritz, of which my shiny little house was part, promised many things, most of which were frivolous and quite a few false. But the sea and the mountains, as

I returned to them year after year, promised nothing whatsoever. All you could say about them was that they were there, they were beautiful and whatever it was they were waiting for, it had precious little to do with you. To someone working in the theatre, with its short-lived victories and bitter defeats, its busy self-importance, the sight of them each year was a kind of rebuke which, like an eloquent but cautionary sermon, I gradually came to welcome as once again I put the theatre to one side and occupied myself with counting the days of summer.

However, our first stay in the house was to come to an unexpectedly abrupt end. We'd only been there a couple of days when one morning I found a telegram pushed through the surround of the front door. It was from Ken Tynan and said that yesterday's *Observer* had leaked the news that Peter Hall was to be the next director of the National Theatre. He asked me to ring him as soon as I could. This took an entire morning because it involved going to the post office, booking a call, then waiting patiently in a queue of other callers for my turn. When we eventually spoke Ken was in an extremely excited state, and urged me to come back at once. Larry apparently had been informed of the Board's decision some six weeks previously but had been sworn to silence. Ken insisted there was still a chance of challenging the appointment, and said he was backing me as an alternative candidate.

This made me uneasy on a number of counts. The first was that his plan didn't stand a chance; the second was that I wasn't sure I wanted the job; and the third was what it said about Ken's own vulnerability. He had been the best critic of his generation but he had changed sides, and now that he had learnt how the theatre actually worked he had forfeited that innocence which enables a gifted critic to believe in the sweep of his judgements. There could be no going back. On the other hand if he wanted to continue working in the theatre at the level he had enjoyed for the past ten years, he had few options – in fact only one, an ongoing job at the National Theatre. This would not be forth-coming under Peter Hall. In a sense my appointment was his one hope. With his health now seriously under threat from his emphysema Ken faced the prospect of doors closing everywhere he looked.

We packed our bags and headed for the railway station. Already my mind had begun sifting through the events of the past year for neglected clues that might have pointed to this totally un-expected turn of events. I remembered things which had seemed of no consequence at the time but which now stared me in the face demanding attention, such as Lord Goodman's demeanour on the first night of *Long Day's Journey*. However, what I particularly remembered was a story I had read in that same *Observer* newspaper around the middle of the previous year when the National was at its lowest ebb and Olivier's health and his competence were under question. At that time Peter Hall and the conductor Colin Davis were under contract to the Royal Opera House and were at work on a programme that would tie them both to the organisation for years to come. Then suddenly, and without a word to his colleague, Peter Hall had resigned. The opera world was in uproar and a bewildered Colin Davis declared himself betrayed. Eventually we would learn that within days of this resignation Peter had had a meeting with Lord Goodman during which he was sounded out about running the National. Peter has always insisted that the two events were unrelated but if so it was an extraordinary coincidence.

Now the National was back on top, and this only served to underline the shoddy and underhand way Olivier had been treated. The man who more than any other had made the National a reality remains to this day the only artistic director not to be consulted about his successor until after the appointment was a fait accompli. And yet, as Tynan was now insisting, part of the blame attached to Larry himself. For years now he had had the entire theatrical profession from which to choose his successor. In his autobiography, published some years later, he says that when he objected to the fact that Hall had been appointed over his head, he was challenged by the Chairman. Sir Max Rayne, to propose an alternative. He made two eccentric suggestions, Joan Plowright and Richard Attenborough, both undoubtedly gifted, but the one unsuitable because she was his wife, and the other because he had worked almost exclusively in films. From my own point of view the strangest revelation to come out of his book was that he had championed a third candidate – me. This had been something about which I knew nothing until the book was published, and it amazed me because at the time it was a matter that had never once been broached between us, nor so much as hinted at. It was the discussion we had never had. Perhaps he didn't want to raise my hopes; perhaps he guessed it was a job I didn't really want; perhaps he couldn't quite bring himself to see me (or anyone else for that matter) as his proper successor.

The theatre I returned to was like a clock that had stopped. No one had been expecting such an abrupt succession. It was a little like a putsch, and people were separated from one another by private concerns: what did the future hold and would they still keep their jobs? Everyone in the organisation seemed to have retreated inward. Only Ken Tynan remained passionately ticking and on the move. He was furious with Larry for not confiding in his colleagues about the Hall appointment; surely his first loyalty should have been to us, not to the Board! And he had been in touch with the Chairman, Sir Max Rayne, demanding a meeting between the Board and the present artistic directorate, at which the one would explain to the other why they had seen fit to leave us in the dark about a decision of such vital importance. With two smash hits in the repertoire business was booming, and we were in a strong position to make our case, in all respects save the contractual. An offer to Peter Hall had already been made and accepted and we would be wasting our breath. However at least we could make righteous noises and jump up and down. The Chairman granted us our wish and we were invited to join a Board meeting one evening a few days later. A subdued Larry was already present but now had little to say; he'd already said what he had to. Ken went straight into battle with a stammered but well-argued defence of the present artistic regime, whose achievements spoke for themselves, and who could reasonably expect to have been consulted about plans affecting the leadership and their own futures. However his credibility with Board members was still at a low point, and no one was listening when he issued a string of demands. I decided to weigh in.

'How can we possibly plan ahead,' I asked, 'if we don't know from one day to the next who will be leading the organisation? We had a positive right to be kept informed!'

With quite startling force and authority Max Rayne snapped back at me, 'Are you suggesting the Board has acted in any way improperly?'

Wondering if I had been guilty of defamation, I beat a hasty retreat. 'Of course not. But perhaps foolishly.' He had given me, as he intended, quite a shock, and I now knew why he was a multi-millionaire property developer and I was not. However, I also grasped that he had come down to the Aquinas Street boardroom at seven o'clock at night and acceded to Ken's request when he could have made life much easier for himself by simply saying no. And moreover I realised that the Board were as much captives of their decision to appoint Hall as we were. Months ago when he and Lord Goodman had secretly offered Peter the job they were rescuing a theatre in crisis and could have expected to be applauded for their boldness. But that crisis had passed and their judgement now appeared to have been compromised by a common fallacy – the doctrine of the Indispensable Man. Peter had been positioned virtually to write his own contract, and not unnaturally he had been busy doing so.

Having had our say, we now had to accept reality, and it was surprising how quickly we and the organisation adapted to the new future. Larry would continue to be in charge for a further year and hopefully would be able to lead the company into the new building. There would then be a period of around six months when he and Peter would run the theatre jointly, after which, as 1974 approached, Peter Hall would take sole charge. In the meantime, even for Ken, there were things to look forward to. His name was already attached to two successes, and with luck he might even take some credit for another, *The Front Page*. He had a further year and a half ahead of him to leave his mark on an institution which as a journalist he had fought to bring into being and as Literary Manager had helped to define. For my own part I had a wonderful comedy to direct, which if we could pull it off, would show the National in a wholly unexpected light. Beyond that I had other productions pencilled in. *Macbeth* was a play about which I'd always had some strong ideas and in two National Theatre actors, Anthony Hopkins and Diana Rigg, I thought I had the performers to help me realise them. Then at the beginning of the following year I would be directing *The Cherry Orchard* with Constance Cummings. Larry's future, too, was about to take a most fortunate turn. He had landed the lead in the film version of *Sleuth*, and Morty Gottlieb's production began shooting at Pinewood in April. With this he would re-establish himself as an international film star and could leave the National with a new career trajectory in place.

The matter of the succession had been so much on people's minds, and for so long, that it was almost a relief to have it behind us. All we had to think about now was our work, and that was going better than any of us could have imagined only a few months previously. We had just opened *Richard II* with Ronnie Pickup as the King, a workmanlike production but seriously under-budgeted, having been planned when the National was at its lowest ebb and broke. However, it was doing well. The next show in the repertoire would be Jonathan Miller's production of *The School for Scandal*, which he had already directed to acclaim at the Nottingham Playhouse. There was no reason to believe that the National's production would be any less successful. We now had a trim and dedicated troupe of about forty performers and we were beginning to fulfil Olivier's ideal of a true company of actors, able to demonstrate the full range of their talents in a wide variety of plays. In any one week you could see, say, Denis Quilley playing an outrageous fop in *The School for Scandal*, Bolingbroke in *Richard II* and the easy-going Hildy Johnson in *The Front Page*. Our audiences now packing the Old Vic could track the work of the company rather as they might a favoured sports team, exhilarated by a brilliant manoeuvre on one night, indulgent when the ball was fumbled on another. Larry's reign was ending as he would have wanted – in an unexpected and spectacular Indian summer. Moreover, the books were balanced and we were achieving a record surplus. As was the case when he took over the Shakespeare Memorial Theatre in 1960, Peter Hall would be inheriting the most successful and financially sound theatre in Britain.

Early one afternoon I was leaving Aquinas Street when Ken Tynan hailed me. He was sitting at the wheel of a brand new, fully automatic Mini. 'Can I give you a lift?' he asked.

'Which way are you going?'

'Any way you like, I'm practising.' I climbed in and he explained that he'd just got his driving licence. I was interested because I didn't drive myself and felt inadequate about it. 'But you must learn!' insisted Ken. 'I feel as if only now have I joined the human race.'

To me, on the contrary, he had always seemed a most conspicuous member of it, with his high and often controversial profile, his famous friends on both sides of the Atlantic and his numerous glamorous liaisons. We had been tenuously acquainted since our early twenties, when at some party thrown by actors in a basement flat, Ken would unexpectedly sweep in with a good-looking woman and perhaps an American celebrity in tow, take one look at the gathering, then sweep out again. We didn't properly engage with each other until I directed *A Day in the Death of Joe Egg* at the Glasgow Citizens Theatre. Ken wanted to buy the rights for the National but, in order to keep our Glasgow cast intact, Peter Nichols had given the rights to Albert Finney's Memorial Enterprises. However, Ken asked me when I was next in town to visit him to discuss other projects. We fixed a date one Sunday at three thirty in the afternoon at his house in Thurloe Square, not far from the Victoria and Albert Museum. It was a handsome early nineteenth-century building and when I rang the bell it was answered by a small, cheerful person from the Third World who conducted me up a sweep of sandstone stairs to a large drawing room on the first floor. Not only did Ken have a house, it seemed he had staff! She told me Mr Tynan would be descending shortly, then returned down the steps to wherever she had come from.

I sat and looked about me. The room was exactly what one of Ken's enemies would have considered the appropriate setting for a champagne socialist – an extremely stylish room at a fashion-able address. Five minutes passed; then fifteen; then twenty-five. After half an hour I began to feel uncomfortable and I was just about to stand up and stretch my legs when Ken made his entrance. He was courteous and pleasant but made no mention of having kept me waiting. Without a scrap of evidence to support the notion, I had the feeling that he'd just risen from his bed, maybe leaving someone else between the sheets. It felt rather as if I was participating unawares in a site-specific theatrical happening.

We chatted in a lively manner for about an hour with me won-dering from time to time whether I seemed interesting enough to this man who knew everybody. The one thing I remember from our conversation was Ken's account of his visit to Cuba with

Tennessee Williams. Castro had asked them whether they would like to attend an execution, and Tennessee had shown great interest. Ken was appalled. 'He's going to be shot anyway,' argued the playwright, but Ken insisted that if you watched an abomination like that you become complicit in it. Telling the story seemed to re-ignite his indignation and I found his sincerity impressive and in marked contrast to the more studied events of the afternoon.

My next visit to the house was some four years later. *Tyger* was just about to go into rehearsal and to celebrate Ken had invited a few of us around to drink a glass of champagne one Saturday lunchtime. The author, Adrian Mitchell, and his wife Celia, who were also close friends, were there, and another friend unconnected to the show, the poet Christopher Logue. I had my first inkling of the importance of friendship to this man who previously I had thought of as a determined celebrity hunter. It was a beautiful summer's day and the drawing room was flooded with sunshine. Kathleen, his wife, was pregnant with their second child, Matthew, expected within days, but she was one of those beautiful women to whom pregnancy adds a greater radiance. Seeing Ken in this setting with his wife and among staunch friends, he seemed both fortunate and surprisingly likeable.

Working so closely with him at the theatre we soon became friends, and I was to become a regular visitor at the Thurloe Square house. Ken was compulsively hospitable, and I was invited to events large and small. There were cocktail parties where every well-known face in London seemed to be packed into the drawing room, and the sustained noise as you ascended the stone steps to join the party was like a swarming. There were Saturday-night parties that spread across two or three rooms where you were inclined to drink more because there were seats to sit down on, and informal Sunday lunches which would conclude with Ken involving his guests in quizzes and games. The Tynans were dedicated hosts and worked to keep their guests not just entertained but on their toes. Ken had a way of giving you his full attention that was both intimate and a step away from the judgemental. It made you craft your jokes carefully and think before you spoke. I marvelled at the generosity and energy with which this couple set about entertaining the rest of the world. And occasionally wondered how they could afford it, both in money and in time.

SIX

After *Long Day's Journey* Michael Annals' next job was in Canada at the theatre in Stratford, Ontario. I had already asked him to design the set for *The Front Page* and he now proposed coming back to London via Chicago so that he could visit the actual Press Room in the Criminal Courts building where the play is meant to be taking place. He returned to London with a wealth of references and a piece of information that would have delighted Hecht and MacArthur – the old Press Room was now a VD clinic. His set and costumes for *The Front Page* represented Michael's work at its very best. It was lucky we were mounting the play at the Old Vic because in 1963, when the National Theatre took it over, the stage had been reconfigured so that it extended into the auditorium about ten feet further than before. This meant that the depth of the playing area, always generous, was now enormous, and it was possible for Michael to conceive of something with the complexity and realism of a film set, exactly what I wanted.

He put his Press Room on the diagonal with, to the right, a bank of big sash windows looking into the well of the building beyond which were the distant windows of the cell block. To the left there were sturdy double doors in varnished mahogany that led out to a corridor. When fully opened they revealed an old birdcage elevator from which visitors to the Press Room would emerge. Further up the hall a short flight of steps led to a covered bridge which spanned the well of the building and connected one side with the other. At a glance an audience member could understand the layout of the entire building and see what was happening in several places at once – lights in the cell block coming on one at a time during the jail-break; the reporters, hot on the trail of a scoop, rushing from the Press Room and over the bridge; Hildy Johnson's future mother-in-law arriving in stately fashion by elevator. The trick would be to keep every corner of the stage alive with interlocking action while maintaining a clear focus on what was important.

The Press Room itself was a marvel of witty and imaginative detail, scrupulously vetted for period accuracy. Dominating the space were two long, battered tables with turned legs, set at right angles to each other, on which stood the numerous pedestal telephones connecting the reporters directly to their respective newspapers. Upstage was the roll-top desk belonging to the effete Bensinger which, in the third act, figures prominently as the hiding place of the fugitive. Everywhere you looked on the set there was some small detail that told you something fresh about Chicago in the twenties. Even in the small rest room downstage of the double doors was a detail visible occasionally to the cast, but only to one member of the audience – someone sitting in the seat at the extreme left of the Circle. When the door was opened this spectator had a view of the lavatory bowl within which it was clear that someone had forgotten to pull the chain. 'A signature touch,' said Michael Annals, with schoolboy glee.

First however we had to get the play cast, and in this we had one huge advantage: the perfect Hildy Johnson was already a member of the company – Denis Quilley. With his battered good looks, masculine good nature and quick, rather nervy sense of comedy I felt we couldn't do better. His professionalism was immaculate: he was always first to know his lines, always on time, something encouraged perhaps by his years in musical theatre. Miscast he could sometimes be a little predictable, but Hildy was a part he understood in his bones. He had the physical co-ordination of an athlete, and he was a delight to work with because he was so responsive to direction and so skilled in implementing it. You suggested something, and at once he improved on it and made it his own. In the second act Hildy has a telephone call from his bride-to-be, whom he is supposed to have joined at the railway station. Instead he's pursuing one last story too juicy to resist. The telephone was on a very long cord, and I had an agitated Hildy move back and forth as he tries to appease his outraged fiancée on the other end of the line. Denis as always was on top of his text, which he was taking at a furious speed, but this was the first time we had run the scene, and his legs became caught up in the cord which then became further entangled with the legs of a chair. The rehearsal broke up when, stumbling and tripping, he started laughing so much he had to sit down.

However, what had happened by accident was exactly what might have happened in life. It both illustrated and compounded Hildy's dilemma. I asked Denis if there was any chance of his being able to repeat it. Like a dancer retracing his steps he immediately began to work out the mechanics of the tangle – how he had stepped by accident into a coil of telephone cable and how that cable had been pulled under the legs of the chair. Within ten minutes the information was stored in his muscular memory, and he was able to replicate it exactly at every rehearsal thereafter. These happy accidents transcend invention, because their truth is self-evident, and unlike traditional comic business they are always fresh and specific to the situation. Particularly in comedy a director needs to keep a sharp eye open for them.

Here's another example from *The Front Page*. In the second act the reporters all rush from the Press Room in pursuit of a new lead. But first they have to collect their top coats, a motley collection of dun-coloured gabardine hanging from a bentwood stand. At one rehearsal the reporters all dived for their coats and two of them by accident grabbed the same garment. Simultaneously one put his arm in the left sleeve and one in the right and, tugging, both came to an abrupt halt. It looked so ridiculous and induced so much laughter that the rehearsal came to a stop. Once again we analysed exactly what had happened, and the next time we did the scene it had become part of the performance – but with a further refinement: the central seam of the coat was replaced with Velcro so that the coat ripped apart and hung in two limp sections from the arms of the astonished reporters. The audience loved it, the more so because they were laughing at something that could actually have happened.

For the other leading part in the play, the managing editor, Walter Burns, there seemed to be no contender available in the company, and we thought we would have to cast someone from outside. Then one morning I slipped in to catch a flavour of the rehearsals for *Richard II*. The scene in progress involved the King being berated by an angry cleric played by Alan MacNaughtan, a Scots actor of very English mien. I had associated him with more buttoned-down roles, but his fulminating Bishop was displaying much the same righteous indignation as Walter Burns when he starts to manipulate or bamboozle someone who has made the mistake of getting in his way. On a hunch I gave Alan the part.

The rest of the casting fell effortlessly into place. The role of the infatuated tart, Mollie Malloy, required real feeling rather than comic skill and went to the young Maureen Lipman, who had both. Within the National we had a group of senior character actors who had been with the company for some time and had a place in the affections of our audience not unlike that felt for the contract players at the old Hollywood film studios. Paul Curran supplied us with our Mayor and Harry Lomax was an incomparable Mr Pinkus. For the reporters we had a splendid batch of younger actors some of them new recruits. They now joined Ben Whitrow, David Ryall and Allan Mitchell to take their places in front of a pedestal telephone. The only actor to be brought in from the outside was a real American, David Bauer, another member of that influx of talent into Britain taking refuge from the McCarthyite witch hunts. He played the Sheriff brilliantly.

Very few of our company had had any direct experience of the United States. One of those who did was Stephen Greif, who, dressed in chalk-striped suit and grey fedora, played the hoodlum Diamond Louie with authentic sleazy aplomb. Most of the others, however, derived their knowledge of America mainly from its films and television. But unlike an earlier generation of British actors, America had become a place in which they had a passionate interest. Marlon Brando and the Actors Studio, playwrights like Arthur Miller and Tennessee Williams, had cast long shadows from across the Atlantic. When I had first arrived in London the West End would occasionally mount a Broadway comedy such as *Affairs of State*, but its star actors, Hugh Williams and Wilfrid Hyde-White, didn't bother with an accent. They strolled through the evening in their own accomplished way as if British English was the lingua franca of the civilised world.

Since our touchstone was the movies I decided to kick-start the rehearsals by showing a couple of early talkies roughly contemporaneous with the play. I chose *42nd Street* because of its swift, savvy dialogue and relentless pace, and *Scarface* because it had a script by one of our authors, Ben Hecht, and like *The Front Page* was set in Chicago with a story that might have sprung straight from the headlines of Hildy's own paper, *The Enquirer*.

The Front Page is not an easy play to read, at least initially. There are so many characters on stage it's difficult to identify which reporter is which as the focus shifts around the room from the group playing cards at one of the tables to someone making a string of telephone calls to someone somewhere else filling in time practising on his ukulele. Others sit around grumbling. With each character having only a couple of lines per page our cast imagined it would be an easy learn, but it was soon clear that without the shape of the entire text in their heads it was impossible to play. If a cue was missed or picked up a second too late the string snapped and the play went dead. Convincing the cast of the absolute necessity of keeping alert as they passed the ball back and forth was my first task. My second was to suggest that we played it absolutely for real. These were men who had families to provide for and mortgages to pay. A scoop could mean advancement and a pay increase. In fact for everyone in the play, from the crooked Mayor to the incorruptible Mr Pinkus, something important is at stake. I was sure that the more plausible we made their world the better the comedy would be served. As in life, laughter would be the dividend; but it had to be earned.

On the page the tart, Mollie Malloy, can be read as a somewhat sentimental cliché from another age who meets a contrived and improbable ending. Not, however, the way Maureen Lipman played her. We first meet Mollie when she makes an unwelcome visit to the Press Room to berate the reporters for the callousness with which they are approaching the imminent hanging. They make cruel fun of her, their mockery soon turning to impatience, then to violence as they forcibly eject her from the room and lock the door behind her. Maureen played Mollie's emotional fragility and her distress at being manhandled with startling conviction. Having locked her out, the reporters now had to listen to her desperate sobs diminishing along the corridor as she staggers out of hearing. They lapsed into silence as each began to feel something distinctly unfamiliar – shame.

Maureen's second act topped her first. It is after the jail-break and Mollie has encountered the fugitive in the empty Press Room and tried to hide him. The returning reporters find her alone and immediately become suspicious. They are now hunting as a pack, and, sensing that she knows the whereabouts of the condemned man, they make threatening advances towards her. 'Tell us or we'll beat it out of you,' says one of them. Terrified, for herself and also because of what she knows, Mollie scrambles on to the ledge of an open window, and on a sudden impulse throws herself out.

How could we make this moment absolutely convincing? In charge of the Sound Department at that time was a Canadian,

Sylvia Carter, who loved the play and was throwing all her resources behind it. I asked her if it would be possible to record a long scream from Maureen and then treat it so that it had the descending pitch of someone falling from a height. Sylvia obliged and added a chilling thump as the body hits the ground and the scream cuts off. I then asked Maureen if, just before she leapt, she could begin to scream for real. The idea was that, as she disappeared from sight, her actual scream would dovetail seamlessly with the one on the tape. In performance the effect was quite astonishing, as if she had fallen forty feet below the stage. The reporters stood stock-still, their mouths open, unable to believe what they had just seen. I had them count to five before anyone moved, then they raced to the window and crowded together to look down at the hapless Mollie. The moment had been so unexpected and realistically rendered that the audience responded to it in much the same way as the characters on stage. Thus from one peak of farce to another of melodrama the show swung like a switchback towards its famous last line.

Sound brought the environment of the play to life in all sorts of ways. Just beyond the windowsill were a couple of hidden mics, so that anyone having a shouted conversation with someone below would hear its echo reverberating within the well of the building. Sylvia had also devised a marvellous sound for the approach of the ancient elevator, the outer cage of which Michael Annals had discovered for real in a junkyard. Its creaking approach on tape blended in perfectly with the genuine rattle of its concertina doors. We were still scratching our heads about how to convey realistically the arrival of the elevator from below when I remembered from my time as a child-conjuror the way black velvet could be used to make a box seem empty. Our elevator, on the diagonal, was also a box, so from the flies we hung two sheets of black velvet which reached the floor and fitted snugly against the two visible sides of the elevator shaft. When the sheets were slowly raised light was revealed progressively from the bottom up. Seen through the ironwork of the cage, and accompanied by the sound effect, you could have sworn that an elevator had just risen up from the bowels of the theatre.

However, our most impressive effect was something that again came about by happy accident. Before rehearsals I had been discussing the set with Richard Bullimore of the Production Department, and I asked him idly what he thought of the play. He was very enthusiastic but couldn't believe we hadn't updated it, since it still seemed so relevant to the America we were reading about in the papers and watching on television. However, what he particularly liked was that moment when the fugitive 'comes crashing through the window'. I didn't correct him but the play describes something rather different: Earl Williams merely 'enters through the open window'.

Afterwards I began to think – but what if he *did* come crashing through the window? What if Earl Williams had been on a ledge somewhere clinging to a drainpipe and the drainpipe had come loose from the wall, and he'd swung in a great arc to come crashing through the glass? I went straight back to Richard. It was possible, yes, but you'd need a new window for every performance, probably with a balsa wood frame and sugar-glass panes. This was the sort of challenge the prop department of a film studio was familiar with, so we went out to Pinewood. They were extremely co-operative and answered additional questions about how we could make a line of machine-gun bullets perforate the back wall of the Press Room during the jail-break.

The crash through the window became the talking point of the show and its biggest surprise. Clive Merrison, who played the fugitive, executed it with real daring when, to the accompaniment of splintering wood and shattering window panes, he pitched himself headlong into the room. There was one problem; when the reporters returned there was sugar-glass all over the floor and they couldn't take a step without an audible crunch. It needed a line from someone and there were numerous suggestions.

James Hayes, playing Murphy, came up with the best one. A reporter picks up a piece of glass and says, 'What happened?' and Murphy replies drily, 'Bensinger broke his glasses'. It got as big a laugh as anything in the evening.

We were now about three-quarters of the way through rehearsals, and, as so often happens, particularly in comedy, the laughs and surprises of the play had become blurred with familiarity. We had temporarily sailed into the doldrums. The repertoire was making heavy demands on the company at this time, with many of them working twelve hours a day – on call for practically every rehearsal, then playing their other parts at night. What is usually needed from the actor at this point is a return to the text on the page – an hour or two of reflection to sharpen up his precise knowledge of the words and with luck to unearth an imaginative detail missed the first time round. This is easier to do when the actor has a two-handed scene to play rather than being, as most of the reporters were, one of an ensemble. We would run parts of Act One and the same hiccups would recur – cues missed or picked up a beat late.

I begged the actors to go back to the text, and there was some improvement but not enough, so I brought a small gong into rehearsals and struck it every time a cue was picked up late. This did not endear me to the actors, but it helped a little. Up till now we had been working in the rehearsal room at Aquinas Street with sunlight streaming into the room or, when it was raining, buckets strategically placed in the playing area to catch the drips from the leaking roof. What I thought might help was a rehearsal on the stage of the theatre in which the actors would soon be confronting an audience. This would concentrate all our minds. And the following week the Old Vic became available for just one afternoon.

The scene I particularly wanted to rehearse was one which had already consumed hours of time. Earl has crashed through the window and is having his scene with Mollie when the reporters return to find the doors of the Press Room locked. Perplexed, and desperate to get to their phones, they rap loudly and demand to be let in, at the same time as Mollie and Earl are having a frantic whispered discussion about where he might hide. The scene, though brief, was technically difficult. The reporters had to time their knocking on the door and their scraps of angry dialogue to cues from their fellow actors they could neither see nor were meant to be able to hear. It required alertness and dogged practice, so these few hours on the stage of the Vic would be important. I'd asked the cast to revise the scene and had arranged for the flimsy double doors of plywood that had been knocked up for rehearsals to be brought over to the theatre from Aquinas Street.

On my way down to the stage that afternoon I called in at the men's room in the basement of the theatre. John Dexter was there washing his hands. 'How's it going?' he asked.

'Not bad, we're a bit becalmed at the moment.'

'Be careful, there's been a lot of grumbling in the canteen,' said John and left. Immediately my mood, already nervy, went black. Was I the only person in the organisation who knew the risk the National was taking doing this play at all? If we didn't do everything we could to get the thing right we would be inviting laughter of an unexpected and unpleasant sort. And did the company really think I enjoyed being a taskmaster rather than a director? With a head like a pressure-cooker I made my way to the auditorium to rehearse the scene.

It's always difficult gauging exactly the impression you make on other people, but I'd been told that as a director I had a reputation for staying calm through all the ups and downs of staging a play and that I had a knack for getting my way without anyone particularly noticing. That reputation was about to undergo a major revision.

We started to rehearse, and almost at once there was an all-too-familiar pocket of silence when there should have been a rap on the door. Without realising it was about to happen, I did what I have only done three times in my professional career: I completely lost my temper. It was more than anger; my rage was echoing round the auditorium of the Vic with a volume and intensity enough to challenge the howls of every Othello who had ever played there. It went on and on. I can't remember what I said except that it was intended to be graphic and devastating. John Shrapnel, an excellent and conscientious actor who had had the misfortune to become the target of my fury now appeared from behind the double doors, ashen with shock. In the wings I saw Maureen Lipman looking at me as if Jekyll had turned into Hyde right before her eyes.

Eventually I must have calmed down because the rehearsal resumed and we limped our way through the rest of the afternoon. Exposing my anxieties in this manner had been exhausting and hideous but the company, once they had got over the surprise of my behaviour, were remarkably grown-up about it. They knew that what I was asking of them was also what they wanted – to be part of a fresh, exciting show that would not easily be forgotten, and the final weeks of rehearsal were characterised by harmony and resolve. When I scheduled a run-through of the first act it was with confidence.

Ken Tynan heard about it and asked if he could attend. An audience – somebody to please – was just what the company needed, so I told him that he was more than welcome. That afternoon the actors gave as wonderful and as focused a performance as I was ever to see, and I watched them with shivering excitement and enormous pride. There is something uncanny about a play coming completely to life in a makeshift space with only words and resourceful acting to conjure it up. You watch the genie coming out of the bottle almost with disbelief. At the end of the act I looked across the room at Ken, and saw all I needed to see. Not only was he smiling but tears were streaming down his cheeks and his chest was vibrating with sobs. I couldn't have hoped for a better commendation. We had passed what would subsequently be referred to as the 'Ken Tynan Blub Test'.

However there would be one more hurdle to clear and it would almost be our undoing. The rights to *The Front Page* resided with the widows of the two authors. Months ago we had received permission from Helen Hayes, who was very excited and surprised about the National doing her husband's play, but from Rose Hecht, despite the reassurances of intermediaries, we had heard not a word.

Then, a week before the play was due to be performed, Olivier received a long and erratically typed letter from her. It rambled all over the place, at one point invoking a Beethoven string quartet with a couple of bars of score inscribed on the page. She reminded Olivier of Ben Hecht's fervent Zionism and his hatred of the British during the bloodshed that preceded the foundation of the Jewish State. Hecht had declared publicly that there was 'a song in his heart' every time a British soldier was killed. Despite its lack of cogency, the import of the letter was beyond doubt. Mrs Hecht would never allow the National Theatre of Great Britain to stage her husband's play.

This was a matter that needed to be referred to the Chairman of the Board forthwith. Max Rayne was remarkably sympathetic to our plight because word was already out that the National might have another hit on the way. However, before he could advise us he needed to consult the full Board, whose members included a couple of legal hot-shots. An emergency meeting was called, the outcome of which was extremely discouraging. Legally, the National didn't have a leg to stand on. In the US if two people jointly own the rights to a play it is enough for one of them to give permission for a production. In the UK, alas, you needed the agreement of both parties. The show would have to be abandoned. However, before a final decision was reached the Board agreed to hold one further meeting to which Lord

Goodman, legal genius and supreme fixer for the British Establishment, would be invited to give his sage advice.

In the meantime invitations had already gone out for a public dress rehearsal. Would this too have to be cancelled? The Board thought not, since we were not charging for admission. A few nights later a full house took their seats at the Vic, unaware that they might be the only people ever to bear witness to this production. When the curtain rose to reveal Michael Annals' sleazy Press Room, seen through a haze of stale tobacco smoke, there was a gasp of pleasure and surprise from the audience, and we knew they had taken the bait in one big gulp. The laughter that followed was the best sort, rapt and expectant. A young man in the very front row of the stalls got so excited during the big laughs that he started pounding on the front of the stage with his feet like someone at a football game.

What I particularly wanted to see in front of an audience, because it was my favourite bit of staging, was the jail-break at the end of Act One. Hildy Johnson, on his way to a well-paid job in New York and a honeymoon with his lovely bride, has called in at the newsroom to bid his erstwhile colleagues a mocking farewell. He is barely out of the door with his suitcase when there comes the sound of raised voices and gunfire from the well of the building. The reporters crowd at the open window and, when they learn what has happened, dive for the telephones connecting them to their news desks. Suddenly there is the sound of machine-gun fire, some panes in the downstage window shatter and we see a line of bullets blowing holes in the wall just above the reporters' heads. (Pinewood Studios helped us with this last effect, and the smashing of the windowpanes was achieved by the stage management using black hammers wielded by hands in black gloves.)

The reporters hurl themselves to the floor, one of them on the way down having the forethought to turn out the lights which have apparently made them a target. During the melee I'd asked one of the actors surreptitiously to topple over the pedestal phone connected to Hildy's newspaper, *The Enquirer*, so that the ear-piece hung over the front of the table and swung from side to side like a pendulum. There's now a lull in the gunfire, and the men scramble to their feet and thunder out of the room in pursuit of a scoop, leaving behind a paralysed Hildy. In the suddenly empty, silent Press Room the only thing moving is the earpiece swinging on its cord, back and forth in a shaft of light. I'd asked Sylvia, our sound expert, to wire it up so that you could just hear the rasp of the operator at the other end of the line repeating 'Hello? . . . Enquirer! . . . Hello? . . . Hello? . . . Enquirer! . . . *Enquirer!*' Hildy looks repeatedly between the phone and the direction in which his colleagues have disappeared, then with a howl of capitulation drops his bag, runs to the phone, tells his paper he's back on the job, and hurtles out of the room in pursuit of an irresistible story.

The curtain fell and a ripple of incredulous laughter rose up from the house, astonished that the National should be attempting such a play, and more astonished that the National should be actually pulling it off. The audience rose from their seats and, hugging the walls like a spy, I moved among them. In the circle I was spotted by Peter Shaffer, who approached with delight and surprise written all over his face.

I had an elaborate curtain call planned, but had not found time to rehearse it, so at the end the cast stood in a single ragged line to take their bows. It didn't matter, the audience went wild. I'd asked the company to stay on stage so that I could give them notes behind the curtain, but when I came on to the set I had nothing for them but a huge smile. Instead they gave me a note of their own, a long round of applause. I was extremely touched, and couldn't bring myself to tell them that this performance might be the only one they would ever give.

The meeting with Lord Goodman took place around six o'clock in the evening at Max Rayne's office off Baker Street. It was sug-gested I wait in the reception area for the outcome. So I sat there very still preparing myself for the worst. However, when the meeting ended and the members of the Board emerged in dribs and drabs I noticed they were all smiles. I was about to have some first-hand experience of why Arnold Goodman had the reputation of being a modern Solomon. It was true, he had apparently summed up, that Mrs Hecht had the law totally on her side. However, in order to bring an action she would have to leave the United States and take up temporary residence in the United Kingdom. Abroad her hands were tied. Given that she was a very old lady and a confused one, given that she detested Britain and all its works, Lord Goodman was of the opinion that never in a million years would she consider making the trip. Trusting that once she started to receive her royalties her attitude would soften, he advised that we should proceed with the opening.

We sailed through a week of previews and opened like a fireworks display. On my way backstage after the protracted ovation, I ran into Larry who greeted me with generous words but a complexity of emotion with which I was beginning to become all too familiar. I detected admiration, a touch of jealousy, and something else, which always touched me because it was so unexpected, the wistfulness of someone now outside looking in. 'It's been a long time since I've heard a reception like that in this theatre,' he said. (Not strictly accurate, since *Jumpers* had had a splendid opening night.) I wondered if he'd been thinking that this was the way *Guys and Dolls* might have been received if his plans for it had not been scuppered by the Board.

The following morning all the papers gave us raves, except for the *Daily Telegraph* whose review epitomised those self-regarding British constraints from which American egalitarian culture had always been my escape. This was something Ken Tynan and I had in common, and the National's successes first with a great American tragedy and now with its most remarkable comedy were triumphs we could share. In a way we were repaying a debt from our growing-up, Ken's in Birmingham, mine in Sydney.

At the age of nine I had spotted the first appearance of *Action Comics* in the news-stand of the shop at the Rose Bay Pier, on the cover of which Superman was making his debut, lifting an entire automobile over his head to hurl to destruction. Even the '10 cents' in the lower right hand corner had a glamour for me, that same ten cents having come out of the radio in scraps of song – 'Ten Cents a Dance' and Bing Crosby crooning 'The Million Dollar Baby at the Five and Ten Cents Store'. For my copy of *Action Comics* I was charged ninepence, a sum I continued to dish out for weeks on end, assembling a collection which if auctioned today would secure the retirement of my entire extended family. As it was my mother threw the lot out when my taste improved.

Ken and I, twelve thousand miles apart, were then going to the same movies, watching spellbound as James Cagney shot his way to a gangster's death or Orson Welles introduced us to the dead heart at the centre of American success. During the war we opened *Life* magazine to see its graphic coverage of the cost of battle, a huge photograph of a dead GI sprawled in the shallows of a Pacific beach, and in the *New Yorker* we read John Hersey's account of the aftermath of Hiroshima. We gulped down without question both Hemingway's romantic pessimism and Steinbeck's dogged indignation, and if we wanted laughter we turned to S. J. Perelman or to a cinema where they were running an old Marx Brothers movie. And all this fervour and yearning from long ago had now made its way on to the stage of a British theatre.

The Front Page was up and running, and my next production would be *Macbeth* in the autumn. Michael Annals and I had some preparatory work ahead of us and the best place to do it was clearly Biarritz. So two days after the first night a party of us took up residence at my French house for a week. Notwithstanding the stern intentions of this present visit, there was no resisting the enormous pleasure of seeing the building for the first time resurrected under a fresh coat of paint or experiencing

Biarritz in the perfect weather of early July. I would set the alarm and work on the text until breakfast. Afterwards Michael and I would spend a couple of hours discussing the play and moving towards ways of staging it – how it should look and move. Then we would throw down our pencils, give up and go down to the beach.

The way to the ocean from the house was down a path which zig-zagged through an elaborate cliff garden abounding in terraces, castellated lookout points and carefully positioned benches that allowed you to savour the changing views at each stage of the descent. It was planted with a forest of tamarisk trees, one of the few species of vegetation that can withstand the harsh Atlantic winters. These rather stunted trees with their twisted arthritic trunks would be ugly if it weren't for their foliage – delicate clusters of very fine needles which in early summer are like puffs of brilliant green smoke. That year the trees were somewhat overgrown and the descent was through emerald tunnels pierced by sunlight. The view between the trees was a canvas of enormous horizontal brushstrokes, one above the other, first the sable of the beach, then the turquoise of the ocean and, above, the powdery blue of the sky tinged with pink along the horizon.

And this feast of the senses was merely the preliminary to the big event – wading into that swaying ocean, breasting its surges, then striking out for the deep water where the bigger waves were breaking. To feel once again every muscle in my body, from the tips of my fingers down to my toes, strive against and yet collaborate with the water in which I was suspended, so that with a couple of strokes and a kick from my flippered feet I could harness one of those walls of water and slide down its front, was for me the closest thing to bliss that physical life affords. In an instant I was connected to my boyhood, not as a memory but as something being relived.

If I seem to have idealised that first week of summer in this place in which I had now staked a claim, it is because that's how

I experienced it. There were, of course, other aspects of Biarritz with which I would later become acquainted, not the least meteorological ones. I had yet to experience the operatic storms that came down from the mountains, and rain that fell like water being emptied out of a jug. From the Bay of Biscay there would come winds which tore the roofs off houses, and which you had to lean into at an angle of forty-five degrees just to stay on your feet; and tempests which would transform the Atlantic into a chaos about as hospitable as an active volcano. There would be weeks at a time when rain clouds hovered unmoving over the town until all its colours seemed to drain away to grey; then, in August, humid muggy days with a dull sun suspended over a choppy soiled sea. The *Illustrated London News* of 19 August 1854 described Biarritz thus: 'Beyond its sea bathing, its rocks and its views Biarritz must be the dullest place on earth.' The writer had obviously visited the town during the wrong week.

The many variations of the place were inscribed on the year like the numbers on the roulette wheels spinning in the casinos, and during the course of any summer they came around again to make their random visitations. I've been coming to Biarritz now for forty years, and if you stay in any house long enough sooner or later some unhappiness will seep under the front door or through the keyhole to catch you unawares. Rooms that during those early days enclosed an almost blatant contentment have since seen something of its opposite. But the perfect days, though they seem rarer, keep spinning round, and when they come they are as pristine as the feathery new green on the tamarisk trees I passed under the first time I set off for the beach.

When I returned to the National all the news was good. *The Front Page* was selling out, and waiting for me was a letter from Helen Hayes praising the show and asking if her son, James MacArthur, who was directing the play in Hawaii, could borrow the crash through the window for his own production. In addition, Lew

Grade's proposal that his television company record *Long Day's Journey* for transmission on ITV had reached the contractual stage, and in Larry's absence (he was away filming *Sleuth* at Pinewood), Paddy Donnell, the Administrator, had proposed that I speak for the National on all artistic matters. But because I was not a member of the appropriate union I could receive a credit only as the director of the stage production. The TV credit would have to go to a union member, though I would retain overall artistic control. There were two ways of going about this. One was to collaborate with a young TV director, who would offer me guidance with the technical aspects of the medium, but leave the actual direction to me; the other was a partnership with someone who already had a reputation in both mediums. Peter Wood, who had directed *Jumpers* for the National and had recently won an Emmy for his *Hamlet* on TV with Richard Chamberlain, had apparently expressed an interest, and had already had some success with O'Neill, having directed on stage a much praised production of *The Iceman Cometh*.

The first option was the more attractive to me except for the dilemma posed by the upcoming production of *Macbeth*. This would be my first shot at directing a Shakespeare, and the production would open immediately before the TV went into rehearsals. I doubted whether I would have the spare capacity to be deeply involved in both at once. With some misgiving I opted for the participation of Peter Wood, but with a proviso that he accept the limits of his brief – namely to bring the National's production to the small screen, not a new version of his own. The executive producer, Cecil Clark, said he would speak to Peter Wood to see if this was acceptable. Word came back that it was and contracts were drawn up and signed. In the meantime Peter Wood agreed to have frequent planning meetings with me whenever our other professional commitments permitted.

The National was expanding in other ways. With Larry's encouragement our new young director, Roland Joffé, had been given a free hand to create a touring wing for the organisation, called 'Mobiles'. The productions he planned were designed for communities without access to a traditional theatre. They were to be strongly cast from within the company but with minimal sets so that they could play virtually anywhere – church halls, school gymnasia, any space that could accommodate a few hundred chairs. The first show, directed by Roland, John Ford's 'Tis Pity She's a Whore, was about to open, and others were planned.

One morning I was just about to enter the Aquinas Street building when I met Peter Hall coming out. We hadn't seen each other since I'd been an actor in the company at Stratford thirteen years before, and I experienced the slight shock you have when you re-encounter someone who once figured prominently in your life, as enemy perhaps or lover, and you realise that the memory you have been carrying around in your mind doesn't quite tally with the person now standing in front of you – Peter, for example, was taller than I remembered. The Stratford period had been painful for me. Peter and I had competed for the affections of the young Vanessa Redgrave and in the process we had both lost her. Then at the end of the season he had dispensed with my services as an actor.

These experiences, transmuted by fiction, had made their way into my novel *Next Season*, which I was pretty certain he must have read. Had it bothered him? He certainly wasn't giving me that impression; in fact he couldn't have been more engaging. In any case our lives had moved on to different places, mine perhaps more dramatically than Peter's. Barely six years ago I'd been a working actor. Now I was a successful director with a book to my name, and any lingering resentment had long ago been soaked up in its pages. We had a wry, pleasant conversation, and parted like friends.

The following day Paddy Donnell beckoned me into his office. His manner was that of someone who has inside knowledge of a prize you're up for. 'Peter *very much* wants me to arrange a time when you two can talk.'

'About staying on?'

'You'd best talk to Peter, but he'd like to see you as soon as possible.'

'There may be a problem,' I said, and then told Paddy about the novel I'd written. I explained it contained an unsympathetic portrayal of a director that some readers had been known to confuse with Peter. Paddy smiled knowingly. 'I'm sure that won't be a problem.'

There were, however, from my own point of view problems of a different sort. As a theatre director my reputation at that time was at its peak and this was unlikely to last. If I wanted to do films, which I emphatically did, this was the time to make my move. Also, as a director working in the subsidised theatre I knew I had a string to my bow that my colleagues perhaps didn't; I was interested in the possibilities of popular entertainment – the comedies and the musicals which at their best could epitomise their own time more vividly than more earnest endeavours. This meant I was fairly confident I could survive in the theatre as a freelance; I was less dependent on an organisation to provide me with the work that attracted me.

I went to see Peter at ten in the morning on the last day of July in 1972. He sat me down at once and started speaking in a steady purr. I had heard a great deal about his remarkable powers of persuasion, but before had never been important enough to become their focus. Now I was receiving the full treatment, and very pleasant it was.

'Michael,' he said, his brows puckered with sincerity, 'I've always thought of you as a good director, but after *The Front Page* I think you might be . . . a great director.'

I didn't believe him, but how comforting it was to hear. Or rather, I didn't think such categorisations were useful to anyone except critics and academics. For someone on my side of the business even the most illustrious track record is no guarantee that on your next project you won't fall flat on your face. Peter continued by saying that he was in the process of choosing his associate directors, that Jonathan Miller was already on board and that he hoped I would consider joining him. When the National moved to the new building it would require two companies, an A and a B, and what he was proposing was that I should be in charge of one company and Jonathan of the other, and that we should work together in partnership. This interested me. It would mean continuity for the acting company I'd helped put in place, as well as the chance of at last working alongside someone with whom I felt entirely compatible. Peter went on to say that he had in mind Harold Pinter and John Schlesinger becoming part of the team.

'Wow,' I murmured.

'And another thing,' he continued. 'You seem to have a wonderful rapport with the company, and I see you as having a special role among the associates which will set you apart and above them. You'd be in a category of your own.'

I didn't know exactly what he meant by this but it sounded to me as if he was offering me the position of second-in-command. Had I known the things he knew, as later revealed in his published *Diaries*, it would have been a great deal clearer – for instance that Larry had proposed me to Max Rayne as his successor, and that just three weeks previously Ken Tynan had argued strongly with the Board that I should be appointed Deputy Director. But of all this I was ignorant. Had I known, the advantages of recruiting me to a key position would have been obvious. It would send a message that the transition from Larry's regime to his own was harmonious and had the unequivocal blessings of his great predecessor. This of course was not the case.

I responded that though I was pleased to be asked to be part of the new regime, there were impediments to my accepting. I wasn't much interested in theatre administration, indeed had

149

little talent for it and suspected that temperamentally I was more of a freelance than a player on a large team. I added that this was also the time when I had my best chance of breaking into film.

'But, Michael,' he replied, 'I see film as very much part of the National's future. There should be a record made of all of our best work, and we should be the ones to do it. With full artistic control! The rehearsal rooms in the new building are big enough to become sound studios, and it's quite possible that one day we'll be making our own in-house movies.'

The meeting came to an end. He had unerringly pressed all the right buttons and though I didn't commit then and there, I said that yes, I was very very interested. I was halfway out of the door when he said, not looking up, but attending to something on his desk, 'Are you doing any writing at the moment, Michael?' I said, 'At the moment, no. There hasn't been time,' and he replied, still not looking at me but with the suggestion of a smile, 'You should. You're very good at it.'

I closed the door behind me. That clinched it! The man had humour and more than that, magnanimity. I had worked hard at the National; why should I not be part of the triumphant move to the new building? I would accept! But that was the last I would ever hear about an A and a B company, nor was my 'special role' among the associates ever elucidated.

It may be interesting to compare my account of this meeting with the one on page 15 of Peter Hall's *Diaries*. His is briefer and much, much cooler. In the proof copy it concludes 'He said . . . what he wanted out of life was to direct plays and films, not run theatres. I was not convinced.' Later, in the published edition, the last sentence 'I was not convinced' is improved to 'I wonder,' a more succinct way of suggesting trouble ahead.

The school holidays had begun. Shirley, Conrad and I went off to Biarritz for four weeks, and I enjoyed the best holiday I had had since my arrival in England.

SEVEN

Waiting for me on my return was *Macbeth*. I knew my leading man, Anthony Hopkins, slightly and regarded him as the most exciting of all the younger actors at present coming to the fore. However, there were things we had yet to learn about each other, so I suggested a dinner one evening during which I could explain my ideas for the production. Of all Shakespeare's plays, *Macbeth* seemed to me to be the one that continued to be seen through a cloud of Victorian historicism, and many produtions were still located in a primitive world of coarse bloodshed and Wagnerian spectres. To its original audience, however, it must have seemed rather more up to date, and its central murder may well have had echoes of another Scottish bloodletting, that of Darnley, husband of Mary, Queen of Scots, a despatch no less ghastly for being implemented with engraved and gilded steel. The play's language and its references belong to the High Renaissance, and as for the presence of the supernatural it would have had the immediacy of a news bulletin. King James himself had written a treatise on modern witchcraft and it had been widely read. I wanted the three witches to be as ordinary as an African witch-doctor might seem to the villagers with whom he mixes – no less malign for being so everyday.

The verbal sophistication of Shakespeare's England is not mirrored in its visual arts, if you exclude the work of visitors from abroad such as Holbein. The portraiture often has a hypnotised, flat look, as if the subjects, in their elaborate constricting costumes, had been ironed to the canvas. I felt this was a primitivism we could justly make use of – the Macbeths as they accumulate

151

power becoming increasingly weighed down by the emblematic finery that records their ascent.

In a small museum in Edinburgh I had once stumbled on a sixteenth-century portrait of Mary, Queen of Scots, that seemed like a key to the production. It was crudely painted on a surface made up of very narrow slats of wood, set at right angles to one another, so that in cross section it would have looked like a succession of tiny troughs and peaks. On the left hand aspect of these slats was painted Mary's portrait, on the right a death's head. This meant that standing slightly to one side of the picture you saw the Queen's likeness; then as you walked slowly to the other side that likeness cross-faded into a skull. The trick of the thing was crude but very telling, and it reminded me of the grim and ironic surprises of the promises made by the witches. I wanted to stage the play with the same simple boldness.

Over dinner at a small Italian restaurant off the Edgware Road, recommended by Tony, we discussed these and other matters related to the play. He had been consulting a stack of academic commentaries, but it wasn't clear whether they were proving helpful or confusing. I found him friendly but rather edgy and on his guard. We didn't drink much – maybe a bottle of red wine between us – but at the end of the meal when we ordered coffee, Tony started to gulp it down by the pint. At least ten small cups, strong and black, went rapidly down his throat. I wondered if he was what I had once heard described as 'an addictive personality'?

The answer to that, unfortunately, was yes. Anthony Hopkins has long ago gone public about his alcoholism and his eventual salvation as a member of AA, since when he has shown himself to be the best British screen actor since Charles Laughton, with at least four quite exceptional performances to his name, in *Howard's End*, *The Silence of the Lambs*, *The Remains of the Day* and *Shadowlands*. What follows does not really describe that immensely talented individual. It relates to a more general group, anyone who has the misfortune to be an unreformed alcoholic, and whose salient characteristic is the lengths he or she will go to in order to satisfy, conceal and justify their dependence on drink.

On the first day of rehearsal, when we read the play Tony spoke his part in an almost inaudible mutter, and this reluctance to show his hand continued into later rehearsals. Though I'd never directed a Shakespeare before, I'd appeared in enough of his plays as an actor to know that performing them carried a double obligation: good acting as it is generally understood – that is to say truthful behaviour and honest feeling – but also fidelity to the requirements of the verse. Tony could deliver the first but seemed unwilling to acknowledge the challenge of the second, and when we came to Macbeth's soliloquies he quickly became lost in the thickets of the language. There were passages in the play that simply could not be played solely out of an imaginative under-standing of the moment. The words needed to be analysed for meaning and a shape found for them so that at the worst mid-week matinee, playing to an unresponsive house, the actor could still hold the stage.

When I attempted to coax Tony in this direction he would change the subject matter to the commentaries he had been study-ing, and I suggested that the time had come to close the book on other people's opinions and decide on our own. That, after all, is what the audience come to see: a text brought to life by gifted actors and fresh direction. At lunchtime Tony would make for the pub, all too conveniently located next to the stage door, and complain loudly to other members of the company about the constraints he was working under. Scraps of his conversation reached me. 'Nobody's going to bloody tell me what I can and cannot read!' he had thundered before ordering another round, and of course nobody had. What I was trying to do was encour-age him to believe in himself.

The best thing to emerge from the first week of rehearsals was the certainty that Diana Rigg was going to be a superb Lady

Macbeth. Her many seasons at Stratford meant that dealing with the language was second nature to her, and she enthusiastically took on board the assumptions of the production. In the banquet scene, as later staged, she appeared dressed in a costume as elaborate and rigid as those worn in the Elizabeth I portraits, looking like some enamelled insect. She wore the same chalk-white make-up with a circle of rouge on each cheek. Her rigid smile was a parody of welcome for her uneasy guests, and she played the beginning of the scene like someone already on her way to breakdown, as her husband pulled her around the stage like a broken doll. When Banquo's ghost appears and Macbeth is suddenly once again the weaker of the two, Diana ferociously recovered Lady Macbeth's strength. And her later sleepwalking scene, the character now divested of her finery but with a smudge of clown's make-up still soiling her face, was mesmeric.

The only other Lady Macbeth I have seen to match hers was to be Judi Dench's in Trevor Nunn's ground-breaking studio production which began its life at The Other Place in Stratford in 1976. This changed the course of Shakespeare in performance towards pared-down productions in intimate spaces, where the entire audience are so close to the action that they have no choice but to listen to every word, and where the expression on the faces of the actors gives them everything they need to look at. My own production, fully mounted in a proscenium arch, and augmented with a lofty set, spectacular costumes, music, theatrical effects and projected acting, had its strengths, but it was coming at the tail end of the tradition I'd grown up in. And it may be that Anthony Hopkins' reluctance to accept the assumptions of the show was at least partly an intuitive understanding of what he would have been able to do in a chamber production.

I caught a glimpse of this one afternoon when we had a run-through of the first half of the play. Only eight feet away from where I was sitting, Tony and Diana were playing the scene leading up to the murder of the King. Their performances had that sense of the absolute present moment that the best film acting conveys, and everyone in the rehearsal room was watching them, rapt. 'Print it!' a film director might have said at the end of the scene. In the theatre, alas, all one can say, with one's fingers crossed, is 'Repeat it,' and the ability to do so is the mark of a good stage actor.

Anyone attempting the part of Macbeth is negotiating a mine-field. The play reads with the grip of a thriller, each scene proceeding inexorably from the one before, but in performance the headlong advance of the narrative stumbles against blocks of language which need the utmost skill to negotiate. Moreover, the supernatural elements of the story when particularised on stage can demolish credibility in an instant. An unruly audience of schoolchildren will undermine an inadequate production with the voraciousness of termites. This means that the physical demands made on the actor who plays the name part are doubly onerous as he climbs the mountain of one particularly demanding scene only to confront another beyond it. And another. And another.

Aware of this I became very protective of Tony, and indulgent when I would have served him better by being firm. It didn't help when, in the second week of rehearsals, I developed a heavy cold, a sign perhaps of anxieties I was not yet prepared to acknowledge. I was so concerned about not passing on the infection to my leading actor that for the next two weeks we didn't communicate without at least ten feet between us. Tony's growing discontents had no difficulty traversing the distance. He was particularly exercised about the climactic swordfight with Macduff: it was too complicated, he complained, too long and (something he knew but did not express) it was not a fight to attempt unless one was entirely sober. This was something I had not yet grasped. Our fight director was among the best in the country, but to placate Tony I felt I had to replace him. Fortunately we had an actor in the company with some experience as a fight choreo-grapher, Desmond McNamara, and he took over. Having some-times been in the pub next door at the same time as Tony he had a rather better understanding of the problem than I did.

Otherwise the production was coming together much as I had planned, with everything in place except the one element that mattered most – a secure central performance. Then, at the final dress rehearsal, the afternoon before the press night, something remarkable happened. Under no immediate pressure and playing to an empty auditorium, Tony began giving the performance I had hoped for. As I watched I suddenly recalled an incident in Tyrone Guthrie's book, *A Life in the Theatre*. Some forty years before in this same auditorium Charles Laughton, playing the same part, had been magnificent at the dress rehearsal but had fallen apart that night in front of an audience. Theatrical history was about to repeat itself. The inspiration that had come to Tony in the afternoon deserted him in the evening. About to embark on a soliloquy he would walk around the stage like someone psyching themselves up for a dive into freezing water. Once in and thrashing about, he waited for the audience to offer a help-ing hand, but none was forthcoming. The performance became unfocused and sweaty. He got through the evening honourably and was well received at the curtain, but I knew he had grievously disappointed himself.

The notices the following morning were mainly favourable, with one mocking dissenter countered by a couple of enthusiasts. The assumptions of the production were widely discussed but even in our better reviews the response to Tony's performance was muted. This worried me. No leading actor enjoys playing second fiddle to a production, and in any case there is something amiss in a *Macbeth* when there is more praise for the director that there is for the star. The critic of the *Evening News* disgraced himself with an attack of such malice that I dreaded the effect it would have on subsequent performances. When a newspaper savages a book or a painting the work is already done, but the performer is in the middle of his task. He has to continue working with the critic's judgement ringing not only in his own head but in the heads of the people watching him.

This is what Tony had to read in the *Evening News*: 'He frequently gives the impression that he is a Rotarian pork butcher about to tell the stalls a dirty story.' To the ordinary reader this was merely a journalistic cheap shot of questionable amusement. To the actor it was an invitation to slit his throat.

There was better news in *The Times* where everything about the show, including Tony's performance, was extolled. What pleased me more than the praise was that the critic, Irving Wardle, had understood the intentions behind the production. During his long tenure as drama critic of the paper he reviewed me many times, and not always favourably, but it was when I was working at Olivier's National, attempting to bring a fresh eye to four classic plays, that I became grateful to him for the record his notices provide of a particularly rich period in my career. I daresay I was over-praised, but it is not for this reason that I put a special value on his words. It is for their prescience about what I was trying to do.

I had only just finished reading the *Times* review the morning after the first night when the telephone rang. It was Larry who had also just read it. He launched into a long, unexpectedly humble speech of congratulations. 'Well, you really got it out of them,' he said, and sighed. 'I suppose you got it out of me too when we did *Long Day's Journey into Night*.'

I was quick to demur, and soon to regret it. 'No Larry, you're a self-directing actor. I won't take any credit for your performance.' This was exactly what he wanted to hear; he abruptly cheered up and became the person I usually dealt with. He was the boss and I was one of his boys.

That evening before the show I went backstage in search of Tony, hoping to find him not too cast down. He had an adjoining dressing room to Diana and, when I arrived in their corridor, her door was open but his was closed, so I decided to test the waters by visiting her first.

'I'm absolutely furious!' she exclaimed the moment she saw me, and I wondered what I'd done.

'What is it?' I asked.

'Tony arrived fifteen minutes ago. He's been drinking all afternoon!' (This was the last thing I wanted to be told.) 'So I was very very angry. Until he told me why!'

'Why?'

'Would you believe it, Larry rang him this morning and told him he was giving a "very middle-class performance". Isn't that absolutely disgraceful?' I agreed that it was, though a weirder criticism of Tony's performance was hard to imagine.

'I'd better go and see him,' I said.

When I knocked on Tony's door it opened a crack, then, seeing who it was, he whisked me inside and closed it firmly behind us. I'd already worked up some indignant sympathy on his behalf.

'Di's just told me that unforgivable thing Larry said to you,' I began.

But he quickly interrupted me. 'No, no, no, no,' he said.

'About you giving a very middle-class performance?'

'No, no, he didn't actually say that. I made it up. It's just that I'd had a few drinks, and when Diana saw me she got a bit angry with me so I said that just to calm her down.'

I looked at him in disbelief. This was something beyond my capacity to deal with. I went out front and watched as much of the show as I could bear. There a pause of two or three seconds before Tony's every line, and that night the show overran by twenty minutes. The second-night critics were in front.

In the morning there was an emergency meeting in Larry's office. Being drunk on stage is a sackable offence, but it was a step

158

we were reluctant to take – I, because it would confirm that I had failed a very talented man, and Larry, because of his instinctive sympathy for an actor in trouble. However, I wondered if a short sharp shock of this sort might be just the thing to stop him destroying himself. Denis Quilley, whose Banquo had been one of the successes of the evening, had already played Macbeth at the Nottingham Playhouse and could be rehearsed in a matter of days. Meanwhile we had an excellent understudy in John Shrapnel standing by. We discussed it but in the end made what turned out to be the wrong decision. Tony stayed on.

Thereafter, any pleasure or pride I might have derived from my work was replaced by the anxiety of never knowing, from one performance to the next, exactly what we would be offering an audience. At one matinee, an ambulance drove past the Old Vic with its siren wailing during the murder scene, and the audience started to titter. Tony simply walked offstage, leaving the play twisting in the wind. Some years later in an interview with *Time* magazine, he referred to this incident, but with certain interesting adjustments. Now the ambulance had passed the theatre during a rehearsal, not a performance, and it was the company who tittered, not the audience. The person who strode out of the room had become the affronted director. This tale was offered as an illustration of how important a sense of humour is in the theatre, and it is true to the extent that by the time I read this I'd certainly lost mine.

Macbeth came to the end of its initial run. It would return to the repertoire after a break of a couple of months. Tony went off to make a film, and when we next saw him he was happier, considerably richer and, it seemed, genuinely determined to avail himself of this second chance to crack the part. There was one small technical hitch for which we already had a solution: at one point in the production the Macbeths are shown standing in front of a huge double portrait of themselves, dressed in regal finery. Because for the film he had had to shave off the beard he had grown for the Shakespeare, Tony was no longer a match to the picture. However, we'd had a new beard made for him, hand-stitched onto fine gauze. This he was now gluing to his face in preparation for the dress rehearsal prior to his reappearance in the role that evening. The curtain rose and he launched into his part with confidence. For a while I thought I was going to see something new. However his problems with the formal demands of the text had not gone away, and he was soon in the middle of an experience he had forgotten how much he hated – playing this part. Halfway through the dress rehearsal he suddenly stopped and bellowed: 'How can I possibly act with this bloody thing stuck to my face!' And he tore off his beard and threw it on the floor. That was it. I'd had enough. I held my peace until after the performance that night, then I went back to his dressing room and without any anger, but explicitly, said all the things I should have said months before.

A few days later I was called in again to Larry's office. 'The little shit,' he said, as I entered.

'What is it?' I said.

Larry waved the envelope he was holding. 'Doctor's certificate. Nervous exhaustion. He's withdrawing from the show.'

So Denis Quilley took over. We found some time to rehearse, allowed him a few performances to settle in, then we invited the press back. This time all the notices were good. They reiterated their praise for Diana, and gave Denis as clean a sweep of super-latives as I've seen any *Macbeth* receive. So at the end I had the show I wanted.

Some years later I received a letter from Tony apologising for his behaviour during our association on *Macbeth*. It is a require-ment of Alcoholics Anonymous that new members write to all the people they may have offended during their drinking years, but I was still touched that he had decided to include me on the list. Away from the rehearsal room I had always found him an

The National Health
The Senior Consultant (Paul Curran) making his rounds
while staff and patients hold their breath.

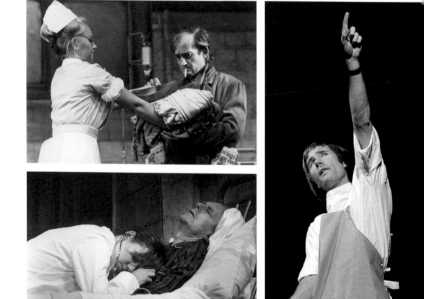

Above, top left: Nurse Sweet (Anna Carteret) kitting out a new arrival
(Charles Kay); bottom left: the overworked houseman Dr Bird (Gillian Barge)
falling asleep over a dying patient (Brian Oulton). Above, right: the Orderly, Barnet
(Jim Dale), reminding the audience of their mortality.

Long Day's Journey into Night
The last moment of the play. A second later the curtain will fall like a blade.

Laurence Olivier rising to the fourth act.

Long Day's Journey into Night
Jamie (Denis Quilley) to his brother Edmond (Ronald Pickup):
'But you'd better be on your guard. Because I'll do my damndest to see you fail.'

Mary Tyrone (Constance Cummings): 'Oh James, I'm so frightened.
I know he's going to die.'

The Front Page

Opposite page, top: the police reporters (John Shrapnel, David Bradley, Allen Mitchell and James Hayes) killing time as they wait for the hanging in the morning.

Bottom: Hildy Johnson (Denis Quilley) and his boss, Walter Burns (Alan MacNaughtan), hot on the trail of the biggest scoop since the last one.

This page, right: Kruger (David Ryall) reporter for the *Journal of Commerce*, appraising the charms of the Clark Street tart, Molly Molloy (Maureen Lipman).

Below: the incorruptible Mr Pinkus (Harry Lomax) arriving with the reprieve which the Mayor has tried to suppress.

Macbeth
Macbeth (Anthony Hopkins) and his Queen (Diana Rigg) after the banquet.

The Cherry Orchard

Top left: Ranevskaya, intent on enjoyment, with her old servant Firs (Harry Lomax) taken for granted in the background. Top right: Trofimov (David Bradley) and Lopakhin (Denis Quilley) stop squabbling for a moment to say an affectionate goodbye. Below: A disconsolate Gaev (Michael Hordern) being observed by the family – Varya (Gillian Barge), Ranevskya (Constance Cummings) and Anya (Anna Carteret).

With Ronald Pickup, Constance Cummings and Denis Quilley,
rehearsing *Long Day's Journey* at Aquinas Street. It isn't raining,
so no buckets are needed to catch the drips.

With Olivier, going back to the script for a moment.

engaging companion. He was a good storyteller and a brilliant mimic, and even at the lowest point of our professional relationship he had still invited me to his wedding. We like to think of gifted people as being friendly and approachable, and many are, but that part of them we call talent is shark-like in its implacable focus and need.

Tony revered Olivier and Gielgud who had spent much of their professional lives gluing tufts of hair to their chins, but I don't think he had any real ambition to be a classical actor. That path had been too well trodden by the previous generation, and the skills it required didn't really interest him. As a boy in Wales it had been the movies that had awakened him to his own abilities, and it was a movie star that he wanted to be. Once sober, that's what he rapidly and brilliantly became, though on the way he made a spectacular return to the stage, directed by David Hare in the play he and Howard Brenton had written satirising Rupert Murdoch, *Pravda*. On the strength of this performance he was offered the lead in *The Silence of the Lambs* . . . and he was on his way.

Long Day's Journey was now back in the National Theatre repertoire but at a new home, the Old Vic. Ahead of us was the television version of the play, about which I'd hardly given a thought during the turbulence of the *Macbeth* rehearsals. Now suddenly it was uppermost in my mind. Michael Annals and I had had a preliminary meeting with Peter Wood as agreed, which Peter rather grandly suggested we have over breakfast at the Connaught Hotel. It had been a pleasant enough occasion, but it was impossible to get him to talk specifically about how we would adapt the play from the stage to the screen. Instead he gave us a meandering lecture about how different a medium television was. It was true neither Michael nor I had worked in TV, but we both had a set at home and had watched enough plays on the small screen to grasp the difference. Some weeks later I asked

161

for another meeting, which we had in the *Macbeth* rehearsal room at the end of a long day. We discussed possible cuts in the text, a task which was left to me, but otherwise the conversation covered the same ground as before. Union rules meant that Peter was working with his own designer, and I had no idea to what extent he was incorporating Michael Annals' work into his own. Or mine for that matter.

It was only after I was free of *Macbeth* that I realised how unsatisfactory the situation had become. I asked for yet another meeting, which Peter declined because he was just about to tape a television play at Teddington Studios. It so happened that my agent, Terry Owen, had a client who was in the cast of this play, and Terry reported back to me that Peter Wood was making no secret of the fact that his TV version of the O'Neill would be a complete rethink of the one on stage at the National. All this, of course, was hearsay, but it was enough to leave me spluttering with rage. I went straight to Paddy Donnell and asked him to arrange a meeting on behalf of the National Theatre with the TV producer, Cecil Clark, during which Peter Wood and I would thrash out what the lines of authority actually were.

A day or two later I caught sight of Peter Wood at the far end of the Aquinas Street corridor. When he saw me he vanished sideways through an office door, and I guessed he must have been there to see Larry. They already had an association, having worked together on Peter's production of *Love for Love*.

The following day I ran into Larry in that same corridor. 'I hear you've asked for a meeting with Cecil Clark at the end of the week,' he said.

Assuming he had been apprised of the situation I replied, 'Yes, I think things need to be sorted out.'

Sounding almost offhand, he said, 'Would you mind very much if I came along?'

'Of course not. No, I'd like you to be there.' Any support he could give me would be welcome.

The meeting took place at eleven o'clock one morning in Cecil Clark's office near Marble Arch. There were a number of us present: a group from the television company, most of whom I didn't know, Larry, Paddy Donnell and I representing the National, and Peter Wood. Since I had asked for the meeting it fell to me to explain what it was about, and as tactfully as possible I gave a full account of my concerns. There was a polite murmur of understanding from Cecil Clark, then Larry, who so far had remained silent, turned to me and almost casually put in, 'You were thinking of coming to rehearsals, were you?'

'Well, yes!' I said, hardly understanding what he was saying.

'And to the studio when we do the recording?' I glanced along the table to Peter Wood, whose gaze flicked downward to a study of the backs of his hands.

'Because,' continued Larry, 'in the past when we've filmed National Theatre productions, the original theatre director has usually stayed away.'

I could hardly believe what I was hearing. Larry had come to the meeting to take Peter Wood's side! I felt a complete fool. I had just spoken in defence of the National Theatre's interests only to have my case shot from under me by the boss of the National Theatre. There was nothing further I could say. I could feel sympathy for my embarrassment emanating from Cecil Clark at the head of the table. He was an excellent producer and a decent man, but he knew that any contractual strengths I had meant nothing without Olivier's endorsement.

Though outwardly I remained mute throughout the rest of the meeting, internally, I was angrier with Larry than I thought it possible to be. He had not only embarrassed me but utterly betrayed me! For a year I had worked unstintingly supporting his vision of what the National Theatre should be; I had delivered three hits which were all selling out and which had turned around our financial situation; I had held the fort for him when he went off to star in his film, one in which his participation (though this was something I could never tell him because I had no way of knowing if it was true) may have depended on the advice I had given the film's producer, Morton Gottlieb. And yet he still mistrusted me, was still wary of a power-grab, still refused to confide in me. What enraged me perhaps most of all was his complacent assumption that *Long Day's Journey* belonged entirely to him, to do what he liked with – that as the play's director I was no more than an employee. I began to think I had no choice but to resign.

The meeting came to an end, by which time my silence felt as conspicuous as if I had leapt on top of the table howling. Without saying anything Larry, Paddy and I made our way to the lift. The doors opened, we stepped inside, the doors closed, and immediately we were alone I exploded. 'You treacherous old bugger!' Larry flinched and looked quite shaken. 'Don't talk to me like that,' he said weakly. But I was unstoppable. We descended past four floors, the elevator shaft ringing with angry noise. The moment the doors opened on the reception area the yelling came to an abrupt stop, and in a lock-step of silence the three of us made our way towards Larry's waiting purple taxi.

It was a journey of perhaps twenty-five yards, during which I had one of those stress-induced emotional switches in which rage flip-flops into its opposite. Olivier had been a presence in my life since my teens – first on screen, then on stage, then as the leading actor of a company of which I was a member, then as a colleague running a theatre. I felt as bereft as a child disowned by a parent, and as I stepped into the cab I was on the point of tears. Larry spotted this immediately and I saw him relax; this would be something much easier to deal with. In turn I responded to his expression by making a quick recovery, and the cab sped back to Aquinas Street.

We gathered in his office and Paddy Donnell produced the contract assigning me artistic control. 'Why did you give him that?' Larry asked, and Paddy replied, with a touch of exasperation, 'Larry, you weren't here! You were off doing your film!' There had been bad blood between the two men ever since Paddy had gone behind his back to the Board to have the production of *Guys and Dolls* scuppered.

Larry took a moment to study the contract. 'Well, that's that. It's a contract,' he said. 'And a contract is a contract.' He then apologised to me for not observing it, and I wondered why no one had told him about it at the time. His mood was very conciliatory; he was offering me friendship and resignation now seemed out of the question.

I had won the battle, though alas too late. The war was already lost. Peter Wood's new set was in the process of being built, and the TV version would be in rehearsal in a matter of days. It is possible for two directors to co-direct a show, but only if they are in general agreement, which I doubted that Peter and I were. I decided that the only thing I could do was keep well out of the way and hope for the best. I avoided rehearsals but visited the studio during the filming to see the set. It bore no relation to anything that Michael Annals and I had dreamt up. The unadorned spaces of a house that was maintained but not loved were now replaced by a small, dinky interior overdressed with theatrical memorabilia. The fanlight separating the rooms was gone, so the power of Mary Tyrone's last entrance went for nothing. The costumes were, to my mind, similarly ill-considered. Edmund was dressed in cloth cap and knickerbockers, a self-conscious reference to the familiar photograph of the young James Joyce in Dublin. It seemed unlikely to me that an aspiring writer of such seriousness and insecurity would ever dress up as a young member of the literati.

I kept my mouth shut because nothing could be achieved by opening it. Later that week, Cecil Clark invited me to his office to see the tape of Larry's fourth act, which they had recorded the day before. He had asked that the scene be shot first thing in the morning when his energies were at their peak. It proved to be a fair record of the stage performance but, to my mind, was too big and too shaped for the screen. I couldn't help but remember that day just over a year before when he had first shown us his hand, that astonishing sketch of all the thoughts and feelings he had found for the part; and the advice which I had wanted to give him but which I had superstitiously withheld because I did not want to take success for granted.

When the show was aired on television it was respectfully received. The actors managed to cling on to the outline of their original performances, but after playing their parts on stage for a year they now lacked a certain spontaneity and daring. The rhythms of my production were entirely gone, the sense of the story 'furling and unfurling' under the watching eye of the Connecticut home that enclosed the lives of the family. However, a long scene between James Tyrone and his elder son was distinctly improved. It came early in the play and in the stage production Larry had insisted on roaming around the set like a caged animal. For TV Peter Wood had relocated the duologue to the exterior veranda where the two men were anchored to chairs. The playing became more intimate and telling. However, I am the last person who should arbitrate on the merits or demerits of the television version. All I could see was that something had been nicked from me and then spoilt.

Directors are unforgiving people and rarely acknowledge merit in the work of their peers. To direct a show successfully you have to become passionate about your view of the material, and this involves a resistance to other perspectives. And although the director works closely as part of a group, he is an isolated figure who rarely gets the chance to see the way others go about the same job. His fellow directors are essentially his competitors, with whom he sometimes has to growl and squabble over the precious scraps thrown into their midst by writers. A director has to harbour within himself two warring identities – a selfless concern for the talented people with whom he is entrusted and who

166

look to him for leadership, and on the other hand the steely egotism that has prompted him to seek out this particular job in the first place.

In general, however, as 1972 drew to a close the National Theatre could look back on an exceptional year. We were playing to full houses, our coffers were overflowing and we were running away with most of the year's awards. Those given by the magazine *Plays and Players* carried a certain weight because they were voted for by the London critics, and leading the winners at the end of the year were Olivier and Constance Cummings, with a special award for Denis Quilley's year's work at the National. *Jumpers* won best play and *The Front Page* best production with *Long Day's Journey* the runner-up. We were entitled to feel a little smug – entitled, but not advised. With only a few weeks to run, the year still had a sting in its tail.

There had been one particular critic who declined to participate in the *Plays and Players* awards. This was Robert Brustein, Professor of Drama and English Literature at Yale University, and now in London for six months as visiting critic for the *Observer* newspaper. In America he had written extensively about the theatre for the *New Republic*, and had effectively spearheaded a movement questioning the reputation of Arthur Miller. (Ironically it would take a string of successful British revivals beginning in the eighties to rehabilitate Miller's name in his own country.) Brustein was an accomplished and persuasive essayist, but he was too oracular and incurious to be a good critic.

What he seemed to expect from a visit to the theatre was a validation of his own doctrines. Practically nothing he had seen so far in London had pleased him. The only evening which had received his wholehearted endorsement was a visiting Polish production, based on a novel by Dostoevsky and spoken in a language which I presumed he didn't understand. My *Macbeth* had been reviewed with unseemly condescension so I was already wary of him. As a theatre practitioner I am not automatically hostile to critics, even when they reject what I have to offer. What is intolerable, however, is when the critic, simply by virtue of a byline, writes on the assumption that he has more intelligence and insight than the people whose work he judges; and that the purpose of his words is to provide a shining apex to that pyramid of work that goes into the making of any stage production. I have known many playwrights and some actors who, if asked, could turn out an engaging column about an evening in the theatre; few columnists who could write or perform in a play. Being a critic is a calling where a little modesty does not go amiss.

One Sunday in December I opened the arts pages of the *Observer* to confront a piece by Brustein two or three times the length of the slot usually given to the paper's drama critic. It was entitled 'The Great American Tragedy' and began with a rather touchy analysis of Britain's changing attitudes to America in the wake of racial strife and the Vietnam War. It concluded with the thesis that because of its civic organisation and public order Britain had lost a sense of the tragic, which was now better understood in America as it struggled to deal with its accumulating woes.

However, sandwiched between these two positions, and taking up more space than either, was a devastating attack on both the American plays in the National Theatre's repertoire. He didn't like anything about them, not the acting, nor the direction: *Long Day's Journey* lacked pain and passion for a tragedy, *The Front Page* was too laborious and slow for a farce. He was particularly agitated that English actors could not catch the authentic cadences of American speech, a complaint which would have been more reasonable if we had been performing the plays in New York. However, our audiences were English, and what we were offering them could not be otherwise than an English take on two rich and remarkable plays, a homage if you like, to American drama. None of us assumed we were doing the plays better than they would have been done in their own country. On Broadway I have seen a number of Noël Coward revivals which, even as I watched and enjoyed them, I knew would never have passed muster on Shaftesbury Avenue. It wasn't that they lacked talent; what was missing was that shared knowledge of English life that audiences and actors in London simply take for granted. Occasionally a good play can actually gain focus by the absence of these specifics. This was true of an excellent off-Broadway production of Simon Gray's *The Common Pursuit*, which, when stripped of its Oxbridge social detail, became a story about any group of bright, ambitious young men as they moved into the world and were slowly picked apart by it.

What I most mistrusted about the Brustein notice was its timing. The *Observer* had already reviewed both productions with overwhelming enthusiasm, and there was no justification for another visit beyond the opportunity it provided of implying that virtually every drama critic in the British Isles was a jackass. This provocation had the smell of the strategies and feuds of a university Liberal Arts Department. In essence what he was saying was that *The Front Page* hadn't been funny, and *Long Day's Journey* hadn't been moving. I've never believed you can, or should, argue with a critic's opinion because, like anyone else, he's entitled to it. However, if he chooses to go ostentatiously on to the attack he needs to be very careful when arbitrating over matters about which there can be no two opinions. Such as facts. In his piece Brustein made two assertions, one about his evening at *The Front Page* and the other about *Long Day's Journey*, which showed that on neither occasion had he been paying due attention. I decided to do what I've rarely done when faced with a panning, and respond. This is the letter I despatched to the Editor of the *Observer*:

If Robert Brustein is going to persist in his role of scourge to a run-down British theatre, I think he must take a little more trouble checking his facts. His evening at *The Front Page* did not last 'almost three and a half hours' but two hours, forty-seven minutes. Without intervals the running time of the play is two hours, eighteen minutes. In *Long Day's Journey into Night* he deplores the absence of New England accents. This is an odd complaint since none of the characters is a New Englander. The mother tells us she was born and brought up in the Middle West. Likewise the father, born in Ireland, was raised elsewhere in America, and in any case has 'the famous beautiful voice' common to leading actors of the period. The idiom of the sons, whose growing up has been spent on the road, in New York hotels and at a succession of boarding schools and colleges, is, if anything, the 'rotten Broadway lingo' the father so frequently deplores. The house in New England is a holiday home to which the family repairs in the summer when the father's theatrical season is in recess. The play provides us with this information not once but many times.

It becomes increasingly clear that Mr Brustein is one of those critics for whom the definitive performance of a play is the one staged in his head before he sets out for the theatre. The circle of his disapproval grows week by week. In his piece not only the National Theatre but the nation at large fell within its compass. It seems we lack a sense of the tragic, and the fault, as I understand him, lies with the Welfare State. There may be some hope for us, he asserts, if Northern Ireland gets sufficiently bloody and unpleasant, but meanwhile the tragic muse, though alive and well, has moved with her somewhat battered Aristotelian baggage of pity, terror and purgation to take out papers in the United States: one can imagine university drama departments all over the country eagerly waiting to receive her.

I would like to ask Mr Brustein this: if the tragic sense is so dependent on social catastrophe, then why has his catalogue of Vietnam, the deteriorating cities, racial strife, drug abuse and civic violence produced hardly one great play among them, or, indeed, how did O'Neill's masterpiece come to be written at a time when, in Mr Brustein's phrase, the nation 'smiled at itself in the mirror'? His thesis is as intellectually confused as it is presumptuous.

Spirits had risen in the tiny press office at Aquinas Street run by Craig Macdonald and his assistant Caroline Keeley at the possibility of a counter-attack. Ken had read and approved of my letter, and Craig had been in touch with the Editor of the *Observer* who had undertaken to publish it the following Sunday. We sent it off by special messenger, giggling like children. Sunday came, I opened the paper and there was no letter. I scoured the arts pages twice. It was twenty-four hours before Craig could telephone the Editor and find out what had happened. We were told that Brustein had insisted on more time to frame his reply.

A week passed and still my letter remained unpublished; Brustein needed more time. At last, on 31 December, Christmas having intervened, the letter made it to the pages of the *Observer*, but the delay had robbed it of much of its force. Brustein's rejoinder, for which he had required three weeks of thought, was another long piece of a thousand words entitled 'The View from My Window'. He sidestepped the two specific points I had raised by dismissing them as trivial. In the case of *The Front Page* he simply reiterated that the running time of the show was well over three hours, notwithstanding that the timesheet of the performance he had attended said otherwise. He then revisited his low opinion of both productions and followed that with a further discourse on the nature of tragedy. His piece concluded with a paean to his own integrity.

This was a critic playing dirty and so would I. It was time for another letter. Ken Tynan suggested I begin with a one-liner of Groucho Marx's – 'Either this man is dead or my watch has stopped' – after which I galloped through a couple of fairly disgraceful paragraphs. This time Brustein's reply was prompt and apoplectic. The correspondence was becoming genuinely nasty, and the Editor stepped in and stopped the fight.

It was soon apparent I could never have won; you can't with a critic, the paper he works for is obliged to support him. Soon another visiting American journalist, writing for the same paper, John Crosby, alert perhaps to what he perceived as creeping anti-Americanism, wrote a second piece supporting Brustein. Up till then I'd enjoyed the skirmish but this shadow which had unexpectedly fallen over a wonderful year was lengthening, and bringing with it an aftertaste of regret. These ego-driven feuds about art are the polar opposite of the quiet perseverance, swinging between belief and doubt, that brings art into existence in the first place. It was best to walk away.

The new year of 1973, the last year of Larry's reign, became an Indian summer for us all. It began modestly with a 'Mobile' production of *Twelfth Night* which opened at the Old Vic before setting out on tour. John Dexter, back on form, returned to the National with two smash hits. The first was *The Misanthrope* in a translation by a young poet new to the theatre, Tony Harrison, and with Diana Rigg giving the performance of her career. John followed this with what proved to be his greatest success, and one which went worldwide, Peter Shaffer's *Equus*. Coming between these two first nights was my own production of *The Cherry Orchard* which, though there were a few carping reviews, rapidly sold out. My other productions were still coming up in the repertoire and during one booking period all four of the shows the National was offering the public were mine, and all were doing wonderful business. In the autumn we had another major hit, Franco Zeffirelli's production of the Italian comedy, *Saturday Sunday Monday*, in which Joan Plowright returned to the sort of work in which she had first made her name at the Royal Court.

For an actor the person nearest to you is not always the best career counsellor. The drawing room of the Oliviers' Brighton house was dominated by two idealised portraits, one from the thirties of Larry as Romeo and a matching one, commissioned by him, of Joan as Masha in his own production of *Three Sisters*. She had given a good performance in the role, but not the superb one had she played the part for which she was ideally suitable – Natasha. At the beginning of their love affair Larry had been drawn to her because she was the very opposite of Vivien Leigh. Now his drawing room suggested he was trying to turn her into the thing she was not, and artistically I suspected she had begun to lose her way.

When Eduardo de Filippo's play first arrived on our desks at the National I had thought immediately of Joan for the leading part and said so to Larry.

'Oh, I don't think so, baby,' he said. 'It's a middle-aged role.'

I was not a close friend of Joan but I was fairly certain that she would be quick to recognise a cracking part of whatever age. Besides, she was now the mother of three, and might relish the chance of playing the matriarch.

'Well, you can try to persuade her,' said Larry, then followed it with, 'But you know women . . .'

So it was arranged: I would travel down to Brighton ostensibly to accompany Joan to the theatre to see John Gielgud, who was on tour there with *Veterans*, but actually to attempt to persuade her to play in *Saturday Sunday Monday*. Larry had to go up to London that night but he was still at the house when I arrived. He poured me a drink and then took me on a tour of the room in which he kept his theatrical memorabilia. When inclined he could be a beguiling host, taking you unexpectedly through a door into the intimate and unguarded spaces of his personality.

The centrepiece of the collection was the sword Edmund Kean had worn as Richard III in the early nineteenth century. This weapon was later presented to the next great Richard, Henry

Irving, and from there made its way into Ellen Terry's family and on to her great-nephew, John Gielgud. When Olivier's Richard III likewise took London by storm in the forties, Gielgud generously presented it to him with a further inscription engraved along one side of the blade. As I watched, Larry turned the sword, first one way then another, to read each inscription in turn. In keeping with theatrical budgets it was a very modest weapon, but he handled it with the balanced care appropriate to something precious. It was impossible not to fall under the spell of the moment.

Later that evening my conversation with Joan about *Saturday Sunday Monday* lasted all of two minutes. She hadn't read the play, but would do so at once, because the part sounded marvellous. It was to be her penultimate performance for the National, and one of her best. And our visit to the theatre that night was also memorable. John Gielgud was giving a funny and singularly brave performance in which he virtually outed himself on stage, playing a homosexual actor filling in time between takes on an epic film being shot on location. It was among the first of a string of elegant comedy performances with which the actor would renew and add lustre to the last years of a very civilised career.

EIGHT

At the beginning of 1973 we had some news which would become wearisomely familiar over the next few years: because of building delays the opening of the new theatre on the South Bank would have to be postponed until spring 1975. The plan had always been for Olivier to stay on until he had led the company into the new building but, with this moment becoming increasingly distant and uncertain, he decided to hand over the running of the National to Peter Hall in the coming autumn.

Peter was now a regular presence at Aquinas Street. He had just returned from New York where his musical, the enormously expensive *Via Galactica*, had gone down in flames. Anyone would have found this discouraging, but Peter had the true entrepreneur's gift of making his failures, when they came along, events on such a scale that they became as newsworthy as his successes. With time people forgot the context but remembered the name. One could not but admire his resilience. I felt I was getting to know him better, and found much that I liked. He had a clarity of purpose, reflected I thought in his handwriting, which was large, fluent and easily read, the sort that gets you a few extra marks in examinations.

One morning at the end of January Peter took me aside and asked if he could have a few private words with me. I followed him to the small office which was his temporary accommodation at the far end of the Aquinas Street corridor. We settled in our chairs and I waited. 'I have a problem, Michael,' he began. 'And I need your advice. Your counsel . . .' I assumed an appropriate expression. 'You've worked with Larry, you know him as well as anyone . . .' I nodded. 'As you know, he's asked me to take over the reins sooner than we planned, but now I'm not sure that's what he wants.'

I'd had plenty of experience of Larry's unpredictability and made sympathetic noises. 'How do you mean?'

'He keeps threatening to resign at once. He keeps using the threat of resignation to get his way. Then he withdraws it. Then he threatens to resign again.'

I thought I understood the problem. 'Well,' I said, 'the next time he wants to resign what you could always do is just say okay and accept his resignation.' At that precise moment, without any knock, the door of the office swung open and there stood Larry, his face a mask of suspicion and hurt. It was almost as if from the other end of the corridor he'd picked up on this betrayal by clairvoyance. In the presence of both men I knew immediately where my first loyalty lay, and I was now consumed with guilt. Since the blow-up about the TV version of *Long Day's Journey* we had been getting on particularly well, and I was angry, not so much with Peter, but rather with myself that I had been so easily manoeuvred into taking his side. I did not doubt that Peter's problems were real, but they were not yet mine, and it would be months before they were.

However, there was a back-story to this event about which I knew nothing until ten years later, when Peter Hall's *Diaries* were published. The previous July Hall had embarked on a secret strategy to merge the National with his old home, the Royal Shakespeare Company. This was not a new idea; it had first been floated some twelve years earlier, when the National was coming into existence under Larry, and those with long memories at the Arts Council and elsewhere recalled that at the time Peter, only recently appointed to run Stratford, had been adamantly opposed. He had always been a brilliant advocate, and it was unclear why the arguments he had marshalled then had suddenly become invalid, beyond the fact that he, not Larry, would soon be running the National. Olivier himself had been kept in the dark about the revival of this proposal until the day he decided to hand over the reins ahead of time. Only then did Peter confide in him.

To begin with Larry was not opposed, but the more he thought about it the less he liked it. The two big subsidised organisations were very different. The National had its roots in the work done at the Royal Court under George Devine and in the values Olivier had espoused even earlier, in the great Old Vic seasons at the end of the war – namely, a belief in the importance of company and the centrality of the actor. The ideas that guided the RSC, on the other hand, were director-driven and derived from academia, particularly Cambridge, and they aspired to a certain rigid correctness. 'Cavaliers and Roundheads' was how Ken Tynan distinguished between the two organisations. Larry was quick to realise that the sort of theatre he had fought to establish over thirty years would not survive this particular Civil War once the present directorate of the RSC had been absorbed into the National.

Hall's successor at Stratford, Trevor Nunn, would have become his deputy, and Olivier's men would be either removed to the periphery or eased out. Hall's *Diaries* record that at a meeting on 22 January to discuss the merger Larry had just speculated on where this would leave Michael Blakemore, and Peter replied, 'If the coming of Trevor means that Michael must go, then Michael must go.' Just two days later he is confiding in me about his difficulties with the man who is still my boss, and, as it happens, my champion. The political implications of this speak for themselves.

Much later I was to identify this meeting as the one in which my relationship with the National began to change, a point where the river divided. In the previous two years there had been arguments and spats, anger and hurt feelings aplenty, but even in my dealings with John Dexter I knew we were both agreed that the argument would be won or lost by what was delivered on the stage. Now another track was beginning to appear, running parallel to the one already there. This new track had to do with what happened away from the stage. It was about power and who had it, about the perception of achievement rather than the thing itself.

It was the fashion in the sixties and seventies for artistic supremos to build empires. The German conductor, Herbert von Karajan, had his symphony orchestra in Berlin, his opera house in the mountains and a private jet in which he could pilot himself between destinations – plus, it hardly needs saying, an extremely healthy income. Later during his time at the National, Peter Hall would convince the Board that he had enough spare capacity to undertake the artistic direction of the Glyndebourne Opera in addition to his existing responsibilities. This was an extraordinary feat of persuasion, tantamount to the Editor of *The Times* insisting he could edit *The Spectator* in his spare moments. Had he succeeded in amalgamating the National and the RSC, and then adding an opera house to his portfolio, Peter would have created an empire that far outshone von Karajan's. But mergers and acquisitions were in the air. And the prospect of big money that went with them.

Indeed, the new building on the South Bank was itself a sort of empire, the largest theatrical complex ever built in Britain, with three theatres, as many restaurants and bars, and a variety of spaces for exhibitions and concerts. I had been taken on a tour of it in mid-construction, when the new theatre was no more than a draughty shell of damp concrete, but could tell even then that the tiers of public spaces facing the river which beckoned you around corners and up staircases would be an astoundingly successful feature. About the two main theatres I was less sure. Many and often contradictory opinions had been sought during the planning stage, but the sagest counsel had come from Olivier himself. However, he couched it in such quaint traditional terms that the architect, Denys Lasdun, felt free to disregard it: 'No spectator should be further from the focal point of the stage than the length of a cricket pitch.' In the age of the screen close-up no advice could have been more pertinent, but it did not mesh with the architect's vision of a kind of indoor version of one of the great theatres of Ancient Greece, in which spectators had sat in ascending rows of seats scooped out of the curvature of a hill. In Lasdun's Olivier Theatre no second tier would overhang the stalls, but the circle would begin where the stalls left off. Thus in the middle of the twentieth century a theatre was being built where a member of the audience in the back row of the upper level was further from the stage than someone in the gallery of Drury Lane, a theatre built two hundred years earlier.

Similarly in the more conventional house, the Lyttelton, architectural theory collided with theatrical horse sense. Here the upper level did indeed overhang the stalls, but its incline was so calculated that a spectator, though he had an unimpeded view of the stage, could see nothing of the patrons sitting in the lower level. The thinking was that this would allow him to concentrate undisturbed on what was happening on stage. In practice it meant that a play in the Lyttelton would address two separate audiences, and in a comedy, where the pleasure of the evening is reinforced by the subliminal signals you pick up from the people with whom you are surrounded, this matters. Theatre takes place within architecture, but the two forms are at opposite ends of the artistic spectrum, the one having to do with permanence and timelessness, the other with a celebration of what will pass. They relate to each other as does the fireplace to the flame, and a splendid mantel or chimney breast means nothing if warmth does not make its way into the room or smoke go up the chimney. Fortunately the space in which a theatrical event takes place is less crucial than the intensity of the event itself and once it has our attention the physical context in which it is happening melts away.

*

The tour of the 'Mobile' production of *Twelfth Night* was now well advanced, playing a couple of performances here, a one-night stand there. But one morning we received appalling news. David Bauer, who played Sir Toby Belch, had died unexpectedly of a heart attack. He was the American actor who had made a brilliant Sheriff in *The Front Page*, and he was widely admired and liked. But his death also raised an urgent practical consideration. The budget of 'Mobile' productions did not allow for under-studies, and there was a performance scheduled in five days' time.

That afternoon I was sitting in Peggy Gilson's office when we heard Olivier's familiar bellow echoing down the corridor – 'Michael!' This was often the way he communicated and I obeyed the summons, but with considerable dread because I had guessed what it might be about. Eight years before I had played Toby Belch in a touring production, something of which our Casting Director, Ann Robinson, was well aware. I opened the door of Larry's office and he greeted me with two terrifying words: '*You're on!*' In an instant I could feel my tongue sticking to the roof of my completely dry mouth. What made it worse was that Larry and Ann Robinson, who was with him in the office, were both grinning at me as if I had just become the victim of some merciless practical joke. I had no desire to return to acting and hadn't been on stage for six years, but I knew this was precisely the sort of challenge Olivier himself would have embraced, and that he would be expecting me to do likewise. I had no choice but to attempt the part.

Everything else in my life was now on hold. I had a weekend to relearn the text, then two days to rehearse it. At first, seeing the words on the page again, it was as if I was reading them for the first time and I was terrified. However, mysteriously, they had all been retained somewhere in my muscular memory, and mouth-ing them came back like some forgotten physical skill. At rehearsals the company rallied to my support, though they couldn't disguise their relish at the spectacle of a director being thrown into that deep end in which most nights of the week it was their job to stay afloat.

On the big night we travelled by bus to a church hall in Kent where work was still proceeding on arranging the seating and setting up the electrics. It might as well have been the preparations for a hanging. Made up and dressed in a costume several sizes too small for me, with my heart pounding and my entire frame convulsed by an overdose of adrenaline, I was thrown into a whirlpool of light where the only way to survive was to start acting. And vigorously. That night at least I managed to do so with some success. Subsequent performances, not informed with the same desperation, were much less good. The trouble was that my playing had no organic connection to the production of which it was a part. Like a nineteenth-century actor who arrives on tour replete with elements of his costume, a well-worn wig and his own stage business, I had wandered in from somewhere else. Larry came to see me on probably my worst matinee, and all he said about it the following morning was, 'You've had your fun, now it's time to get back to work.' I could have throttled him.

Yet I did not regret the experience. It was instructive to be reminded again of what it is to be a performer, hopping on and off a trolleybus that will not wait for stragglers. I was reminded what a backstage is like during a show, hearing from the darkness of the wings dialogue being bellowed under the bright lights. Once again I was one of a troupe of actors – collaborators and competitors who before each entrance collect themselves in a frozen moment, like a fragment of prayer, before stepping forward and taking their chance under the lights. Or, having exited, make a dash to a designated area in the wings to mark time frantically through a quick-change, substituting one set of clothes for another as if the first were on fire. Riding home in the bus at eleven thirty at night, I felt an understanding with the company that I could not have acquired in any other way.

My first task in approaching *The Cherry Orchard* was to decide on a translation. Ronald Hingley was an Oxford don and fluent Russian speaker who rendered Chekhov in a plain colloquial English that was a mirror to Chekhov's own use of Russian. He purged the text of the literary overtones of the early translations, and even dispensed with the Russian patronymic – that use of double names which for English audiences moves the plays away from the recognisable world and into a rarefied and exotic Russianness. His translation was my first choice but Larry had already approached Moura Budberg, the Russian countess living in London who, when young and plumply ravishing, had been the mistress first of Gorky and then of H. G. Wells. She had done the translation of Larry's production of *Three Sisters* and had already been commissioned for *The Cherry Orchard*. I had only to read a few pages to realise it was the very opposite of what I was looking for – somewhat flowery and with an uncertain feel for spoken English. I told Larry how much more I preferred the Hingley and he conceded graciously, but left to me the awkward task of explaining the situation to Moura.

Not looking forward to it much, I visited her one morning at her large, rambling flat in Cromwell Road. She was now certainly in her late seventies, maybe older, and like many erstwhile beauties didn't much care for it. She was attended by a female servant, also Russian, of about the same age, and equally cranky. The appearance of these two women was a match to the apartment, which looked decorated and empty at the same time; various exotic items of furniture were disposed around the room but each seemed to stand apart, not quite relating to the others. Moura had on a long dress, by no means new, but appropriate to a countess, and her grey hair, its colour improved by the application of some silvery liquid, was swept on top of her head. A tiny metallic trickle ran down the side of her face. With much trepidation I began my explanation of why I wanted to use another translation and Moura's expression became sourer and sourer.

However, I had one good card still to play; would she consider being the Russian adviser to the production, attending rehearsals and tutoring us in all aspects of Russian life? Her eyes flickered with interest, and with relief I realised I was dealing with a realist; the job would get her out of the house and involve her again in the work of artists. She already had a friend on the production, our costume designer Bumble Dawson, and Moura sought out her advice. She accepted the job, in which she proved very helpful and was an interesting presence in the rehearsal room.

The sort of production I aspired to was the very opposite of what at the time was conveyed by the adjective 'Chekhovian'. Though the plays may leave you with a sense of the sadness and bleakness of life, this is not what they describe. Chekhov's characters are for ever on the hunt for amusement of some sort, anything to distract them from the underlying drift of their lives. They play games, stage amateur theatricals, enjoy magic shows, or just sit under the trees in the garden having long circular conversations over their tea. And they are always offering each other hospitality. The first two acts of *Three Sisters* are both extended parties, and the most spectacular party of all, the most absurd, is the ball given by Ranevsky in *The Cherry Orchard* on the day she and her brother put the family home up for auction. Her social equals who would normally have attended such an occasion have all moved away from the district or died. However, so determined is she to cheer herself up with music and company that she makes up the numbers of guests by inviting such people as the Postal Clerk and the Stationmaster. This is surely as funny as it is tragic, and suggests that the playwright was not joking when he described the play as a comedy. Walk past a London pub on a warm summer night, with customers spilling on to the pavement: the intense and jubilant buzz of people absorbed in the pursuit of a good time blocks out any thought that for some of these same people (and for all of us eventually) winter is not far away.

Chekhov allows us, unlike the pub's customers, to see both these realities at once.

I was able to cast the show entirely from the resident company, and the actors played together with a cohesive intimacy that was already there. Constance Cummings never quite lost her mid-western good sense in the part of Ranevsky, but she had some extraordinarily affecting moments. At the time her husband of many years, the playwright Benn Levy, was seriously ill and at the end of the play, when brother and sister bid farewell to the house they grew up in, the tears that streamed down her face belonged as much to the actress as to her part. When Benn died towards the end of the run, Connie found the play so distressing that she had to withdraw. Michael Hordern was wonderful as her brother, Gayev, and the two played together as if they were indeed siblings. I was reminded of my mother and her brother Jim, who had grown up together on a large country property in the Manaro district of New South Wales, and had remained close all their lives. I tried to find moments between Connie and Michael which would evoke a shared childhood, and found one when the two of them made private fun about an intimidating great-aunt. However, the particular success of the evening was Denis Quilley's Lopakhin, who was at last played not as a jumped-up peasant with an inclination to get drunk but, in accord with Chekhov's instructions, as someone gentle, courteous and correctly dressed in a black tailcoat. The playwright knew better than most that a few social graces are among the easier things that an intelligent man on the way up has to learn. And no wonder: the background of the playwright is remarkably similar to that of his character – his father a village shopkeeper and his grandfather a serf.

For a couple of critics the production stumbled badly on an idea I had for its last moments. On the page the family have left their house for the last time and the axes are about to start ringing in the orchard when on comes the old servant, Firs, to give his final speech. This is usually seen as an elegiac lament for the passing of the old order, which to an extent it is; but it has a more immediate and shocking resonance. All his life Firs has been in service to this family, and now he has been left behind by his feckless employers as carelessly as an old pet tortoise. I wanted to remind the audience of this dimension and purge the moment, which in performance can too easily seem like an actor coming on to deliver a final aria, of its comfortable familiarity. But how?

I had noticed that in the script a few pages earlier there is a stage direction in which Lopakhin, now the new owner, goes around locking all the rooms in the house, including a door which opens out of the nursery. What if, at the beginning of the act, when the house is being emptied and luggage and possessions are being taken outside, Firs, now too feeble to be much help, goes into this small room to check for further belongings or perhaps just to have a rest? In the melee it would be unlikely that anyone (including the audience) would notice that he doesn't come out again. Our designer, Alan Tagg, was using a revolving stage to facilitate the scene changes. When I studied the model I realised that there was space beyond the door that Lopakhin had locked, but out of sight of the audience, for a child's small bedroom. The ending of the play could now go like this: everyone has left, and the nursery is now deserted and utterly still. Then one small thing moves – the handle of the door we have just seen Lopakhin lock. The set starts to revolve. It swings round, bringing downstage centre the small room in which the old servant has been accidentally confined. He tries the door then slumps exhausted on to the child's cot to say his last words.

I saw at once how powerful this image could be, possibly too powerful. If this was the first time the audience had seen the set revolve, there was a danger it would have an almost melodramatic impact. We had to acquaint the audience in advance with the mechanics of our scene changes so that there would be no surprises when the stage moved at the end of the play. This would necessitate keeping the curtain up during the two previous scene changes. We would do them in full view of the audience in the manner of the Berliner Ensemble.

However, what I didn't allow for were the days of rehearsal it takes to make such transformations elegant and interesting to watch. At our first preview everything went smoothly except the scene changes, which were ugly and interminable. Peter Hall, who was taking an intelligent and encouraging interest in the production, pleaded with me to bring the curtain down and do them out of sight. Larry concurred. I had no choice but to concede because there wasn't the time available to get them right.

I continued to believe that this solution to the last moments of the play was valid, particularly as played by Harry Lomax, whose Firs was as frail and transparent as an autumn leaf, but I wasn't surprised when I had my knuckles rapped by a few in the press. Chekhov is the one classical dramatist everyone thinks they understand, and any departure from tradition needs to be scrupulously judged. Had I been able to do my scene changes in full view I'm sure the ending of the production would have been more readily acceptable.

There was one critic who understood what I was attempting – Irving Wardle in *The Times*, who wrote with unqualified approval. Someone had pinned his review to the Aquinas Street notice-board and one morning I noticed John Dexter reading it. He turned to me, scowling. 'Well, you've done it again!' he barked in a tone that would have been more appropriate had I been guilty of allowing the bath to overflow for the third time in a week. Then he strode off down the corridor, snorting. Robert Brustein's review was less enthusiastic than either Wardle's or Dexter's, though he did his best to be magnanimous and bury the hatchet; I learnt that I was at least 'a skilled craftsman'. It didn't surprise me that he hadn't much cared for the production because in one of his books I'd read his commentary on *The Cherry Orchard* and disagreed with every word of it. As in his comments on the two American plays, his numerous reprimands contained a couple of bloomers. He regretted that Lopakhin was not being played as he should be, as 'a clumsy, good-hearted peasant who bumps into the furniture and flails his arms about'. He also deplored that the ball scene was staged like something 'from *The Great Waltz* with richly wardrobed guests swirling about', apparently unaware that in Tsarist Russia every civil servant down to the lowliest postal clerk was obliged to wear a uniform. I knew because I'd spent a weekend in Moscow researching such things. In any case, if he'd been watching not the uniforms but the performances inside them, he would have realised that these people could not possibly be archdukes and duchesses. They were having far too good a time. I thought of writing another letter but couldn't be bothered, and not long afterwards Brustein returned to America.

One morning I had a telephone call from Kathleen Tynan asking if we could meet; there was something she needed to discuss with me. We arranged to have tea together that afternoon at Brown's Hotel, not far from where she was having her hair done. She arrived looking extremely chic but with the brittle look of women who have just emerged from the hairdressers. The subject she wanted to discuss was Ken, about whom she said she was extremely concerned. First there was his health, which was much worse than most people supposed; but even more troubling was his state of mind. He seemed incapable of working and would do anything to avoid it, distracting himself with social events, meals in expensive restaurants, reckless purchases and brief trips abroad to recover his health. He was like a man in flight from himself. I knew the way Ken lived but had always assumed it went hand in hand with a rigorous work ethic. 'Not at all,' said Kathy. 'He stays in bed all morning with his secretary in attendance, lingering over his correspondence. Then he gets up, gets dressed and goes off by himself somewhere. He has all these projects, but never gets down to work on any of them.'

Kathleen herself had recently embarked on a novel and I was sufficiently acquainted with her Canadian good sense and application to know that she would finish it. Now she had a further incentive: to encourage (or admonish) her husband. 'Then there's the money,' she continued. Because of the way they both lived I'd never assumed money was a problem. 'No, we're practically broke. When Ken finishes at the National at the end of the year we'll have absolutely nothing coming in.' 'I'd no idea,' I said, adding: 'Well, thank God you have the house.'

'Not for much longer. All we ever had on it is a short lease and it's up in a couple of years.' The house had always seemed so indisputably theirs that I'd taken for granted that they owned it. I remembered drinks there that sunny day before *Tyger* went into rehearsal, and what a stylish couple they presented to the world. Now the entire edifice of their life together was crumbling in front of me. I didn't want to ask how it was personally between them, because I thought I already had some idea. I knew Kathy still loved her husband and believed in his gifts, but they were in the sort of trouble it's beyond an outsider to ameliorate.

Some weeks before I'd been sitting with Ken and his assistant Rosina Adler in the tiny office that served as Literary Department. Ken had been talking about the new show he was planning as a follow-up to his sex revue *Oh! Calcutta!*. With an amused insouciance, which implied that what he was saying was the most natural thing in the world, he remarked, 'I've met someone whose tastes I would love to see incorporated into the show. She's an out-of-work actress who's filling in time in a massage establishment in Pall Mall. I often drop in there on my way home.'

In all aspects of his life – his work, his politics and in the private sphere – Ken had a quixotic compulsion to declare himself, which I both admired because it was brave and deplored because it left him so vulnerable to attack. Ken's enemies did not need to look for ammunition; he handed it to them in boxes. With *Oh! Calcutta!* he had been able simultaneously to strike both a public and a private pose. I'd never discussed his sexual tastes with him, but I hardly needed to; they were already on display in the poster he had chosen for this show – wittily derived from the Man Ray photo of a woman's generous backside decorated with fortissimo symbols. When you entered his house one of the first things you saw was an original painting by the pop artist, Pauline Boty (his friend until her early death in 1966), again featuring a voluptuous bottom. I guessed there was sadomasochism involved, though I knew Ken would never have dreamt of inflicting physical hurt on another person against their will. Games, dressing up, acting things out, however, were another matter. What someone else would have kept hidden, Ken announced. He refused to be socially marginalised by proclivities which, though entirely his own business and relatively harmless, would hardly have been categorised by most people at that time as 'normal'. In his two sex revues, the erotic film he planned, the biography of the sexologist Wilhelm Reich which he never completed, Ken was insisting that they could be.

I had attended the first night of *Oh! Calcutta!* in 1970, when the show was still being taken seriously as a radical event. It opened not in the West End but at the more experimental venue, the Roundhouse, and every fashionable face in London appeared to be in the audience. There was excitement, even a sense of trepidation, about what we might be in for. Would the sight of totally naked men and women and the loud expression of Anglo-Saxon language actually corrupt us? It was a beautiful midsummer evening, still light when we emerged from the theatre, smiling and laughing like disembarking passengers who have come to no harm after a turbulent crossing. On this occasion the show had accomplished exactly what it was meant to – freeing its audience from hang-ups and inhibitions which when confronted were shown to be without substance.

The only corrupting element in the evening was the unevenness of the various sketches. What eventually was to discredit the show was the wishful thinking behind its central premise – that the sexual impulse was exclusively benign. When it moved to the West End and later to Broadway the sort of informed audience that had attended the first night was soon replaced by a more furtive clientele who took their seats still wearing their raincoats. In London the show lingered on at the Duchess Theatre and in New York at the Edison, becoming sleazier with each year of the run. Ken was assumed to be making piles of money, but there were so many contributors taking a cut of the royalties that he actually received very little. And by the time of his departure from the National those pennies had put paid to his reputation.

Ken's other venture into the commercial theatre, a non-sexual one, was similarly misjudged. This was a German play by Rolf Hochhuth, *Soldiers*, which offered a revisionist view of Winston Churchill, who was charged with two crimes: the deliberate targeting of civilians in the aerial bombing of German cities; and collusion in the death of the Polish General Sikorski, whose plane was sabotaged in flight. The British Establishment were outraged that a German playwright should question a national hero and they went on the attack.

For some reason Ken was far more exercised supporting the second charge, for which there existed practically no evidence, than by the first, for which there did. In a television debate, when asked to provide proof he swore that he had a piece of paper in his safe that showed without doubt Churchill's responsibility for Sikorski's death, and which he said he would produce in due course. It was a dramatic gesture and a transparently empty one that made me feel embarrassed for him even as I watched. In the furore he created over Sikorski the far more important matter of destroying heavily populated German cities of historic but no military importance was all but overlooked.

Yet seen from the perspective of forty years later both of Ken's forays into the West End had a certain prophetic edge. The one undoubtedly advanced the cause of sexual tolerance, and prepared the way for the various liberations that have followed. *Soldiers* questioned the role of patriotism in the writing of even-handed history, and asserted the right, indeed the obligation, to challenge official secrecy. It was one of a number of ripples which by the time of the Pentagon Papers and more recently Wikileaks would become an unstoppable wave.

Officially Larry was meant to hand over the artistic directorship in October, but because he had one last part to play at the Old Vic, John Tagg in Trevor Griffiths' *The Party*, Peter Hall encouraged him to retain his office in Aquinas Street until the end of the year. *The Party* would also be Ken Tynan's swan song, and it was an audacious choice for both men, though in the event not an entirely successful one. The play was about a group of middle-class left-wingers who gather in a living room not unlike Ken's in Thurloe Square to discuss in Marxist terms the way forward. The title was therefore a play on words. It described both the gathering and the political party whose cause the guests are there to advance. Getting a serious play about left-wing politics on to the stage of the National Theatre was something of a coup for Ken, but one which, like any other production, needed to be validated by an audience's approval. It was given a lavish staging by John Dexter, and had at its centre an astonishing performance by Olivier as an old, battle-scarred Glaswegian communist, the only truly working-class character on stage.

Having listened dutifully to what the other characters have to say, John Tagg embarks on a speech which reduces everything that precedes it to chatter. It lasts about twenty-five minutes and is expressed entirely in the remorseless and inert language of Marxist argument. Learning it, which Olivier did over many weeks, a certain amount each day, must have been as difficult for him as learning by heart the operating instructions of a Japanese camera, particularly since I doubt he had much sympathy with the views expressed. He had chosen the part as his farewell to the

National Theatre, guided by the same instincts which had always guided his career: to attempt something fresh and unexpected, something with a whiff of the future about it – above all something that challenged him. On this occasion the play was not sufficiently realised to support Ken and Larry in their hopes for it, and their joint departure from the National was something of an anti-climax.

A few days before the first performance I had another call from Kathleen. Elaborate preparations were afoot to mark the end of Olivier's reign – he was going to be presented with a replica in solid silver of the theatre which was to bear his name. However, nothing whatever was being planned to mark Ken's departure and he was very upset. I agreed that this was negligent, and said I would have a word with Larry. I found him sitting in the auditorium of the Old Vic watching the dress rehearsal of the first scene of *The Party*, in the course of which Ronald Pickup had to appear naked. Progress was slow and Ronnie looked cold and uncomfortable. We both agreed that no force on earth would ever persuade either of us to take off our clothes in front of eight hundred people. Eventually I chose my moment to mention Ken. Larry listened carefully, thanked me effusively for bringing it to his attention and said he'd give the matter serious thought.

The following day he told me he'd arrived at the perfect farewell gift, a rare and expensive pot plant to decorate the Tynans' house. I was somewhat taken aback because this seemed hardly appropriate, particularly as Ken was thinking of leaving England for a climate more conducive to his health. A pot plant was not something you could take on board an airplane; in any case it would invariably die. What Ken would have liked was something more permanent that could sit on a shelf. I should have said so, but in the face of Larry's apparent enthusiasm, didn't. He was doing what he often did, giving generously with one hand and slyly taking away with the other. He didn't appear to bear grudges – in the theatre you can hardly afford to – but he had a long memory, and he had not forgotten the harm that Ken, the critic, had once done with his funny but merciless reviews of Vivien Leigh at a time when she was psychologically at her most fragile. When she appeared as Lavinia opposite Olivier in *Titus Andronicus*, Ken had written that she 'receives the news that she is about to be ravaged on her husband's corpse with little more than the mild annoyance of one who would have preferred foam rubber'. Ken's readers were amused, but Larry was left to pick up the pieces. I doubt too whether Olivier had forgotten the letter he received from Ken just before the first night of *Long Day's Journey*.

A few years later, when Ken had become seriously ill, anxious about money and living an exile's life in California, he was offered a substantial advance to write a book about Olivier, but Larry refused to co-operate. It turned out to be a loss for him as much as it was for the general reader, because no critic brought the great actor to life on the page as excitingly as Ken. To read his description of *Coriolanus* in performance is the next best thing to being there. This rejection was a double blow to Ken because he had both a perceptive love of Olivier's art and a troubled, contentious love for the man. This was something that was probably true for all the younger men Larry brought in to help him run the National – John Dexter, Bill Gaskill, Frank Dunlop, Jonathan Miller and myself. He was not content with being *liked*; he wanted to be *loved*, and for the most part love is what we gave him, but it made for turbulent relationships, forever swinging between acquiescence and revolt. He wanted to be challenged, but hated being defied. We were prepared to serve, but not to be taken for granted because it was all too easy to be swallowed up within his myth and vanish. In this emotional to-and-fro Ken was the big loser.

I stayed closely in touch with the Tynans after Ken left the National. Ken had a number of esoteric projects on the go, but only one, his second sex revue, *Carte Blanche*, would come to anything. Kathy on the other hand saw her novel published and moved into film writing, which helped considerably with their finances. Ken continued to see his girlfriend Nicole, who was becoming an acknowledged presence in his life. She was very quiet, watchful and slight, and dressed demurely; more like the girls he had grown up with in Birmingham than the confident and fluent women among whom he ordinarily moved. I met her for the first time one evening when Ken and I were invited to appear on a panel discussion at an Oxford college. He had offered me a lift in the big second-hand Jaguar he had just acquired and in which he took considerable pride. 'The faster you drive, the safer you are,' he announced, with no supporting evidence, as he stepped hard on the accelerator, and the car thundered up the motorway with me in the front seat clutching the leather up-holstery and Nicole, mute, in the back. It was like being taken for a spin by Mr Toad.

Though Kathy continued to show great concern for Ken, it was clear that the couple were going their own ways. He had his lover and she now had hers. One summer they let the Thurloe Square house to make some additional money, and Ken found himself stranded in London for a week without anywhere to live. Know-ing that I was shortly leaving for Biarritz, Kathleen asked me if Ken could make temporary use of our flat, and she indicated that he might not be alone. Indebted as I was to the Tynans for their hospitality, I was pleased by this opportunity to repay it. When some weeks later we returned from France and opened the front door, the first thing I noticed standing on the chest in the hall was a magnum of champagne, and propped up against it a charming note from Ken. It was in his characteristic handwriting, with its flourishes and wavy connecting lines between one word and the next, a style that someone might have assiduously cultivated at fifteen and then continued to use for the rest of their lives almost by default. It was characteristic of the man who had once decided always to hold the cigarette he was smoking between his two middle fingers.

That might have been that but Ken had further surprises waiting for us in the flat. The following morning I noticed that one of the struts at the head of the double brass bed was missing. I discovered it tucked behind a floor-length curtain. This drew my attention to the underneath of the chaise-longue, where a single high-heeled shoe, intended for a woman of suspiciously large feet, stood like an exclamation mark. It was only then that I realised that a full-length mirror of considerable weight had been brought from the other end of the flat and then propped against the wall facing the bed. As in a suggestive treasure hunt, one clue led on to another. The flat was otherwise orderly and clean, nothing was broken and the screws that connected the loose brass strut to the bed-head were still in place so that the repair was a matter of a few minutes. But it was absolutely typical of Ken to indulge in this sly game-playing, this witty exercise in confession.

When a year or so later the Tynans left London for California, Kathleen went ahead with the children to arrange accommodation in Los Angeles and Ken was left behind to say his goodbyes. Since no one else suggested it, his secretary offered to throw a farewell party for him in her basement flat in Primrose Hill. Like most of the people who had worked for Ken – his various part-time secretaries, Rosina Adler at the National Theatre – she had become quite fond and protective of him. Jonathan Miller was one of the guests, but there weren't many of the fashionable faces that had once pressed up the stone steps to the drawing room in Thurloe Square. Nicole was present, dressed as usual in a white lacy cotton blouse and as quiet and enigmatic as ever. Most of the guests arrived in a batch after ten o'clock. They were the cast of *Carte Blanche*, which had just opened at the Phoenix Theatre, to considerable public and critical indifference. People who an hour or two before had been parading around nude now arrived muffled up as working actors, parking their bikes in the hall and looking as wholesome as lumberjacks. Their cheerful arrival seemed to underwrite Ken's belief in the innocence of sex.

Before I'd set out to the party I'd been puzzling about what I could contribute to it, when it occurred to me that Ken's magnum of champagne was lying on its side at the bottom of a cupboard waiting for the right occasion to be uncorked. This was surely it. My gift was enthusiastically received, but at first Ken didn't make the connection between the bottle he'd given me and the one I was giving him back. An hour later he caught my eye from across the room, his expression alight with excited conjecture. Was this the same bottle? Or an identical one specially acquired for the occasion? Did it perhaps come with a twin present of a woman's single shoe? Alas, I had in mind no game in which we could both participate. It had simply been a lazy way of making a gift.

With the Tynans on the other side of the world it was easy to lose touch. I kept track of Ken only through his writing; he appeared frequently in the pages of the *New Yorker,* and had brought out another book, *Show People.* But about his day-to-day life I knew nothing. In the summer of 1980 I was on my way back from Biarritz when I picked up an English newspaper and read that he was dead. I knew he'd been ill but had not suspected that his emphysema was something that could kill him, especially as I'd never once heard him complain about it. He was only one year older than I was. Death had never before seemed such a thief.

During her last tormented years with Ken, Kathleen had survived by making sure she had some sort of a life of her own, both professionally and personally. She had the cool good sense to manage this, though it was never easy because she still loved him and never reneged on her responsibilities to care for him. The evidence for this love is provided by the two books, one written by her, the other edited, in the years after his death. Whereas another widow, once married to a famous name, might have been content with the penning of a memoir, Kathleen embarked on a full-blown, highly professional biography. For the first two hundred pages it is a meticulously researched account of Ken's life up to his mid-thirties; then suddenly the author herself enters the book as the second most important person in it. She continues with the same scrupulousness and honesty she brought to its first part. There is no attempt at myth-making or showing either of the couple as other than they were. On the contrary, we see time stripping away all pretences, and Ken's tragedy becomes something that applies to all of us, but writ large because he was so gifted: that he did much with his life, but nowhere near enough. Perhaps he never had a clear idea of what he really wanted. His brilliance latched on to whatever was at hand, and he could improvise his way round having to make hard choices. Kathleen's unflinching description of his last weeks facing death exiled in Los Angeles make almost unbearable reading.

Her second book was perhaps even more a labour of love – a comprehensive collection, some five hundred pages long, not only of Ken's letters but of memos, notes and the nonsense verse he wrote to delight his children. It reveals a man who could hardly write a sentence that wasn't eloquent and felt, even when wrongheaded. In these two hard-won books Kathleen paid in full the debts she owed to this man she had once so loved.

Kathleen was now making a life for herself and her children in two cities, London and New York. With her wonderful looks and social skills she moved easily among an interesting circle of people in both places. I tried to keep in touch, but I was frequently working abroad myself, and it was a matter of luck if we found ourselves in the same place at the same time. But Ken's memorial service in St Paul's, Covent Garden, drew all the Tynan friends together. Quite a few of his enemies too – the church was packed. Later, Adrian and Celia Mitchell arranged another celebration at the National Theatre, and afterwards I discussed with Richard Eyre, by then the Artistic Director, a way of memorialising Ken in the new building. He seemed to have been written out of its history. We agreed the perfect acknowledgement would be to name the National Theatre bookshop after him and Richard promised to look into it.

One morning in 1995, retrieving some lost information from an outdated pocket diary, I came across an old telephone number for Kathleen written in pencil. We hadn't been in touch in an age so I decided to give it a try. To my surprise she picked up at once and greeted me with that familiar, slightly circumspect friendliness which before long would always turn into a peal of laughter. I asked her if she knew of any movement on the bookshop idea. 'Not so far,' she said. After I'd hung up I impulsively picked up the phone to ring Richard Eyre at the National. I'd expected he'd be in rehearsals, but he was doing a morning's work in his office and again to my astonishment I got straight through. He told me he was still a strong supporter of the bookshop idea but as yet hadn't made much headway. I didn't ask why, but it wouldn't have surprised me if there had been some opposition from the Board. Richard assured me he'd do his best to push it through, and I was then able to ring Kathy straight back and inform her.

'Your good deed for the day,' she said and laughed, and I had the feeling that at last she was moving clear of her husband's shadow; that she'd done her best for him and now it was her turn. However I had misunderstood her detachment. Less than a week later, just as I had with Ken I read in a newspaper that she was dead. Very few of her friends had known that she'd been dealing with cancer for years, living in England but from time to time slipping over to America for treatment. Like her husband she was only in her fifties. No two deaths have so taken me aback as those of the Tynans, or left me with a feeling, not so much of negligence as of some opportunity, something to share, now for ever lost.

NINE

All through 1973 I was being pulled in three directions. *The Cherry Orchard*, which had opened in May, was my last production for the Olivier regime, but I would remain at Larry's disposal until he departed at the end of the year. At the same time I was now committed to his successor, and was attending regular planning meetings to map out the theatre's future. Because of further delays in the opening of the new building we would remain confined to the Old Vic for some time and would have to curtail our repertoire accordingly. There was nothing for me to do beyond attending meetings and I was therefore encouraged to take time off to pursue freelance work.

A year's programme quickly fell into place. I was offered two productions in the West End and these would be followed by an Australian tour of *The Front Page*. In addition the head-hunters were after me. As soon as the Chekhov opened I was on a plane to Canada where the Board of the Festival Theatre, Ontario, wanted to know if one day I would be interested in running their theatre. Later I was invited on another short visit to the Guthrie Theatre, Minneapolis, where I met with a similar offer. However, in both places I soon realised I hadn't left my homeland and spent twenty years making a new life for myself in Europe only to return to another part of the New World.

On 8 March Peter convened the first official meeting of his group of associate directors in Larry's Aquinas Street office, and the champagne corks started to pop. Gathered in this tiny room were not only the first and second artistic directors of the National Theatre but Harold Pinter, John Schlesinger, Jonathan Miller and me. In such an illustrious company and after a second glass of champagne it was impossible not to feel excited about the future. And perhaps a little smug. Jonathan's hold on the conversation was even more brilliant and reckless than usual, and only Harold, though in the most good-natured way, insisted on a little more rigour in the ideas, precedents, gossip and jokes bouncing back and forth. It was the hairline crack, invisible for the moment, which would eventually become a temperamental chasm between the two men, and which Peter Hall would one day use to advantage when he wanted Jonathan out.

My first freelance show was Noël Coward's *Design for Living*, which was to be a co-production between the illustrious management of H. M. Tennent and an American producer, Robert Regester. The supremo of the Tennent organisation was still Hugh 'Binkie' Beaumont, whose successes over three decades had dominated the West End. In the forties and early fifties his productions with John Gielgud and other great stars of the day had challenged the Old Vic as forerunner of the yet-to-be-established National Theatre.

Ever since I'd been in England the H. M. Tennent posters, extremely chic and always the same – no graphics, simply classic typography in black and red – had dotted the West End like badges of established supremacy. One evening I was bidden to have a drink with Binkie at his house in Lord North Street, Westminster. I set off in some trepidation. Binkie had been the Board member of the National Theatre who, after having attended a preview of *Tyger*, had so alarmed Larry by describing the show as 'seditious'. He had also been in the audience on the second, disastrous night of *Macbeth*, so I wasn't sure his curiosity about me was entirely benign.

His Georgian house had a dark but stylish interior, and I was ushered into a first-floor drawing room adorned with an astonishing collection of museum-quality eighteenth-century furniture which he had acquired for pennies during and immediately after the war. Binkie was a small elegant man rather in the Somerset Maugham mould, with the watching eyes of a predator bird assessing you through thick lenses. He offered me a scotch, which I declined because at that time I was supposed to be avoiding alcohol for medical reasons. 'Just a teeny one,' he whispered, before turning and forcefully extending in my direction half a tumbler of whisky. As when Matron handed out a dose of castor oil, I knew I would be under observation until I had downed the lot. I daresay he regarded me as a priggish representative of the new sort of theatre first trumpeted by John Osborne and the Royal Court. In the light of his own achievements he still couldn't quite see what all the fuss was about. Any more, I suppose, than forty years later, when the wheel has turned again, can I.

However, *Design for Living* was firmly rooted in Binkie's world and he'd already staged a revival some years before starring Rex Harrison. I wanted to be involved in this current production because Vanessa Redgrave would be playing Gilda and it would be the first time we had worked together, or indeed seen much of each other, since the Stratford season in 1959. In the intervening fourteen years both our lives had changed beyond recognition and the offer of the job beckoned me like a question mark. Would it be possible to put a fond professional seal on the emotional turbulence of the past? I hoped so. The other two parts would be played by Jeremy Brett and John Stride, both of whom had been members of Larry's National company so, as happens frequently in the theatre, we would be working in the context of a pleasant tangle of private and professional lives.

About the play itself I had to admit to a few reservations. It is stylish, crisply written and frequently amusing, but Coward never really addresses his chosen subject: the sexual equation between the three leading characters, two young men, probably gay, who feel their lives are incomplete without the presence of the remarkable Gilda. In the thirties it would have been unthink-able for Coward to have attempted the more interesting play buried somewhere beneath the one he had written. Not until recently would a change in public attitudes allow a director such as Anthony Page to supply through production the elements Coward had so sedulously avoided. In 1973 such liberty was not available to me.

Some three weeks after my meeting with Binkie, and quite unexpectedly, he was dead. A shocked hush descended on the Tennent Organisation as a door which had been slowly closing on an entire chapter of theatrical history shut fast with an abrupt click.

Meanwhile, back at the National the bright new chapter we hoped to be writing was defaced by a spill of ink. On 16 April the *Daily Telegraph* ran a story that for months plans had been afoot to merge the National with the RSC. I supposed this to be a reporter's scoop, but the Peter Hall *Diaries* would later reveal that it was in fact a leak from Peter himself with the aim apparently of 'testing the waters'. A few days later at our next associates' meeting it was clear that the waters were frozen solid; not one of us was in favour of this amalgamation. In the ten or more years since the two theatres had come into being, both had done excellent, though very contrasting work. You preferred Hall's RSC or Olivier's National according to temperament. The RSC gave critics more to discuss, perhaps; the National more for audiences to feel. It is doubtful whether the RSC would ever have made an offer to the ex-pop singer and stand-up comedian, Jim Dale. At the National he played leading roles. The 'serious' theatre is notoriously subject to the whims of intellectual fashion, and the rivalry between the two companies ensured that more than one notion of talent had somewhere to work.

As all the associates expressed their opposition, Peter nodded sagely. However, none of us said what was at the forefront, certainly of my mind, and presumably of the others'. One had only to cross-check the dates to see that at exactly the same time he was asking us to throw in our lot with him, he was attempting to push through a merger which would drastically alter the terms of our engagement. And yet none of us had been told. From my own point of view this was something either to go on fretting about or to overlook and forget. So far I had enjoyed working with Peter and was appreciative of his many qualities as he moved with a kind of steady purr between the worlds of the boardroom and the numerous departments of the theatre, all clamouring for his attention. In between there were meetings about his own productions, and discussions with his associates about the rest of the repertoire. In the evenings he was going to the theatre and in the mornings getting up early to attack a pile of scripts. I was impressed by his energy but more with the precise way he distributed it, and had become convinced that he was indeed the right man to be running the organisation.

The fact that he passionately wanted to do so, which few others did, was reason enough. Olivier had been an artist who tried to become a politician as and when required. I believed Peter to be a politician first and foremost, but perhaps this was what was required for an organisation with such varied challenges ahead. I'd had enough experience of running theatres to know that an undertaking given in good faith on one day can become impossible to fulfil a day or two later, and Peter had hundreds of supplicants knocking at his door. I made up my mind: I would forget that I had once been offered a role 'above and beyond' my fellow associates, and instead would work to the best of my abilities as one of a team.

And there were distinct advantages to being in the parade of this energetic man. Peter followed one project remorselessly with the next, so that there was a good chance that any failure would soon be painted over by a new success. I was bidden to private screenings, replete with drinks and canapés, of two films he had completed that year, *Akenfield* (dreadful) and *The Homecoming* (good), and had attended a Sunday lunch party in the summer at his house in Wallingford, a modernist structure built in a spacious area of parkland belonging to a nearby stately home. There were contemporary sculptures in primary colours disposed around the grounds looking like the Lego constructs children leave out on the lawn, enormously enlarged.

It was a lovely day, and after lunch young, sleek A-list celebrities splashed each other in the swimming pool, observed, as if from behind the wrong side of a plate-glass window, by Peggy Ashcroft sitting fully clothed in a deckchair. I remembered photographs of her as a beautiful young woman, and the stories about her adventurous love life, first with Komisarjevsky, the Russian director, and later with Paul Robeson. But having lived, it seemed, would always be a poor substitute for living. However, when she gave me a lift back to London at the end of the day (we were neighbours in Hampstead) she soon established that age had its compensations and was alert and delightful company. Being one of Peter's men you soon grasped that you were in the swim.

The American co-producer of *Design for Living* was determined to press on with the production and we rehearsed in October. The show opened on tour in Brighton the following month, and at our first performance I had a demonstration from Vanessa of exactly what it is that makes a stage star: the ability under pressure, with the heart thumping and the mouth dry, to illuminate a performance with a flame of energy that seems to come from nowhere. If you can do this on a succession of first nights when the press are there to record it, you have a career. Larry, to whom this applied more than to any actor I've ever known, came to see the show. Afterwards the National Theatre contingent – Jeremy, John and I – took him out to supper, but it wasn't clear if he had enjoyed it. About work with which he had no involvement he could often be thin-lipped and competitive. Other more enthusiastic visitors from the National came to visit us – Caroline Keeley, one half of the Publicity Office, and Sue Higginson, who did my secretarial work. They made a day trip to offer their support. Sue was a tall, wryly attractive woman whose personal life, about which she gave a long-running and very funny account, always seemed to be in trouble. Over the dictation of many letters and spells of gossip, we had become friends, and sitting having a drink with these two encouraging faces, I would never have believed that by the time I left the National Sue and I would be on opposite sides of the fence. After Brighton, *Design for Living* opened successfully in London at the Phoenix Theatre and settled in for a run.

Within weeks I was rehearsing my second outside show on leave from the National, which I had prepared and cast in tandem with the Coward. Of the two this was the play about which I was most excited, something brand new from a young playwright on the way up, which the West End's shrewdest and most audacious producer, Michael Codron, had commissioned and now proposed bringing straight to London. This was *Knuckle* by David Hare and it tapped into an enthusiasm I shared with the author for the private-eye films of the 1940s such as *The Big Sleep* and *The Maltese Falcon*. David had invented a Raymond Chandler fable and imposed it on the sedate world of Guildford and its environs. Curly, a young arms dealer and a flawed hero in the manner of Sam Spade, is on the hunt for his missing sister, and his search becomes a journey through the undergrowth of English capitalism as a sleazy old country moves away from its deference to old money and prepares to embrace the unapologetic rapaciousness of Thatcherism that is just around the corner. To say the play was radical would be putting it mildly, so it was courageous of Michael Codron to give it his unequivocal backing. He had surrendered to it, as I had, because of its fresh, vivid dialogue and that unmistakable smell of the future that attaches to the work of gifted young writers.

For me it presented a task which I relished – trying to put a movie on stage. Over the summer David came down to Biarritz for a week so that we could discuss his play without distractions. There was one thing that worried me about it: if you are going to pastiche Chandler you need to make sure you can reproduce his narrative grip. David had fashioned an ingenious plot, but his play was inclined to proceed in fits and starts, and there were digressions, always powerfully written but perhaps too personal to engage an audience, during which the tale had to mark time. I wasn't sure enough of my ground to express these reservations with real conviction; more to the point I couldn't find the right language to do so, which with a playwright of my own generation, like Peter Nichols, would have come to me effortlessly. I was twenty years away in both directions from the cast of mind of, on the one hand, David Hare, and, on the other, Binkie Beaumont, and I realised with a slight shock that I must now be middle-aged. I had climbed up the hill; now presumably, I would be descending it. The trick was to do so gradually.

We went into rehearsal with a strong cast, led by Edward Fox fresh from his success in the film of *The Day of the Jackal*, and a stunning newcomer, Kate Nelligan, a determined Canadian with all the attributes of stardom – talent, beauty, intelligence – unhindered I felt by that ambivalence that goes under the name of humour. However this was not required of her in *Knuckle* where she had to be a luminous, impassioned presence, the first of those David Hare heroines who become the moral centre of many of his later plays.

From the start the production had a bumpy ride. Nothing too awful happened but nothing went entirely right. The designer I had chosen, Ralph Koltai, withdrew at the last moment because he was overstretched with other work, but he recommended to replace him an up and coming young talent, John Napier, who would one day make a worldwide name for himself designing *Cats* and *Les Misérables*. *Knuckle* was a play of many scenes and it had to move like a film. John came up with an ingenious arrangement of trucks, one at the back of the stage which glided forward, and two to right and left, out of sight in the wings. Both were attached to long pivoting arms which could swing one or the other to centre stage when a change of scene was required. This was mesmerising to watch the first time you saw it, like something at a funfair, but over the course of an evening it grew repetitive. To cover the scene changes I'd commissioned a full Warner Brothers film score from Marc Wilkinson, a composer with whom I had already worked very productively at the National, but this had run over-budget and Michael Codron was growing nervous. I had another idea which didn't quite come off – to render all the elements of the various sets in film shades of black and white with only the actors and their clothes providing colour, but this too became a little monotonous. However, it was an idea with life in it, which fifteen years later I resurrected with notable success in the Broadway musical *City of Angels*, a show which also owed a debt to Raymond Chandler.

Knuckle opened out of town at the Oxford Playhouse and it was soon apparent that, however much we liked it, this was a play for which the public weren't yet prepared. Both Michael Codron and David's ever-protective agent, Peggy Ramsay, had said as much from the start, but it is one thing to reach this judgement reading the lines on a page, quite another to experience it among other people sitting in a half-empty theatre. We set to work to make improvements, but with an anxiety not present during rehearsals. David tried numerous rewrites and sent me reams of notes. First thing in the morning the telephones would start ringing in the Randolph Hotel where we were all staying, but often they were calls from which you found out later that you'd been excluded. The hunt was on for something or someone to blame. In this regard Peggy, with her passionate concern for her young client, showed herself to be an admirable agent but a dangerous colleague. I began to feel myself being sidelined. It didn't help that in this volatile situation too many people had a crush on Kate Nelligan.

By the time we reached London the show had improved, and on our first night I felt quite proud of it. However, the following morning most of the press reviewed it with the sniffy condescension they save up for work that takes them by surprise. Our opening anticipated by a day the first night of Peter Hall's *The Tempest*. I had been too preoccupied to pay much attention to what was happening across the river at the Old Vic, but news of the show's ups and downs had reached me. One of the actors had a drug problem and occasionally didn't show up, there were huge cost overruns because of the complexity of the set, and at the dress rehearsal John Gielgud, approaching seventy, had fallen down a trapdoor which a stagehand had forgotten to close. Miraculously he escaped injury. In comparison *Knuckle* had had an easy ride.

With my own first night behind me I was able to attend the opening of *The Tempest*, wanting to like it but unable to do so. It is a play much discussed but infrequently realised in performance, being composed of wonderful things which in the simplest story terms don't quite add up to a satisfactory whole. In this production Ariel flew down from the flies like Peter Pan, but without the cover of soaring music the device of flying with its wires and winches can seem extremely earthbound. Denis Quilley, playing Caliban as a savage from the New World with a Mohawk haircut, was the only member of the Olivier resident company that Peter had chosen to use, which worried me, since their welfare was supposed to be one of the reasons he had engaged me. Mostly the show had been cast expensively on the open market. Sir John Gielgud's Prospero was beautifully spoken, which we expected, but wanted more.

Gielgud was the first of the knights, dames and film stars with whom Peter would underwrite his productions during my time there. Sir Ralph Richardson was already pencilled in for *John Gabriel Borkman*, and this casting would be further augmented with two dames.

The only time the performance of *The Tempest* came alight was with the entrance of Captain Mainwaring from *Dad's Army*, Arthur Lowe, who was playing one of the comics, Stephano. The audience briefly sat up in their seats, then relaxed back and gave themselves over to an immaculate comedy performer whose laughs came with the aplomb of a thoroughbred taking hurdles. Otherwise the production landed on the stage of the Old Vic with a dull thud, reflected the following day in the notices. Peter had made the mistake of which all directors are guilty at some time or another, particularly when they are anxious: he had over-produced it, and gone shopping for talent when he might have been better served by the talent under his nose.

Because of the earlier first-night start, the curtain came down on *The Tempest* just in time to nip back across the river and watch the last moments of *Knuckle*. The show suddenly looked wonderful, eloquent, felt and above all, relevant. I couldn't help wondering if we would have been better received by the press had the two first nights been in the reverse order. Even so, trouble lingered over *Knuckle*. Michael Codron kept it on as long as he could, but it never quite caught fire with the public. Our best notice, a rave, was from Frank Marcus in the *Sunday Telegraph* which concluded with some faint praise for me, after which the critic went on to assert that the play would have been better directed by the author.

I sensed a telephone ringing somewhere in the background. Margaret Ramsay, thrilled for her client, persuaded Codron to have the entire review blown up and mounted on a board front-of-house, the first and only time I have ever had a personal bad notice displayed outside a theatre where one of my productions was playing. I was indignant and hurt, a vulnerable combination, and stormed into Codron's office to complain. He listened politely but as I raised my voice I could see him withdraw his sympathy. It would take some six years before we would work together again, but when we did, on Michael Frayn's *Make and*

Break, it was the beginning of a run of quite remarkable success for all three of us.

My thoughts now turned to the Australian tour of *The Front Page*. We had lost a number of our original cast to other work, most grievously Denis Quilley, so we would need a couple of weeks of rehearsal before we left London. There was still time for me to attend associates' meetings and one in particular gave me some concern. The purpose of these meetings was mainly to decide which plays would be included in the repertoire, and the associates were encouraged to propose projects that interested them. Jonathan Miller always had a long list. His restless energetic intelligence propelled him towards work and, because the more humdrum aspects of directing plays bored him, he liked to work fast and frequently. He had once told Peter Hall that, if allowed, he would willingly direct ten plays a year.

One project he was promoting hard was Oscar Wilde's *The Importance of Being Earnest* performed by an all-male cast, and when he brought this up again at an associates' meeting it was icily dismissed by Harold Pinter, who insisted that the director's job was not to play games with the text but to release the intentions of the playwright. Jonathan countered by saying that this might well be the case with a new play, but with a work like *The Importance*, already familiar through a hundred conventional productions, there was room for some interpretive leeway. The worst that could happen was that the director would make a fool of himself. Harold was adamant, and the argument had suddenly become quite hostile.

Those present began to take sides. I was inclined to agree with Jonathan, particularly about this play which was already shadowed by ambiguity. When he wrote it Wilde was known to the public only as an immensely successful playwright and family man, though his intimates knew him also to be a secret, questing homosexual. A recent, much-acclaimed production of the play in

New York, in which the director Brian Bedford also played Lady Bracknell, suggests that Jonathan might well have been on to something. Peter Hall defused the tension in the room by having it both ways; deferring in one direction, he said he would hate to see such a production, but, deferring in the other, would never stand in the way if Jonathan wanted to do it. Only one clear thing emerged from the meeting. In our group of associates these two brilliant men, both Jewish and thus unencumbered by the least suggestion of prejudice, were at liberty to dislike each other heartily.

When I boarded the Qantas jumbo jet to Sydney to mount the Australian tour of *The Front Page* I had other concerns. It would be only my second trip home since arriving in England in 1950, and I had uneasy memories about the first visit some nine years before, when I had confronted with a shock the thing I had forgotten – why I had left home in the first place. Reacquainting myself with Australia then, complicated by the onset of a serious illness, had been extremely disturbing. However, more recently the country and my own fortunes had undergone changes and some dramatic improvements. I hoped I could return this time with a more forgiving eye.

Within twenty-four hours of arrival I was introduced to an aspect of Australia I loved, and an aspect I didn't. I was accommodated at a well-appointed motel at Rushcutters Bay with a ravishing outlook across parkland and through the swaying masts of yachts to the harbour. How could I have survived for so long without this dappled sunlight, these smells and sounds as substantial as butter? That was one side of the equation. The other was the Sydney representative of the J. C. Williamson firm who were presenting the show in Australia. He was one of those authority figures who were all over the country when I was growing up, but who these days, except perhaps in remote pockets of Queensland, seem to have become extinct. He was of medium height, medium in all respects, with the copper badge of a returned serviceman from the Second World War a permanent fixture in his buttonhole. He looked at you with a slow stare, wearing that expression of controlled distaste that you see on the faces of racist policemen, except that in his case the race he disliked was the tribe of theatricals to whom he was obliged to give house room in his theatres. I took an instant dislike to him, and didn't much care for the way he barked orders, 'The day after their plane touches down the company will be expected to be on stage for the dress rehearsal at precisely seven o'clock!'

The jumbo was expected around six a.m., so I rose early to meet the actors and join them on the bus which would take them to their accommodation in the suburbs. They trickled out of the terminal in twos and threes, squinting in the Australian light and ragged with jet lag and sleeplessness, having travelled halfway round the world sitting up in Economy. When we arrived at their motel (this one without a view), they were told they would have to wait in the lobby until noon when their rooms would become available. It seemed that J. C. Williamson had decided to save money by booking their accommodation some six hours after their arrival. These were the sort of travel arrangements Polonius might have made.

The following day the company rallied for the dress rehearsal, which was particularly stressful for those playing important parts for the first time. During a break I was approached by the racist policeman. 'I need to address the entire company. NOW!' he said with unpleasant and unexplained satisfaction. I informed the stage manager, and the actors obediently trooped into the auditorium, wondering what was up. When they had collected in a close group and each found a seat, the policeman raised something above his head, holding it delicately between his thumb and forefinger. 'This,' he said, indicating a bent cigarette butt, 'is what I have just found trodden into our spotless, newly laid carpet. Now I want it clearly understood that this is a brand-new theatre, and I'm not having you people coming in with your cigarettes and your dirty paper cups and making a pigsty of it.' He then reeled off a list of rules and prohibitions as if addressing delinquents in an orphanage. I saw my cast of polite English actors watching him with utter disbelief. In London one of them would have been on his feet at once, protesting, but this was a foreign country, and perhaps all Australians behaved this way.

Afterwards I challenged the policeman about his tone, but he wasn't listening. 'And another thing!' he said, 'On the first night we're going to be honoured by the presence of the State Governor, Sir Roden Cutler, V.C. Sir Roden has got one leg. The moment the vice-regal party has settled, the moment Sir Roden has sat down, *that curtain goes up*! No matter what. I'm not keeping a man with one leg waiting!' I couldn't see why the leg would be a problem once the Governor was seated, but I said I'd do my best. 'Not your best. *Just do it!*' he replied.

The night of our opening there was one of Sydney's spectacular semi-tropical storms, with huge claps of thunder and water falling on to the city in one great block, the sort of natural phenomenon that makes any cultural event seem trivial. I knew that our audience, if they came at all, would arrive late, sopping and ill-tempered. Sir Roden, as befitted his military background, took his seat exactly on schedule, and the curtain rose like a rocket. For the next twenty minutes latecomers dribbled in spasmodically, shaking water from their garments and umbrellas like shivering wet dogs, as they peered along the rows trying to locate their seats. However, the company fought back, and the reception at the end was warm and enthusiastic.

On my second day in Australia I'd bought a daily newspaper, the *Daily Mirror*, to see if any attempt was being made to promote the show. This meant ploughing through a section of largely parochial news, followed by page after page of advertisements for Sydney's department stores and other retail outlets. Dotted randomly among all these ads would be an infrequent news story, presumably there to give credibility to the notion that what I was holding in my hands was, as described, a newspaper. Midway through I turned a page and read the headline – TWO YEAR UNI STUDY SHOWS HALTER-NECKED BRAS MAKE GIRLS ROUND-SHOULDERED. It seemed we'd brought *The Front Page* to the right country. But actually I was wrong. It was a play the tone of which was sufficiently familiar with Australians for them to have made a pretty good job of producing it themselves. What they rightly expected from the National Theatre of Great Britain was something from Europe – a Shakespeare or a Chekhov. I realised, too late, that I would have been on safer ground bringing them something like *The Cherry Orchard*, not an offering which, unintentionally, had a whiff of condescension about it. *The Front Page* was not badly received in Australia; our press was good and we drew an audience, but it wasn't the 'event' I'd hoped it would be. Nor did it mean anything to anybody that an expatriate had directed it. However I was back home for a while, loving the soft warmth of autumn and determined to make the most of my stay.

The physical lushness of Sydney had never seemed more alluring. J. C. Williamson asked me to stay on through the four weeks of the Sydney run, and see the show into its Melbourne theatre, an important date for business. So I decided simply to take it easy and enjoy myself. I saw old friends, ate spectacular food and drank rather too much good wine. I also explored new theatrical venues like the Nimrod Theatre, founded by a resource-ful ex-lawyer, Ken Horler, where I saw shows that didn't need overseas validation to speak to their Australian audiences. I made friends among the actors and directors who worked there, and was instructed in the gulf separating them from Australia's com-mercial theatre, of which I was currently a part. They held it in contempt and I could hardly blame them.

I left Australia reconciled to all the things that had once driven me away, knowing that I would always be imprinted by its beauties but not yet prepared to chance a fulfilling career there. That day would come, year by year, if not for me then for other younger Australians. I took the long way home in a wandering trajectory through the Far East and on to Scandinavia, leaving behind me a Continent and returning to an Island, which on the map was beginning to seem a less significant shade of red.

Back at the National I resumed my attendance at meetings. Indeed my most vivid memories of the Peter Hall years are of meetings, at which not much was done, but sometimes, and inadvertently, a great deal was revealed. These meetings fell into three categories. There were large ones at which the associates would be joined by the heads of departments, like John Goodwin in Publicity, when a crowd of people would be crammed into Peter's Aquinas Street office, some sitting, some standing. There would be smaller meetings of just the associates in the same space, and these Larry would sometimes attend. Finally, there were the associates' dinners at which Larry never made an appearance. These occasions reminded me of a privilege extended to prefects at an expensive private school, and they took place in Peter's new flat, a triplex at the very top of Cromwell Tower, one of a nest of modernist skyscrapers that had just risen out of the new Barbican development. He had chosen to live there originally because of its proximity to the building site of the RSC's projected new London home. Our dinners were catered by a smart young woman from a South Kensington firm who supplied excellent food and even better wines. It was not unusual to see bottles of Château Talbot and Château Palmer gracing the table. Once or twice a month Peter's wife Jackie would make herself scarce and give over her home to these events, leaving the associates, like very large children, to tuck in.

In London at that time it was fun to find oneself enjoying a good dinner so high in the air, and as always it was interesting to be allowed to see the inside of someone else's living quarters. In his first marriage, to Leslie Caron, Peter had lived in a period house on Montpelier Square, replete with Victorian furniture, decorative wallpapers and converted oil lamps. Now, in his second marriage, he had embraced modernism with a vengeance, his past sprayed over by a concrete matching that of the new theatre on the South Bank he was now running. The associates sat on soft modern seats and observed less comfortable ones elsewhere in the room, a Le Corbusier recliner in black-and-white calfskin and a modernist chair constructed of slats of wood painted in primary colours, which, being a museum piece, we were requested not to sit on. There was a lamp like a small willow on which the end of every branch was tipped with illumination. Beyond the living area and running round the outside of the building was a narrow balcony, more like a rampart, with a very thick concrete wall at chest height. One evening we all trooped out to take in the view. It was the sort of place which invited you to pour down boiling oil on your enemies. I looked across the rising urban landscape to St Paul's which seemed so close you could have hit it with a slingshot, and noticed that the balcony where we stood was on an exact level with the gold cross on the top of the cathedral's dome. A mischievous name for Peter's apartment slipped into my mind and stuck: Satan Towers.

The most productive hour or two of any associates' dinner was invariably the one before we sat down to eat and drink, when our sense of well-being would improve but not our focus. The last hour after dinner was pretty much a waste of time.

Our group of associates had grown considerably since Peter had first spoken to me about Harold Pinter and John Schlesinger. There were now three full-time resident directors, Jonathan and I joined by the Scottish playwright–director, Bill Bryden, who was the youngest member of the group. Also included were John Bury, the Head of Design and Peter's most frequent collaborator, and his new right-hand man in charge of business, Peter Stevens. Completing the assembly were John Russell Brown, an academic whose subject was drama and who had written a number of books on the subject, and, Michael Kustow, recently director of the Institute of Contemporary Art and a one-time associate of Peter Brook's at the RSC. He now preferred to be known professionally as Mike, but would one day revert to being a Michael.

It was a diverse collection of people and a voluble one, and I admired the skill with which Peter handled us. He had less to say and less to drink than we did, but skilfully guided the conversation in the direction he wanted it to go. Over coffee, when Jonathan made an amusing assault on some current orthodoxy, or Harold handed down a severe judgement on a person or a piece of work of which he disapproved, or Bill Bryden embarked on an appreciation of an actor he'd liked, with plentiful demotic digressions and the constant use of the phrase 'you know', as if concise speech was somehow a mark of insincerity, I would watch Peter as he watched us, behind a haze of smoke from his small cigars, and see his thoughts circling in his head like planes in a holding pattern over Heathrow Airport. What would we discover, I wondered, when eventually they touched down?

The quietest among us was John Bury, a big teddy-bear of a man whose professorial appearance belied his long association with the radical theatre of Joan Littlewood. He was a born committee man, who could sit patiently for hours holding his peace while others held forth. He had put this talent to productive use sitting on a string of committees which had taken him all over the world – to theatre festivals in Eastern Europe, to symposiums on stage design in America. We were all rather surprised, therefore, when, at one meeting, he raised an important question which none of us had properly considered. 'What we haven't yet discussed,' he said, 'is what's going to be the actual *policy* of the National Theatre.' The room fell silent. This was a difficult question to answer. With three auditoria to fill, six nights a week, the immediate demand on us was simply to find enough good plays of whatever complexion, and enough good actors of whatever style, to fill them. A policy, say, 'to pursue new writing' or 'to re-evaluate the classics' could never be more than part of our overall approach.

'I envisage our policy,' began Peter slowly, 'quite simply to be the pursuit of Excellence. Nothing that appears on any one of our stages should be other than first class. Excellent in all departments – the production, the performances, the design.'

'That's not always possible,' someone put in.

'Well then,' said Peter, 'if something reaches the dress rehearsal stage and is not up to our standards, then the production should be scrapped.'

This would be a radical departure from all previous theatrical practice, but at the time there seemed to be so much money sloshing towards the National that maybe such a thing would be possible. We nodded our heads, unaware that within months our complacency about our finances would be abruptly challenged.

A policy of Excellence: with a good meal inside me it didn't seem such a bad idea, perhaps the only one available to us. However, thinking about it the following day, I realised it wasn't a policy at all; it was an aspiration. You can't have a true policy unless its opposite also has some credibility; a theatre whose policy is the pursuit of new writing will not be attempting old texts, a government whose policy is to lower taxes will not (or should not) be raising them. But what exactly was the alternative to the policy of Excellence – a policy of Mediocrity?

And there were other problems. Who would decide which productions were insufficiently Excellent and had to be scrapped? Peter's standards and those of his mentor, the contentious Cambridge don F. R. Leavis, were not necessarily mine. Moreover, in theatrical history there were innumerable instances of ground-breaking new work coming to birth surrounded by doubt and misgiving. Even talented people can lose heart and err in their judgement. In my own career I knew of well-meaning people in the theatre who had disapproved of Peter Nichols' play *A Day in the Death of Joe Egg* and wouldn't have minded if it had never seen the light of day. In the arts it has always been the case that talent and money and the audacity to employ them in interesting ways have been in short supply. The best new work can hope for is, like tadpoles, to keep wriggling and survive. Was Peter Hall proposing to change this? He seemed hungry for certainties in a field where I wasn't sure they existed.

I suspected this had something to do with Peter's recent, and very successful, excursions into the world of opera, where certainties are easier to come by. There is little dispute about a great voice, a great conductor or an inspired instrumentalist. Whatever the struggles and the luck that have led to their emergence, such gifted individuals can look forward to a busy and sustained career. The bookings pour in often for years ahead, and the bank balance more or less takes care of itself. An established conductor has a much greater security of income than a theatre director, whose failures are absolute and have to be expected about twenty-five per cent of the time.

Peter was an excellent director of opera. I had been to see his production of Monteverdi's *Ulysses* at Glyndebourne and loved it. He was musically educated and with John Bury at his side was adept at finding ways of visually enhancing the score. Working in opera offered prestige, celebrity and, for the elect, an excellent income, and I think Peter looked at the lifestyle enjoyed by his colleagues in the musical world with envy. However, it was a life circumscribed by an acknowledged canon of scores and librettos. What it lacked was the open-endedness of theatre, unpredictable as it is both artistically and in the way it distributes financial rewards. There are so many possibilities – from an acclaimed run of a few weeks in a studio theatre, to four years in the West End, to a Broadway musical playing all over the world, to huge earnings in films. And Peter, I thought, wanted all it offered. But with operatic certainty.

So a quest for certainties began to characterise our associates' dinners, which would often begin with Peter delivering glad tidings. 'The Board have agreed unanimously that salaries for top actors must be improved!' or 'The South Bank Board assure me that the building works are definitely on schedule and that we can plan accordingly!' The associates would greet these announcements with delighted expressions and exaggerated murmurs of assent and congratulations. One evening Peter arrived wreathed in smiles. 'I bring great news!' he said. 'Harold is pregnant!'

'That's *wonderful*!', 'How *marvellous*!', 'When, *when*?!', came the rejoinders. I was reminded of certain news items that in those days were always left to last in BBC bulletins. The announcer, having catalogued a string of worldwide catastrophes with imperturbable detachment, would suddenly break into a broad, teasing smile before saying 'And finally . . . !' At once you knew the kind of story that was coming. Another minor member of the Royal Family was no doubt with child. I sometimes wondered whether I was the only viewer in the British Isles to whom this was not a matter of immediate and joyous interest. Admittedly Harold's pregnancy was of a different order. It would be splendid to have a new Pinter play in the National's repertoire, which of course Peter would direct. A more pressing concern, however, for those of us who were also directors, was exactly what plays we would be doing in the months ahead.

There would be other occasions at our meetings when a huge smile from Peter or one of his deputies would presage a 'royal baby' announcement. And for me at least the cant this encouraged became increasingly hard to bear. However, I still regarded Peter as the proper person to be in charge, and on one occasion he demonstrated real concern for my own artistic development. The 'royal baby' on this occasion was the news that Albert Finney had approached Peter and offered to commit himself to the National for an extended period of time. He wanted to explore some of the great classic parts. and the first role he wished to attempt was Hamlet. His father at the time was far from well and Albert felt that this had given him a particular insight into the part. Having explained this to the associates, Peter then turned to me, 'Michael, you've had a long association with Albert'. (This was true. We'd worked together as actors at the Birmingham Rep and at Stratford, and his production company, Memorial Enterprises, had brought Peter Nichols' early successes to London, with me attached.) 'And I thought a *Hamlet* might be something it would be good for you to do.' I was surprised and touched. This was just the sort of work I'd stayed on at the National to attempt, and Peter was displaying the sort of concern for the artistic well-being of the people under him which had been one of Larry's great virtues.

Hamlet is a play that most directors sometime in their careers would like to attempt, and I'd often thought about it. One idea I'd had was to be unafraid of its length and instead capitalise on it by using a completely uncut text. There were a number of small scenes – for instance the comic exchange between Polonius and Renaldo – that were often dropped in production, but at the National there was rehearsal time enough to bring them to life. Perhaps we could do the play with a long interval of about three quarters of an hour so that the audience would have time to enjoy a light supper out on the terraces of the new building and take in the river while they readied themselves for the second half. I expatiated on this idea to those present and it was agreed that a slot should be found for the production. The next step was arranging a meeting between Albert and me.

This proved difficult. He was very busy and so was I, but we finally arranged an amiable, if brief, encounter in the foyer of the Royal Court Theatre. He had heard about the notion of an uncut version, said he still needed convincing but would continue to think about it. We had known each other in a variety of professional and personal contexts over fifteen years, and I wondered if we were a little too familiar with each other to become partners in the sort of artistic quest he had in mind for himself. But we agreed to keep talking. 'Nice shoes,' said Albert, looking down as we parted.

There had been a slight shadow over this meeting that neither of us had referred to. As producer of Peter Nichols' West End successes, Albert felt almost as proprietorial about the playwright as, for rather better reasons, did I. I had directed his first three London hits and *Joe Egg* had gone on to Broadway with Albert himself in the lead. Two of these plays had been bought for the movies and Peter and his family now lived in a large house in a fashionable street in Blackheath. For both of us acquiring a reputation had been an uphill struggle, and it was pleasant and unusual for two close friends to be able to share in this joint vindication and the prosperity it brought with it. I took it for granted that his next play, *Chez Nous*, the one he had been working on when we stayed at the Nichols' farmhouse in France, would come my way.

And so it did. Peter gave it to me to read, and I was transplanted at once back to the Dordogne. It was set in the same barn attached to the same house as the one we'd stayed in that summer. Living there were the same couple, Peter and Thelma more or less, and visiting them were the same batches of friends, more or less. Like all his plays it drew directly on his own experience rendered with his unrivalled comic observation. However, the big difference between this and his previous plays was that the plot turned on a complete invention; namely, that one of the visitors had impregnated the couple's very young teenage daughter. I knew that of course such things could, and did, happen in life, but on the page, in the context of this particular play, which in all other respects breathed authenticity, I simply couldn't believe it.

Peter and I usually had long discussions before going into rehearsal, in the course of which the play often underwent various revisions. I went out to Blackheath with an overnight bag

222

so that we could begin this process. As tactfully as I could I told him of my principal concern, but as always made it clear that I would direct whatever text he finally decided to put in front of me. This proved to be the first occasion on which he responded with sharp impatience. I thought I understood. He had worked long and hard on this play. However, I couldn't help wondering if his response had something to do with the nude swim we had taken that summer in France. Had the sexual connotation he had imposed on this relatively innocent event somehow been transmuted into the far graver transgression at the centre of the play?

A week or two went by during which we weren't in touch, then one morning I had a call from Albert, who as usual would be producing. He came to the point with almost unseemly relish. Peter Nichols, he said, had been thinking about it and he now wanted to try going with another director. I was shocked into silence. 'Yes,' continued Albert, 'we thought we'd approach Lindsay Anderson. Then if he says no, go to Ronnie Eyre. And if *he* says no, come back to you.' If ever a response merited a sharp expletive this was it, but instead I responded with a lifeless murmur, 'I don't think that's a good idea.' Albert's call had been crass, but it was not him I was angry with. This was surely a conversation Peter should have screwed up his courage and initiated himself.

Rather as I expected, first Lindsay and then Ronnie Eyre turned down the play, but it came to the West End ably directed by Robert Chetwyn. It was well received in the press but failed to draw an audience and was soon taken off. It has never been revived. In Peter's earlier work, which portrays his own extended family or, say, the working-class patients of *The National Health*, he observes his characters with a sharp but always understanding eye. With success he was now moving in middle-class and occasionally upper-class circles, and when he put these new acquaintances on stage they were not charitably presented. The general audience picked up on this slight but unmistakable whiff of misanthropy, disliked it and decided to stay away. Indeed, this may have been the thing to which I had instinctively responded when I first read *Chez Nous*.

In his next play, *The Freeway*, Peter took as a model for one of his characters his near-neighbour and new friend, John Grigg, the ex-peer who, as Lord Altrincham, had dared to question the usefulness of the monarchy, and later (second only to Tony Benn) renounced his title when this was made possible in 1963. In the play he is transformed into a mother-fixated, cowardly politician – which, with much well-bred amusement, Grigg later suggested to Peter that he wasn't. *The Freeway* was one of a number of plays at that time – another was John Osborne's *Watch It Come Down* – that anticipated the total breakdown of society, and occasionally you had the feeling that both playwrights were rather rubbing their hands at the prospect.

In Peter's play the metaphor for society's collapse was a huge traffic jam lasting weeks on one of the new freeways criss-crossing Britain. An ordinary family in a motor-home sit stranded on the hard shoulder, waiting for rescue which never comes. It was a play with a large cast and considerable scenic demands and Peter offered it to the National Theatre in the expectation that I would direct it. I might have done had I liked it, but I read it and didn't. And with loyalty no longer a factor, I turned it down. Peter wrote me a long aggrieved letter which particularly exasperated me when he wondered why I needed to 'feel strongly' about a play before agreeing to direct it. He then went on to question whether I had ever felt strongly about the earlier plays we had done together. I said 'no' once again, with more firmness and some satisfaction.

Jonathan Miller, who at the time was directing the original play by Beaumarchais on which the Mozart opera *The Marriage of Figaro* was based, and who had three further productions in prospect, stepped in and offered his services. I was glad that someone else at the National had agreed to do it but a little concerned for Jonathan. Even if I'd liked the play I knew it would not support that second agenda of fresh ideas and invention that had made his *School for Scandal* so interesting. Nichols' plays could only come to life on their own terms, and this meant patient, demanding work getting all the people on stage so arranged that the focus was precise while meticulously rehearsing the naturalistic dialogue until its rhythms and hesitations seem to happen of their own accord. This was the sort of work that bored Jonathan, and for the most part he left his cast to sort it out for themselves.

One morning I looked in on rehearsals of *Figaro*. He always welcomed visitors because he took pride in creating an environment where actors could enjoy their work and he could enjoy showing off. Notwithstanding his formidable intellect and some understandable snobbishness about it, around the theatre he was the complete democrat, encountering everyone as an equal. I once found him deep in conversation with a maintenance man whose hobby was body-building and who lifted weights in a space beneath the stage of the Old Vic. He had sprained a muscle in his neck and Jonathan was having a comprehensive discussion with him about the anatomy of the area, as detailed as if he was conferring with a fellow doctor.

For most people in the theatre their knowledge and curiosity is constrained by its usefulness to their work. Not in Jonathan's case. Half the time he fretted that he was wasting his life in the theatre when he could have been pursuing his medical career, or doing research in a Cambridge laboratory, or taking a new direction entirely to become a lecturer in Fine Art. As well as a director he was a natural teacher and scholar; but what was to set him at odds with Peter Hall was that he was also seditiously funny.

With people for whom it is really important, humour is its own justification. It does not, as Peter writes in his *Diaries*, need to be 'about' something. Sometimes all it is about is a person exercising a facility to make other people laugh. At our associates' dinners Peter was quite able to appreciate another's joke, but

I never heard him make one himself. Nor, for that matter, do I ever remember him indulging in mischievous gossip, probably because neither served any useful purpose. On the contrary, all they did was risk making enemies. Peter did a great deal of public smiling, and loved to be photographed with his face creased in mirth. Where Jonathan was concerned Peter was right to be wary because he deployed his wit with absolute recklessness and to anyone who would listen.

His descriptions of people who had irked him had a weird, hilarious accuracy. For instance, Caryl Brahms, the detective story writer, was a regular presence at London openings, which she attended as the companion of Ned Sherrin, and during the interval neither hesitated to broadcast their opinions about the show they were seeing. Doubtless Caryl Brahms had once said something adverse about one of Jonathan's productions. She was a tiny woman, no beauty, with a large head and hooded eyes which slanted downwards. 'Caryl Brahms . . .' I heard Jonathan meditate one day. 'Yes, Caryl Brahms . . . She reminds me of a small boy holding aloft on a platter the severed head of John the Baptist.'

Despite its surrealism and unkindness, his description was uncannily precise. Harold Pinter, of course, was regularly mocked, for his consistently black wardrobe, his flawlessly laundered cricketing gear, and his gnomic silences whenever he was asked to explain his own work. And yet, though there may have been a degree of malice in the things Jonathan said, there was never a sense of grudge. Invented on the spot, proclaimed to whatever audience was available, they were then allowed to be blown away on the wind and forgotten – at least by Jonathan. However, others remembered them, particularly the things that were said about Peter Hall, which Hall's deputy Peter Stevens regularly reported back to his boss.

TEN

At our various meetings and our dinners the quest for certainties continued. Occasionally there was a specific agenda; at one dinner we co-opted the Casting Director, Gillian Diamond, so that we could sort out the actors we liked and the actors we didn't. The idea was that once we'd drawn up our lists, we would be free to cross-cast with confidence among our various productions. This proved an exercise of dubious value since none of us felt comfortable putting a cross against an actor's name. In any case there were certain people no one dared categorise, because they were considered to be beyond criticism – the knights and dames who featured so regularly in Peter's productions. There was a rumour that this select few would in future be paid a salary appropriate to their special status, and that differentials in compensation between one actor and another were getting wider.

Similarly, when the discussion was about playwrights there were three names that had a place all to themselves. One was Samuel Beckett, another Edward Bond, and the third was with us in this very room. About playwrights like Arnold Wesker or Michael Frayn you could say what you liked, but these three were somehow exempt from all opinion. I think Jonathan and I were alone in finding this a little ridiculous. No matter how exceptional, they were still writers like other writers who, in doing what they did, invited comment. None of us would have dreamt of criticising Harold's work to his face, but surely there were small reservations that could be made about any playwright, even Sam Beckett. For instance, wasn't his pessimism a little too absolute to be a comprehensive reflection of life? Wasn't *Happy*

Days, now proposed by Peter as one of his future productions, more an extraordinary metaphor wrapped in language than a play? However, even thinking such things, let alone expressing them, was somehow off limits.

One evening before the beginning of a dinner I was standing chatting with Harold and Mike Kustow. 'I'll never forget the first time I saw *The Birthday Party*,' said Mike. 'It changed my life. Literally.' Harold gave us his guarded smile. I didn't doubt Mike's sincerity but found the expression of it, in this particular context, a little uncomfortable. Harold nodded, then extricated himself from the praise with practised ease, and I realised that such moments must occur frequently in the life he was now living, inside a bubble of unassailable reputation. We too, the associates, seemed to be in a bubble, waiting to go in to dinner, appetite undiminished, high above London at the top of Satan Towers.

During Larry's regime all our meetings had been in the daytime, and if they overran into the lunch hour he would order coffee and a plate of smoked salmon sandwiches from the canteen. I was the only associate present who had any memory of the previous administration, in which Olivier had been confident enough about his crown to delegate power to others. Peter, though apparently more egalitarian, was always careful to keep the people he worked with at arms' length from real influence. We were allowed to talk a great deal but we decided very little.

The only area where we exercised any control was in the plays we chose to direct. Both Harold and John Schlesinger of course had their primary careers as playwright and film-maker to attend to, so their impact on the organisation was confined to only one production a year. Bill Bryden, however, had been busy with a number of productions, and Jonathan had *The Freeway* and no less than three other shows planned for the coming year, *The Importance of Being Earnest*, then *She Would If She Could*, a period comedy he had discovered, and *Measure for Measure*. Peter himself had lined up three irreproachable texts performed by irreproachable casts: *John Gabriel Borkman*, *Happy Days* and the new Pinter play, *No Man's Land*.

I, however, was in something of a quandary. Since returning from Australia my most pressing concern had been finding a play to direct which would establish my association with the new regime. I was looking for something fresh and lively, a match to *The National Health*, and there was one script I found in the cupboard in the Literary Department that I thought might be a possibility. What had drawn me to it at once was the name of the author on the title page, A. E. Ellis. Some ten years before I had read his one extraordinary novel, *The Rack*, about a TB sanatorium in Switzerland, and had never forgotten it. The problem was that his new script, though an absorbing read, wasn't yet a play. It was a history, and a very comprehensive one, and on a subject which I found riveting – the story of Alfred Dreyfus, the Jewish officer whom the French High Command persecuted over many years for a crime of which they knew him to be innocent. The 'Dreyfus Affair' had divided Europe and its repercussions would end only in the general devastation that concluded the Second World War.

Peter Hall himself had read the play and had submitted an intelligent but damning report, the case for the prosecution cogently expressed in a paragraph. It was difficult to refute his judgement but I still found myself drawn to the material. John Russell Brown, the literary adviser among the associates, was more encouraging about the play's possibilities and urged further exploration. I had become acquainted with the author, whose real name was Derek Lindsay, and liked him, though he was the most pessimistic man I had ever met. Like Peter Nichols and John Osborne, he too had premonitions of a total social breakdown and spoke ominously of untreated sewage belching out into the streets. He was a man of anguished courtesy who dressed in a city suit and tie like a literary figure of T. S. Eliot's generation. I guessed he had a private income, and this, combined with his temperament, had allowed him to work away for years without compromises, first producing his singular novel, and now this play. I felt, as did John Russell Brown, that it was one of the National's responsibilities to identify such writers and offer them a welcome, so I accepted Derek's invitation to visit him in Suffolk for a few days when we could discuss his play at length.

I was in for some pleasant surprises. He had rented a thatched cottage for the summer in which he lived with his attractive French girlfriend, Marianne. It was beautiful weather and in this environment he was a far more humorous and expansive man than I had been expecting. Sitting in the sun, we discussed the background to the play, about which he had encyclopaedic knowledge. For a number of years the Dreyfus Affair had obsessed him and he had amassed a room full of research material, including newspaper cuttings and a collection of the anti-Semitic cartoons which had appeared in the anti-Dreyfusard periodicals of the time.

All of this intrigued me, but it also defined the problem with his play. Like a cupboard in a small flat, it had so much hanging in it you couldn't shut the door. I had some suggestions to make, a number of which he accepted, but about the most important he wouldn't budge: namely to reduce the play from three acts to two with only one interval. Audiences were getting impatient with the old three-act form, and in any case I thought that if we could start thinking about the material in two halves it would begin to slim down of its own accord. He had called his play *The Jew of Mulhouse*, a play on the title of Marlowe's anti-Semitic *The Jew of Malta*. However, I thought few of our audience would make this connection, so we agreed on *Grand Manoeuvres*, a better title because it located the subject of the play in the machinations employed by the French army in defence of a bogus honour.

I was not convinced we were doing nearly enough on the text, but as we worked our way through it I kept on having ideas about how to put it on stage. The play had a lively sense of theatre and the subject matter allowed for some great moments, such as the ceremony of Dreyfus' dishonourable discharge from the French Army early one grey Parisian morning, when the buttons of his uniform were torn off and his sword broken across the knee of a presiding officer. It was a tale of surpassing official wickedness, and the more I thought about it, the more I wanted to get it up and running. However, I returned to London not yet convinced that we were ready to go.

I passed the amended script on to John Russell Brown for an opinion. A few days later we caught sight of each other down the length of the Aquinas Street corridor, and he was smiling broadly. If I'd had my wits about me I would have suspected the imminence of a royal baby, but I heard what I wanted to hear. 'He's done it!' John announced joyously. A few days later I ran into Peter, also smiling with enthusiasm, and he greeted me with the identical usage, 'He's done it!' Again I should have asked myself if so busy a man had really found the time to study in any detail a new draft of a play which he had already emphatically rejected. However, what both my colleagues were offering me was genuine encouragement and the belief that I could pull it off. After all, had I not had four successes in a row? The other associates were given the play to read and endorsed it as a project which I, if not they, should direct. For them, as for me, it was the subject of *Grand Manoeuvres* rather than its rendering that attracted them. Mike Kustow was the only one to express a prudent doubt or two, but it was decided: the production would go ahead.

I began to assemble my team. Michael Annals wasn't free, so I asked John Bury to do the set, and he modelled a splendidly architectural design centred on a monumental arch. Our costume designer, Deirdre Clancy, produced sketches of the peacock uniforms of the French top brass, and Marc Wilkinson set about composing a score for shrill brass instruments and drums. We were going to give this show the works. Something that particularly pleased me was that the production provided excellent parts for the remnants of the company that had helped give the last few years of the Olivier regime its Indian summer.

A few weeks before rehearsals were due to start any complacency we might have been feeling about the future of the National was buried under an avalanche of bad news. On 11 September Peter told the associates that we had to prepare ourselves for a forty per cent reduction of our proposed South Bank budget. On the 21st came word that the completion of the new building would be delayed by a further year. On 1 October *The Freeway* opened to disastrous reviews, and on the 3rd, at a troubled and argumentative midday meeting of the associates, we learnt that the National would soon be under attack in the press. Oscar Lewenstein, a West End producer with a particular association with the Royal Court, was canvassing other distinguished theatre people to be co-signatories of a letter he was proposing to have published in *The Times*, strongly critical of the National.

Larry attended this meeting, in the course of which he deplored the erosion of the idea of a true company of actors. We were all taken aback by his appearance. He was supervising the West End transfer of *Saturday Sunday Monday* and had been struck down by a mysterious complaint that left one side of his face swollen as if it had been stung by a swarm of bees. Another symptom was a painful sensitivity at the tips of his fingers. This would prove to be dermatomyositis, the worst of the diseases that plagued the last two decades of his life, and the same illness that had killed the shipping magnate Onassis. It was a rare degenerative condition that attacked the muscles of the body, and which, in Onassis' case, left him so weak that in order to see he had to have his eyelids propped open.

Larry was self-conscious about his appearance, and worse, something which I hated to see, he carried the shame of illness. Nor was I happy about Jonathan's state of mind. Like all of us, he hated failure, and he and Peter Nichols were blaming each other for what had happened to *The Freeway*. Around the building he was also recklessly bad-mouthing the organisation, and muttering about resignation.

On 7 October I started rehearsing *Grand Manoeuvres* and was too busy to attend the associates' dinner two days later. Nor did Jonathan make an appearance. The following day I learnt that on the agenda had been the surprise announcement of the forthcoming productions which would have to be cancelled in the light of the necessary cutbacks. All three of Jonathan's shows in the New Year were to be axed. The work of other directors would not be affected. This, a matter absolutely central to future planning, had been decided by Peter Hall and Peter Stevens without any consultation with the associates. Coming on top of a flop it was impossible for Jonathan to regard it as other than an invitation to resign, and it had a devastating effect on him. I spoke to Peter Hall for clarification but he insisted he had no wish for Jonathan to go.

When the next associates' dinner came along I made sure I was free to attend, and to my surprise Jonathan was also there. However he was no longer the person we were familiar with. By the strangest of coincidences he now shared the disfigurement we had seen on Larry's face only a few weeks before. In Jonathan's case it was apparently the result of an allergy, but the symptoms were identical, the same puffed top lip and swollen nose that had given both men the look of people who had just suffered a beating. During the course of the entire evening this compulsively articulate man said hardly one word.

The Lewenstein letter was published in *The Times* as I began the second week of rehearsals. He had assembled a remarkable group of co-signatories, thirteen people in all, running theatres all over the country, including Lindsay Anderson, Joan Littlewood, Richard Eyre and Michael Elliott. The thrust of the letter was that the National was absorbing so much government money and poaching so many personnel away from other theatres that their very existence was under threat. In his *Diaries* Peter Hall declares he was 'terribly upset' by the letter and describes Lewenstein as a 'classic moralist', but I found the views expressed extremely persuasive. Just as I was the only person among the associates to have experienced the Olivier regime, so I was the only one to have worked extensively in the provinces. As an actor I had had two seasons at the Birmingham Rep when Sir Barry Jackson, who had funded and presided over it for thirty years, was still alive; and I had worked all over the country in reputable theatres such as the Bristol Old Vic and Nottingham Playhouse. As a director, moreover, I owed my career to work that had originated in Glasgow, and I knew that the health of the theatre in the metropolis was intimately connected with the work done in the provinces which provided, not only a training ground, but a place where, if you were prepared to accept budgetary constraints, you could enjoy striking artistic freedom.

Since the war the British theatre had experienced an extraordinary resurgence. By the time the National was under construction it could boast a catalogue of star actors who were famous all over the world, and it had a greater abundance of new writing than the rest of Europe put together. Where once we had looked enviously towards America, where Tennessee Williams and Arthur Miller were writing plays and Kazan and Brando were directing and acting in them, now New York was looking towards us. The British stage had a place in the national imagination not unlike that enjoyed by British art at the beginning of the new century, and as always bricks and mortar followed fashion – the Tate Modern now, the National Theatre then. Indeed it could be said that without the successes of the forties and the fifties, seeded before the war at the Old Vic and at the better provincial theatres, the will to memorialise the idea of a National Theatre in a vast new building would never have been found. Now the building was almost completed and about to open its doors to the public.

It was a little as if we had constructed a huge concrete dam in the middle of an existing and very successful ecosystem and it would have consequences very difficult to predict.

That pre-existing and abundant ecosystem had consisted of the two leading theatres, the Old Vic and the Royal Shakespeare Company, offering an alternative and a balance to each other. Co-existing with them were the more radical London theatres, the Royal Court and Joan Littlewood's Theatre Workshop, as well as established theatres in the regions, which regularly enriched London with transfers of their most interesting work. Finally, and quite as significant as the subsidised sector, was a thriving commercial West End where astute and dedicated producers such as Michael Codron could both make money and launch the careers of new playwrights like Harold Pinter, Simon Gray and Michael Frayn. Now the concrete dam was threatening to divert resources and talent away from this ecosystem on a huge scale. Were those of us perched atop the dam giving this enough thought?

With the failure of *The Freeway*, 1974 was beginning to look a fairly dismal year for the National. Though not unusual at the start of a new regime, it was still a cause for anxiety. Neither Harold's production of *Next of Kin* nor Bill Bryden's of *Spring Awakening* had done well at the box office, and the hunt was on for a sure-fire hit. I was pressured to direct Ben Travers' farce from the twenties, *Plunder*, which I'd read and was in two minds about. 'After *The Front Page*, you're the ideal man to do it!' insisted John Russell Brown with his usual enthusiasm. But they were very different plays, the one a transcription of raw American life made palatable by uninhibited humour, the other a comedy which related to the way the English lived about as indirectly as *Alice in Wonderland*. However, the theatre appeared to be in trouble so, without thinking about it too much because I was so preoccupied with *Grand Manoeuvres*, I agreed to do it.

Rehearsals I thought were going well. The company were committed and the play gave me all sorts of opportunities for invention. I was aware of the risks we were running and hoped I could steer around them. One afternoon we were working on a scene derived from Dreyfus' correspondence when he was imprisoned on Devil's Island. It was being well played by Alan MacNaughtan as the hapless officer, but as I watched a little worm of doubt crept into my mind that this was not so much a play as a pageant. Scenes followed each other like floats in a parade, each interesting and informative in itself, but not vitally connected to what went before or came after. Most directors have had this experience of misgiving in mid-rehearsal. The thought slips uninvited into your mind, and there is nothing you can do about it except banish it as soon as possible, and do everything you can to forget you ever had it.

At the final run-through in the rehearsal room the company were so good and the show unrolled with such elegance that my faith returned. Peter Hall attended, praised the cast and said admiring things to me about the production. I did not doubt his sincerity. He wanted a success, not only for the show, but for me personally. On the first night he sent every member of the company a handwritten note, a time-consuming exercise with benefits to the organisation which are no less real for being intangible. This was one of the occasions when he was doing exactly what is expected of an artistic director and I admired him for it.

The notices after our first night were of a hostility I had never before experienced. Some of them were so indignant that it was almost as if they, the critics, rather than the French High Command were the ones coming under attack. Which of course to an extent was true, because Derek Lindsay's wrath was directed as much at the apathetic general public that had stood by watching as it was at Dreyfus' persecutors – in the same way that a similarly apathetic public in Germany in the thirties stood by watching, as later did many Americans during the McCarthy witch-hunts. We had our defenders among the press, as passionate as our detractors, but there weren't enough of them to make a difference.

The following Monday I was told that *Grand Manoeuvres* was to be taken off. This was again decided by Peter Hall and Peter Stevens without reference to me or any of the other associates, and it had ramifications beyond the hurt to my own self-esteem. An entire company of actors would be put out of work. Alas, I was in the worst possible position to be the one to come to their defence. Along the corridors of the theatre, like a wire cable snapping thread by thread, I could sense my run of luck coming to an end, my influence diminishing, and I had no one to blame for this but myself.

I was particularly concerned for the state of mind of our playwright, but Derek accepted the rejection of his work with a dignified stoicism. As a true pessimist he did not exempt himself from the bad things one should expect from life. And there was one pleasant and surprising development. During our run of a few weeks our audiences began to build and increasingly they were greeting the show with partisan enthusiasm. At the end of the final performance, which had gone extremely well, Derek asked me if he could address the company. We gathered on stage behind the curtain and, in a few eloquent words, he thanked the actors and all of us involved for bringing his play to life in a way which exceeded his best expectations. It was a very impressive display and a healing gesture for all of us.

Meanwhile there were still meetings to attend. One such was a large planning meeting with, once again, the associates and the heads of departments all crammed into the Artistic Director's office. Peter had an important announcement to make: there would be a change of policy with regard to commercial transfers of the National's work. Before, such transfers had often been in partnership with a West End management, but now the National itself would become its own producer, renting the theatre and attending to all matters of advertising and promotion. Such a move would improve the National's stake in any success. 'Moreover,' said Peter, 'the Board strongly believes that the actors and the artistic team should be properly compensated for their work when it moves across the river.'

This was a departure; in the past, when the National played the West End, the company did so on their National salaries, and no royalties were paid to directors and designers. Had that not been the case then the run of *Long Day's Journey*, which had played to capacity for four months, would have considerably enriched me. There weren't many people among those gathered in Peter's office – only the directors and our Head of Design, John Bury – who would gain from this new policy, so we quickly assumed those solemn expressions of disinterest and integrity which I imagine are replicated in the boardrooms of banks every time the matter of bonuses comes up for discussion. Among ourselves afterwards, however, we were all broad smiles.

Jonathan Miller was still a presence in our midst, though an increasingly unhappy one. Months had passed since the postponement of all his productions and as yet he had been given no assurances of future work. He spoke often to me about resigning and on a number of occasions I tried interceding on his behalf. I told Peter that even in Olivier's day, Jonathan had let his tongue run loose, but that Larry, because he liked him and valued what uniquely he had to contribute, always overlooked his indiscretions. When I warned Peter that Jonathan was on the cusp of resigning he insisted, as he had always done with Jonathan himself, that this was not something he wanted.

The situation was becoming unendurable, and inevitably the day came when Jonathan sat down and wrote a brief letter of resignation. Copies of this letter and Peter's reply to it, which began 'My dear Jonathan' and expressed much 'sadness', were circulated to the associates. To anyone coming after, who chose to follow the paper-trail of this resignation, it would seem self-evident which of the two men was the more magnanimous and long-suffering.

Someone had once told me that Peter Hall was proud of the fact that in the course of his career he had never sacked anyone. He always managed it that the person he wanted to see the back of departed of their own accord. Was this what he had just done to Jonathan? It made me extremely uneasy to think so. In any case, Peter had chosen the wrong man on whom to impose this strategy. Once Jonathan had resigned, once he realised to what extent he had been manipulated out of the building, he became absolutely consumed by a prolonged rage. Peter had made an implacable, extremely vocal and well-connected enemy. The cost to Jonathan was to have the next two years of his life given over to an obsession that, at times, came to seem almost deranged. The one thing no gifted individual can ever forgive is to have someone undermine his belief in his gift.

Occasions when Peter's behaviour was a cause for misgiving were turning up with disconcerting frequency. Earlier that year, he had told the associates of an offer he had received to edit and front a new television arts programme, *Aquarius*, and that he was thinking about accepting. We could hardly believe what we were hearing; running the new National Theatre was surely a full-time job. If done properly, its demands were virtually unending. Like the painting of the Sydney Harbour Bridge, once you got to one end, it was time to start again at the other. It wasn't simply a matter of administering the theatre, putting in place a repertoire of plays and directing a number of them yourself; there were the intangibles of becoming a real presence for all the people who worked in the organisation, visiting the various departments, earning their trust and keeping the lines of communication open with the unions.

One by one the associates expressed their polite opposition to the idea. 'But it would only be one day a week,' argued Peter. Surely two, I thought: one day to prepare the programme and another to broadcast it. In the event, it was often three, as when Peter flew to Paris to interview Peter Brook, or even four when he and Denys Lasdun went to Athens to visit the ancient Greek amphitheatre at Epidaurus. What on earth was the Board doing allowing him even to entertain such an idea? What the associates didn't discuss, though it was on the minds of all of us, was how much Peter would be paid for this part-time job – doubtless a healthy sum to add to the unquestionably generous though mysteriously confidential salary he received as Artistic Director.

Prior to the *Aquarius* affair, Peter had made another proposal which had had the uniform opposition of the associates but which still went ahead. This was the decision to create a new post, that of Deputy Director. Peter broached this at one of our dinners and again it was met with silence and evasive glances. 'You don't understand,' he said. 'What I want to do is to provide all of you, the directors particularly, with a producer figure they can depend on if for some reason I'm not available.' However few of us had needed a producer figure in the past and, when we were rehearsing, rather preferred our producers to stay out of the way. John Schlesinger gave me a long, sympathetic look from across the room, which it was easy to interpret: if a deputy director was a real requirement surely there was enough spare capacity among those of us present to fill the role. I could see that Bill Bryden was thinking much the same thing. Peter continued to sell his idea, 'And to be perfectly honest I would like a deputy director in place so that, frankly, I could pursue the same sort of outside work that, for instance, you do, Michael.' Again none of us said what was in our minds. At least one of the reasons Peter was being paid probably four times what the rest of us were, was to relieve him of any need to find extra work.

Despite our objections a deputy director was appointed. This was Michael Birkett, the son of a famous jurist from whom he had inherited a peerage and an impressive pair of eyebrows. He came from the cinema and had no experience of theatre, but he proved to be fair-minded and enthusiastic, a gent in a three-piece suit, well placed to be entrusted with the announcement of several royal babies. He was impossible to dislike, but one needed to remind oneself that he was Peter's man; that's what he'd been hired for, and he and Peter Stevens became essentially a Praetorian Guard for the Emperor.

More and more, especially after Jonathan's departure, it was John Schlesinger with whom among the associates I found I had most in common. He was an amusing, generous man whom the rough and tumble of the film world had made an outspoken realist. Our association had turned into a friendship and I'd gone to a dinner party at his Kensington house in honour of a close mutual friend over from New York, Rosemary Harris. He was the person I most trusted to share my anxieties about the direction the National was going, but this was not always possible because he was often away shooting or planning a movie.

In my pocket diary for 1975 there are eleven occasions on which I have made a note of an associates' dinner. In Peter Hall's published *Diaries* only two of these dinners find a place, which may give some indication of their relevance to the running of the theatre. I began to wonder what exactly our dinners were *for*. Was it perhaps that they were an instrument for Peter to get his own way? Just as so many of our gatherings began with an announcement along the lines of 'The Board strongly recommends that top actors should be properly paid,' I wondered, when he went to Board meetings, did he begin by making similar declarations: 'All the associates are strongly of the opinion that such-and-such should be done'?

Looking back, there was only one occasion I can remember when something I said made a practical difference to the running of the organisation. This was when we were first informed by the builders that they would be completing their work in stages; first the administrative offices would be ready for occupancy, then the

Lyttelton Theatre and some months later the Olivier. The question then arose: should we wait until the whole building was in working order before we moved in, or should we occupy it by stealth, stage by stage? I strongly advocated the opportunistic approach, taking over, like insects, whatever space became available. This was what we did, and I believe our presence helped motivate the contractors to get the job behind them. At our other meetings, however, apart from having a say over which plays I would be directing, all I could do was listen closely and think hard about what was being said.

There was soon an occasion when I was not only listening closely, I was sitting rigid with attention. It was at one of our dinners, well attended, though not on this particular night by Harold, who by now had delivered his new play, *No Man's Land*. We had eaten well, Bill Bryden had risen a second time to replenish his brandy from the sideboard, and the focus of our discourse was pleasantly blurred. I thought it would be only a matter of minutes before we all went home. Suddenly Peter was addressing us and we looked down the table in his direction, mildly surprised.

'About Harold's new play . . . As you know, when we did Harold's new work at the RSC they were part of an Aldwych Theatre season, and when the season was over the actors dispersed and the play came off. At the box office we had to turn people away. Well, Harold doesn't want this to happen all over again with *No Man's Land*. He wants us to curtail the run of *No Man's Land* at the Vic to a single booking period so that we can then take it to the West End and offer it to as many people as possible.' Hang on, I thought, the way Olivier had organised it, there had been no 'seasons' at the National, and a success could play for as long as there was an audience for it. *The Royal Hunt of the Sun* had been in the Old Vic's repertoire for over two years. Peter expanded on the point that what Harold was asking for (not Peter, we were to understand, but Harold) would be good for the

National because of the extra revenue it would bring in, more than ever now that such transfers were being organised in house.

I could more or less accept Harold's proposal from Harold's point of view. As a playwright his first responsibility was for the widest possible dissemination of his work, and it could be argued that this took precedence over any responsibilities he had as an associate director. But what of Peter? His prime responsibility, surely, was not to Harold's play, but to the National Theatre and to our audiences at the Old Vic who enjoyed lower seat prices than they would have to pay in the West End.

My mind was racing. If the author of a new play – not necessarily Harold, any playwright – knew that by giving his script to the National Theatre he could be assured, not only of a rehearsal period of seven weeks as opposed to the West End's four, but a budget for the production at least twice what a commercial management could afford; if, moreover, he knew his play would be cast with stars from the open market and that if it succeeded it would move in no time to the West End, why would he be offering his play to anyone but the National Theatre? Would the West End now wither away? Or be forced to become something else – a purveyor of down-market entertainment.

The concrete dam was taking its first toll on the ecosystem. While Peter still paid lip service to the idea of a permanent company, the important parts in his own productions continued to be cast from the profession at large. I was now seeing a very good reason why this might be so. In a true company actors are cross-cast throughout the repertoire, and it becomes extremely difficult to extract any one production from the mix for the purposes of a transfer. Peter's productions could move effortlessly.

And what royalty, I wondered, would he be paying himself? In the commercial theatre a director customarily earns his money from a royalty based on a percentage of the weekly box-office takings. This is on a sliding scale: a certain percentage before the costs of a production are recouped, a slightly improved one when the show moves into profit – typically in the case of a successful director, three per cent rising to four per cent. What would Peter pay himself? Would the assumption be that during the run of thirty or forty performances at the Vic the show had recovered its costs? This was a clear impossibility. The investor in our case was the taxpayer, though he probably didn't realise it, and in any case had no representative beyond Peter to go through the books on his behalf.

Could I really believe what I was beginning to think: that Peter Hall intended to use the National to enrich himself? At the moment I had no proof of this, only a disturbing hunch. By the time I left the National that hunch was supported by a trend. By the end of the decade it would become an established fact, documented, for those who care to look, in Peter's own published *Diaries* covering the period 1972–1980. In this remarkable volume he manages both to come clean about himself and simultaneously to cover his tracks. In the first half of the book there are four descriptions of visits to his accountant, Bernard Kimble, during which he is lectured repeatedly about his debts and the need to earn a greater sum of money than his already considerable National salary if he is to continue supporting his many dependents and living his usual life. On page 286 he confides, 'Can I have my cake and eat it? I think I must.'

Later, discussing a Broadway transfer, he comes right out with it. 'It may be my one last chance of making money, real money.' However, exactly the scale on which he manages to do this is so buried under an avalanche of material relating to the daily running of the theatre that the ordinary reader is hardly aware of it. During the eight years covered by the *Diaries*, three National Theatre productions transferred first to the West End, and then to Broadway. These were *No Man's Land*, *Bedroom Farce* and *Amadeus*. A fourth, *Betrayal*, went straight to Broadway. All four shows were directed by Peter Hall and together they earned him a small fortune. This could not have happened simply by chance.

Peter was not only the director of these productions; as head of the National he was also in some sense the producer who controlled the rights. This put him in an unassailable position when it came to negotiations. For the Broadway run of *Amadeus* he negotiated five per cent of the profits, on top of four per cent rising to five per cent of the weekly gross – extraordinary figures. What he failed to do at this point, according to the New York producers, the Shubert Organisation, was to secure a single cent of income for the National itself. The organisation undoubtedly had a stream of revenue from *Amadeus*, but my understanding is that this came from the author, Peter Shaffer. Three of his previous plays had been staged at the National during Larry's regime and to show his appreciation of this support he had now gifted the organisation with one of his own percentage points. Peter Hall's admitted earnings from the Broadway production amounted to £720,000. To get some idea of what that figure means in today's terms you need to multiply it by eight.

To a certain extent all artistic directors cherry-pick from among the plays and projects that come their way; it is one of the just compensations of a demanding job. But running the theatre and pursuing their own career are usually seen as part of a single transparent agenda. Peter behaved as if he was running two unconnected businesses; one on behalf of the National, the other on behalf of himself.

Undoubtedly he brought high levels of energy and focus to the first of these concerns, which acted as a kind of smokescreen to the second; and in the months ahead I'd forget about his self-interest until something happened that brought it back into my mind with a jolt. Most of the time I was still finding him an impressive artistic director, though it must be said I no longer trusted him.

The trouble was that a somewhat puritan attitude to money was there at the heart of the National Theatre ethos. At least one of the reasons why the institution was so slow in coming to Britain compared to its Continental neighbours was that while the profession knew a National Theatre to be desirable, they were also aware it was not strictly necessary. To have a career in the British theatre is to have a market for one's work, a potential for money and celebrity, way beyond the expectations of talent on the Continent. A successful new play in London will probably have a future all over North America and throughout Australasia, and its leading actors, its director and designers will be rewarded accordingly. However, if you are putting on a play in Denmark, performed in Danish, your audience usually ends at the frontier. On mainland Europe the survival of theatre virtually depended on generous government subsidy.

Historically, popular drama has been to the British what opera has been to the Italians, and from the Elizabethans onward there has been a huge public appetite for it. For the gifted and determined there has always been work to be had and a living to be made. From the time of the steamships, leading figures in the British theatre who, had they been born on the Continent, would probably have been running state theatres, made fortunes for themselves and increased their reputations touring the world. However, in the twentieth century, as increasing costs began to narrow the scope of what a commercial management could attempt, a curious, never consciously defined tradition began to evolve. It was accepted that some kind of financial support was necessary for a theatre attempting the classics or an adventurous programme of new writing. Since this money frequently came from private benefactors – the Flower family at Stratford, or Sir Barry Jackson at the Birmingham Rep – some acknowledgement of the principle of charity was now expected of the talent.

Thus in the thirties Charles Laughton and Laurence Olivier put Hollywood careers on hold while they had a shot at some of the great parts offered by a season at the Old Vic. The reward certainly wasn't the salary. The work itself was the inducement.

However, there was also a more subtle incentive. If the actor could pull off his Hamlet or Macbeth, he could return to the market with his prestige enormously enhanced.

For the theatres themselves the custom of low salaries had one self-evident advantage: it permitted them to survive. But they were involved in a constant battle to maintain standards. There was never enough time to plan and rehearse productions with appropriate care, never enough money to mount them without cutting corners, and always they were at the mercy of failure at the box office. Tyrone Guthrie, director of the Old Vic in the early thirties, must have looked across the Channel at the subsidies and conditions enjoyed by someone like Max Reinhardt with disbelief. Poverty however had one harsh benefit. To work in such a theatre you had to have enthusiasm and purpose; when these flagged there was no reason to stay. You went off and improved your income elsewhere.

It was not until the war years that the general public and the politicians began to perceive that a National Theatre was not merely desirable; it might even be useful. The Old Vic seasons at the New Theatre after the company had been bombed out of their Waterloo home blazed as an expression of the national spirit. Even if you'd never been inside a theatre, you knew that the film of *Henry V* playing at the local Odeon had had its genesis in a season at the Old Vic. Soon wildly successful tours of New York and Australasia were promoting Great Britain as effectively as royalty, and by the mid-fifties the necessity for subsidy received growing acceptance in both London and the provinces. With the foundation of the National Theatre the principle was fully conceded, and at last funds were available for extended rehearsal periods and generous design budgets.

One of Olivier's first moves was to improve on the salaries that actors had previously expected at the Old Vic, while still keeping them below West End levels. He knew from first-hand experience how important the ethic of public service had been in arriving at this moment of theatrical history, and the dedication it had demanded from so many people over so many years. Nevertheless he was now able to make an offer to a rising actor sufficiently attractive to persuade him to join the National, not just for a season but for two, three or more years. By carefully staggering holidays it was now possible to do two things: first, abandon the idea of seasons altogether – the National would now play all the year round; and second, keep a production in the repertoire for as long as its success warranted. Transfers to the commercial sector were possible, but they were no longer necessary. The National was a self-sufficient entity.

Was I now being invited to see Larry's model for a National Theatre dismantled? He, as much as anyone, had accepted that there would have to be changes once we had occupied the new building. Even the idea to which he was most attached, that of the permanent company, might find itself challenged by the logistics of having to fill three auditoria nightly. This was something that had always concerned Ken Tynan; with opportunities in film and television work on the increase, expecting the country's best actors to stay together for two or three years might no longer be feasible. Nevertheless the notion of public service which had brought the institution into being in the first place should always be there as an unobtrusive thread in its fabric. The National would be a theatre where you could entertain artistic ambitions impossible to fulfil elsewhere, where you would be justly compensated for your work, but where the work itself would be the truest reward.

Olivier had been such an unpredictable and occasionally infuriating man to work with that it wasn't until he'd gone that I fully appreciated in what a principled way he had run the organisation. It was something everyone in the building took for granted, one of the reasons we liked to work there. Peter Hall's frequent claim in the *Diaries* that he could make so much more money away from the National as a freelance is as doubtful in his case as it is the literal truth in Olivier's, who we all knew was forgoing hundreds of thousands, if not millions, of pounds in film money. When he did occasionally do outside work both he and Ken were meticulous about going off-salary, something that Peter would resist until the Board insisted on it.

This was the ethos in which we were invited to work with Olivier, and we assumed that it was, as it should be, the norm. But benevolent government is never 'normal'; another definition of the word is always waiting for its chance in the long grass. Larry, approaching sixty when he took up his new post, had many of his greatest achievements behind him: his three Shakespeare films, his fame as an international movie star, and not least the many great stage parts on which he had left an indelible mark. Though he might match, he would never top his success in roles as diverse as Oedipus Rex, Archie Rice and Richard III. He would of course continue to act, needed to do so, but was now less driven to perform. His priority had become the welfare of the institution he had been chosen to launch, and he gave a great deal of thought to setting up structures which would safeguard its future. He had always been drawn to projects to which he could uncompromisingly devote himself, and now he was facing the most important of his life, one for which his generation of theatre people had done so much to prepare the way. It would be his last cause and his greatest legacy. Mixed in with this aspiration of course were more common human attributes of rivalry, mistrust and even spite, but it seemed to me that at crucial junctures his gaze went well beyond them.

Now this remarkable man was no longer among us. At an associates' meeting shortly before his resignation, Jonathan had told us, 'Larry may be dying.' This was the trained doctor speaking, and we knew that what he was telling us was the sober truth. The great actor was in a Sussex hospital, undergoing the only treatment available for his disease, enormous doses of cortisone which had the effect of leaving him temporarily deranged. Only the family were allowed access, all other visitors being discouraged. He had vanished into that social limbo occupied by the gravely ill, around which the healthy circulate, averting their eyes, some through tact, others through indifference, as they continue to go about their business.

My business at that moment was trying to make up my mind about *Plunder*. The thing I admired about it was the ingenuity and skill of the farcical plotting. Like *The Front Page*, it was a machine designed to generate gales of laughter, but the trouble was it took half the evening to wind the machine up, and unlike *The Front Page* the characters with whom you were meanwhile keeping company were mostly dated stereotypes from British popular theatre between the wars. Indeed, I had played one of them frequently during my time in rep – the upper-class twit, usually with monocle and buck teeth, who, being posh, it was assumed audiences would find loveable. The second important male role was another twenties stereotype, the gentleman cracksman, who moved in high society and relieved rich middle-aged women of their jewellery at country house weekends. This character had made his debut in the *Raffles* novels, and was last seen played by Cary Grant in Alfred Hitchcock's *To Catch a Thief*. Like Bulldog Drummond he was one of those fictional creations that a couple of generations later it becomes almost impossible to believe anyone ever took seriously. Maybe a similar fate awaits James Bond.

The plot of *Plunder* goes something like this. D'Arcy Tuck (the twit) has come home from a visit to an outpost of the Empire in the company of his fiancée, Joan, also returning to claim her inheritance from a recently deceased uncle. The couple motor down to the house in the country that Joan assumes is now hers, only to find that it is occupied by her uncle's housekeeper and two members of her ghastly family. Before the audience learn that these people are rogues, who inveigled the old uncle into a marriage which has left the housekeeper the beneficiary of his entire estate, it is clear that they are guilty in a more irredeemable way: they are common. However there is another guest staying in the house, and for D'Arcy a very surprising one. This is the suave and debonair Freddy Malone, with whom he was once at public school. When D'Arcy indignantly explains to his old school chum how his fiancée has been swindled, Freddy confesses that he is not there as a proper guest but in his professional capacity as a gentleman jewel thief. Together they conspire to rob the housekeeper of her baubles and thereby retrieve at least a part of Joan's inheritance.

Halfway through the play (and not a moment too soon) comes the brilliant scene of the actual theft, executed entirely in dumb-show. It is the dead of night and up a ladder come the two thieves who climb through the window and into the housekeeper's locked bedroom while she snores on oblivious. However, one of her relatives, out walking, has noticed the ladder propped against the house and he climbs up to take a look. In the scuffle which ensues he falls back into the garden and is knocked unconscious. The robbery now proceeds as planned, but with D'Arcy Tuck a nervous wreck. At the end of the act the two men learn that the relative who fell off the ladder has now died. If caught they will not only be charged with theft but with murder.

'And you know what that means,' says Freddy. 'The rope.'

Suddenly the play has moved to a new place and becomes intensely interesting. Act Three begins with a dramatic scene which is as funny as any in the English language. D'Arcy and Freddy have been summoned to Scotland Yard to be questioned by the investigating detectives, now certain of their guilt. D'Arcy, by the sheer inanity and inconsequentiality of his replies, so baffles his interrogators that they let the men leave. D'Arcy's dialogue has a nonsensical brilliance that harks back to Lewis Carroll and other Victorian surrealists. The play now rollicks to

251

its conclusion. The housekeeper proves to be a bigamist, so Joan retrieves her fortune, and Freddy and D'Arcy escape scot-free of all charges – which is somehow okay because they're both gents.

When I reread the play recently a further forty years had elapsed since its first production, and it seemed so essentially innocent that I wondered why I had been even mildly disturbed by its snobbery. These days it reflects a world almost as remote as that of Restoration comedy, about which it would be equally fatuous to moralise. But in the mid-seventies the British theatre had not long cut free from the tyranny of plays about the upper classes enjoying life in town and country. In fact able authors like William Douglas-Home were still writing them, so there were reasons to be on one's guard.

I had another reservation. Unlike *The Front Page*, *Plunder* was not a National Theatre discovery. It had recently been revived, and very successfully, at the Bristol Old Vic in a production by Nat Brenner, starring Peter O'Toole as D'Arcy Tuck. Though the production, by all accounts excellent, hadn't made it to the West End, it had fingerprints of entitlement all over it. I felt uneasy picking up someone else's discovery. Peter O'Toole was a friend, so I wondered if he would consider reprising the role. We met, but he had had a bad experience some years before at the Royal Shakespeare Company when Peter Hall tried to hold him to a long-term contract which would have put a brake on his burgeoning film career. Hall took him to court, lost, and O'Toole was soon an international movie star. He wanted to play D'Arcy Tuck again but was suspicious of the context and made impossible demands. We would have to look elsewhere.

I felt the casting of the two male leads was absolutely vital to the success of the show, and with the help of Gillian Diamond and Ann Robinson in the Casting Department I trawled through long lists of candidates, but the few who were suitable would not be available until later in the year. The generation of actors to whom these parts would have come easily, performers like Arthur Lowe, now in their sixties or seventies, were no longer contenders. I wondered about the new Oxbridge comedians who were popping up on television; maybe they would have the wits to liven up the heavily expository first act. There was someone who had recently come to the fore in a comedy show with the two Ronnies, Corbett and Barker: this was John Cleese. He had the right qualifications for D'Arcy Tuck and was also an excellent actor. I got in touch, we met, and for a while he showed distinct interest, but a dazzling future in television was beckoning and eventually he, too, made a courteous withdrawal.

We were only a few months away from the start of rehearsals, so I went to Peter Hall and told him that at the moment it was impossible to cast and that we would be best advised to postpone until later in the year. Peter looked irritated. 'We still need a comedy for the summer, Michael,' he said, and I felt like answering, 'Well then, *you* find one, and *you* direct it.' Had I done so he might well have replied, 'I just have.' For some time he had been assiduously wooing Alan Ayckbourn away from the West End, and his latest play, *Bedroom Farce*, had recently landed on Hall's desk. Before any of the associates had read it or even knew of its existence, it was on the list of his future productions. In due course *Bedroom Farce* would have a run at the National, and then rapidly make its way, first to the West End and then to Broadway. However, it was agreed that *Plunder* would be rescheduled for the autumn, and John Russell Brown would help me unearth a suitable comedy for the summer. In the meanwhile I could console myself with the prospect that when Albert Finney became free at the beginning of the new year I had my uncut *Hamlet* to direct.

Or so I thought. One evening at home I had a telephone call from Peter. 'Michael, I'm going to be absolutely straight with you, and I want you to be equally honest with me. Because I'm not going to go ahead with this unless you're a hundred per cent in agreement.' 'What is it?' I asked, and after further assertions of candour and straightforwardness, Peter went on to explain. 'Albert has discovered he'll be free of his commitments some months sooner than expected and he's asked if we can bring the production of *Hamlet* forward. I've explained that with *Plunder* rescheduled you're going to be tied up, but he's very keen to go as soon as possible. And if you're not available he's asked me to consider taking on the production. I, of course said, the first thing I had to do was talk to you. And if you say "No", Michael, then "No" it is. I want to be absolutely straight about this.'

I did not doubt that Peter meant what he said, to the extent that he said it, and had I insisted on my prior claim to the production he would have relinquished it. But he had now released in me some misgivings of my own. If Albert had been so ready for Peter to take over the reins, it meant he wasn't overly excited at the prospect of working with me. I wondered if we both knew each other too well for the kind of honeymoon that the best collaborations can become. Besides, Albert, in common with a number of English actors whose formal education had been fairly rudimentary, had an inflated regard for the Oxbridge mystique which was Peter's stock-in-trade. It was obvious that the two had already had discussions about the play, and I had experienced at first hand Peter's powers of persuasion and his ability to talk up a brilliant production if not always to deliver one. Supposing that Albert had swallowed the bait, he and I would be no use to one another. The telephone conversation concluded with me assuring Peter I would have no objection if he took over the production.

ELEVEN

My future at the National now consisted of two comedies in succession, the first of which we had yet to find. I went through various possibilities with John Russell Brown and one day he produced a copy of *Engaged* by W. S. Gilbert. I hadn't even known that the librettist of the Savoy Operas had written a play. It was a surprising read and a very funny one: a misanthropic comedy in which the Victorians, behind their elaborate courtesies and sentimental avowals, were shown to be as rapacious as sharks. There was a brilliant scene between two ruthlessly competing young women of which Oscar Wilde had clearly been aware when he wrote *The Importance of Being Earnest*. I turned the last page with real pleasure, unaware that what I held in my hand was that deceptive article of which John Dexter had had some experience – a lively text which, in front of an audience, never quite becomes a play. It had some rich parts, and I saw it as an opportunity to reintroduce to the National company the sort of talented actors one would not normally expect to find there. For instance there was a role for someone I considered extremely gifted, Pauline Collins, who had made a name for herself (and an excellent living) in the TV series, *Upstairs, Downstairs*. Once I had decided to direct it, a first-rate cast, led by Pauline, quickly fell into place; Cheryl Campbell was already in the company, playing a tiny part in *John Gabriel Borkman* and the freshest thing in it. She was joined by, among others, Jonathan Pryce, Polly Adams and Peter Egan.

However, *Engaged* got off on the wrong foot. Michael Annals and I concocted two lush Victorian sets overflowing with naturalistic detail, when what was required was something as weirdly schematic as the play itself. Tenniel's original illustrations for *Alice in Wonderland* might have suggested a better approach. Rehearsals, though enjoyable, took place in the hottest July for years, and our opening was on an even hotter night in early August. I knew we were in trouble at the interval, when Lindsay Anderson, who had attended a number of my first nights and who was inclined to grow increasingly scathing the more the evening looked like being a success, approached me in the stalls bar wearing the sympathetic expression of someone pulling up a chair beside a hospital bed. Notices the following day were at best lukewarm but mostly bad. I had now had two flops in a row, and was beginning to question the point of my being at the National if I was there only to supply (unsuccessful) light entertainment.

Two days later I was in France, going to the bakery each morning for fresh bread, then returning to the house by way of the cliffs to see what sort of a surf was running. I spent my days treading water in the blue Atlantic among people who didn't know or care what my job was, and who, like me, were only interested in what was in front of their eyes – the blinding white of a breaking wave or the distant line of the mountains tracking the wide arc of the Bay of Biscay as it melted into the haze of distant Spain. A sense of proportion returned, and the sunlight bleached away any lingering discouragement attached to the failure of *Engaged*. I returned to London ready to make a fresh start.

However, certain concerns about the National, of a general rather than a personal nature, were still stubbornly in place when I got back; and new ones kept piling up. For instance: one morning I ran into a beaming Michael Birkett. 'Wonderful news,' he exclaimed, and I knew that the announcement of a royal birth was imminent. 'When Peter's *Don Giovanni* is staged at Glyndebourne next year he's bringing it to the National for a short London season.' I quite liked the thought of Mozart drifting down the corridors of the Lyttelton Theatre, and I was therefore surprised when I heard that John Schlesinger was passionately opposed to the idea. He argued that opera already consumed far more of the Arts Council cake than it deserved, and that to subsidise it further by giving it expensive house room in a National Theatre auditorium was nothing short of scandalous.

Some months earlier, John's production of *Heartbreak House* had given us our first unqualified hit in fourteen months; but like Harold, who had his plays to write, John with his films was only free to direct at most one production a year. He was much valued by Peter because as a distinguished movie-maker he brought a particular prestige to our group of associates. But he was a man of strong opinions and now there was the possibility of a rift.

At an evening meeting of the associates a few days later the matter was vigorously debated. Not only was it iniquitous that so much as a penny of the National's resources should go to propping up an opera production, argued John, but the auditorium in which it was proposed to stage it had been built with an acoustic to accommodate the spoken word and was quite unsuitable for music. The heated argument went back and forth until we seemed to have reached a stalemate. In the silence that followed Peter Stevens came up with an idea that was so unexpected that it threw us all off balance.

'What if *Don Giovanni* wasn't just a one-off opera production,' he ruminated, 'but part of a Don Juan season? What if we did the opera in conjunction with a string of plays on the same subject?' This was something to think about other than the uncomfortable deadlock that had just silenced the room, so we all screwed up our faces and looked at the ceiling as we competed to think up plays in which Don Juan made an appearance. 'Well, there's the long version of Shaw's *Man and Superman*,' suggested someone. 'And what about Molière's *Don Juan*?' asked someone else. There was also the play by Horváth on the same subject, *Don Juan Comes Back from the War*, which was already being considered for the National. 'That's it!' said Peter Hall excitedly. 'A Don Juan

Season!' And John Schlesinger, while not entirely appeased, conceded that it might make a difference.

However, all this was a year or two in the future, so we moved on to other subjects. I had taken a fairly neutral position during the debate, and it wasn't until I returned home that it dawned on me what all of us had signed up to. The more I thought about it, the more incredulous I became. At the heart of any theatre is its repertoire, the plays it chooses to offer to the public. This will explain its policy, dictate the composition of the acting company, and in the case of the National, involve the expenditure of many hundreds of thousands of pounds of public money. Were we seriously considering theming an entire season of productions because the Emperor Nero wanted to display his aptitude on the fiddle? Had any other director among the associates proposed booking an opera he'd directed elsewhere for another organisation into a National Theatre auditorium, let alone justifying it in this way, he would have been met with stares of disbelief. It was ridiculous, and what was worse, it was not *serious*; it was a frivolous way to run a theatre.

Some time after I'd resigned from the National the 'Don Juan Season' was scheduled to go ahead, but it fell apart because a West End management owned the rights to *Man and Superman* and the Hampstead Theatre had already done a production of the Molière. What did proceed, however, because the Artistic Director, as the saying goes, had a whim of steel, were the performances of the Mozart opera in the Lyttelton Theatre.

Another unsettling surprise, though of a more personal and less significant order, was waiting for me at one of our larger planning meetings, attended, not only by the associates, but by the heads of the departments. We had crammed into Peter's office, some managing to find a seat, some standing. 'As you all know,' Peter began gravely, 'I'm about to embark on a new *Hamlet* with Albert, and I want to do something that many of you may consider madness. Sheer folly. And I don't mind in the least if you tell me so! In fact, I *want* you to share your thoughts with me. Crazy perhaps, but what I want to do is this: I want to do the play *completely uncut.*' He continued to expatiate on the boldness, the absolute recklessness of this decision, as I waited, sitting directly in front of him, for the moment when he would catch my eye. This never came. I had never considered that doing an uncut *Hamlet* was a particularly original proposal, and had Peter mentioned to me beforehand that he wanted to take up the idea I would have nodded my approval without a second thought. But having to sit there, directly in his eye-line, but with our eyes never engaging, and to hear an uncut *Hamlet* blown up into some kind of artistic breakthrough was extremely vexatious.

However, I had yet to learn what Peter had already been told by his press relations officer, John Goodwin, namely that this would be the first uncut *Hamlet* to be staged in London in forty years – the last had been Tyrone Guthrie's production with Alec Guinness in the thirties. This new production would therefore be newsworthy. The two men had found the hook to hang it on, and in John Goodwin's sure hands it would generate many column inches of comment in the press – just as later it would provide material for Peter Hall's *Diaries.* There is an entry for 27 July 1975, that I later read with my mouth agape. 'Broody on Hamlet. There is enormous pressure on me from my colleagues not to do it as I want to, full length.'

I was beginning to have an understanding of the way Peter operated. There would be something you thought of as yours. You would look away for a moment and when you looked back, it wasn't there. It was now Peter's. There had been no unseemly grabbing, no sign of teeth marks. He had simply ingested whatever it was he wanted in one swift, silent swallow, and that would be that. My experience had not been unique. On the eve of rehearsals of his production of *The Cherry Orchard*, Peter took his translator, Michael Frayn, out to dinner to discuss the play, and encouraged him to give a full account of his thinking. The following day in his address to the company, Peter repeated, verbatim, what he had heard the night before, but now expressed entirely as his own thoughts. Michael Frayn was sitting a few feet away and was much amused that he was neither acknowledged nor once looked at.

Often these ingestions were so comparatively trivial that to draw attention to them seemed needlessly disruptive. This is what I felt that day when Peter announced his uncut *Hamlet*. Sometimes they were of more consequence, like his passive appropriation of the direction of *Amadeus* from John Dexter. Sometimes they were so enormous – his ingestion of an entire theatre at Stratford-upon-Avon for instance – that, like the politics of the Middle East, people were expected to accept them as facts on the ground.

I had been an actor in the company the year Peter Hall became director designate of the Shakespeare Memorial Theatre at Stratford. For centuries Shakespeare had been performed in his birthplace, but after the war the existing theatre had been hugely revitalised by Sir Barry Jackson and Anthony Quayle. At the end of the fifties, as Peter prepared to take over, it was the most successful theatre in the country, a Mecca for all the great stars of the British stage and its most notable directors and designers. 'Sold Out' signs were the norm, and for a hot ticket people would queue all night. Now its success was to be acknowledged with the granting of a Royal Charter and henceforth the Shakespeare Memorial Theatre would become the Royal Shakespeare Theatre.

The following year, when Peter took charge, he immediately embarked on some audacious changes of policy. He created a permanent London home for the company where plays other than Shakespeare could be performed, and signed actors, not just for a season, but for periods of two or three years. He had also lobbied hard to change the name not to the Royal Shakespeare

Theatre, but to the Royal Shakespeare *Company*, thereby further severing verbal links with the previous title. Peter's achievements in these early years are by any standard remarkable, but they were only possible because they were sheltered under the umbrella of an existing institution of immense reputation, extensive real estate and enormous reserves of cash. Whatever else this may be, it is not 'founding' a theatre; and yet the claim has been made so often it has now become 'official': 'Peter Hall founded the RSC.' Actually he swallowed it, and the Shakespeare Memorial Theatre's distinguished history went to oblivion down his gullet.

A similarly cavalier attitude to precise language followed Peter into the West End after he left the National. The advertising for all his shows was blazoned with the logo 'The Peter Hall Company'; though, like other commercial productions, his were mostly cast on an ad-hoc basis. During his fifteen years at the National, where he had the opportunity to lead a real company, he showed no inclination to do so. In the West End, however, the formulation he invented allowed him to have his name prominently displayed twice on the same poster, as leader of his company and director of the play. It reached ridiculous levels on Broadway, when the slogan on the T-shirt for his production of *Orpheus Descending* on sale in the lobby mentioned neither the playwright, Tennessee Williams, nor the star, Vanessa Redgrave, but only 'The Peter Hall Company'.

Trumpeting your achievements and making unsubstantiated claims has always been theatre practice, and is perfectly proper, even admirable, in an impresario, and Peter was a great impresario. Such practice sits less comfortably with an artist, who needs an authentic sense of who he is and what he has or hasn't achieved. Olivier accepted the importance of publicity, and the tiny office out of which Craig Macdonald and Caroline Keeley worked was usually buzzing with activity; but he also knew that his true legacy was in the memory of the people who had been there on the nights when he had given his greatest performances. He was suspicious of PR because it blurred as much as it revealed. In any case he had a talent of an order that didn't need help in spreading the word.

One of Peter's first appointments at the National was the sly and brilliant John Goodwin – brought from the RSC, to become not only Head of Press and Publications but his confidant and intelligence officer, and later editor of his *Diaries*. In the new building, the staff of the publicity office increased threefold and now occupied a suite of offices. As I was soon to learn, it became a place of considerable influence in which success always became a matter of public perception.

One piece of good and quite unexpected news had been waiting for me when I returned from France: against all the odds Larry was recovering from his illness. The condition which had killed Onassis he had somehow survived, one of the few people ever to have done so. In life, as he had on stage, he continued to defy expectations. I went down to Brighton to visit him, and found him physically much diminished. The leonine features were gone and instead he resembled one of his notable parts from the forties, Justice Shallow in *Henry IV Part 2*. He had a sharp pointed nose and seemed as grey and precariously intact as the ash on the end of a cigarette. Most distressing of all, the disease had weakened the muscles of his throat and that thrilling voice was now reduced to a high, reedy whisper.

However, the personality was still there and undiminished, as was that same faintly ironic watchfulness that had always put me a little on the back foot. As usual he was an excellent host, and over a light lunch which he'd arranged for us both we chatted amiably. I didn't discuss any of my misgivings about the National, nor at the moment did I intend to, and he, supposing me to be still Peter's man, asked me no leading questions. Instead we talked about *The Cherry Orchard*, which I had been thinking about revisiting in the new Olivier auditorium, and for which Larry would have made a perfect Firs. But the more we talked, the more

I had the feeling that we would never see him on stage again. I made a solemn return to London by train, reflecting on Larry's life as if its final shape had now been revealed, and quite unprepared for the surprises he had yet to spring on the world.

The administrative offices of the National Theatre had now made the move from Aquinas Street to the South Bank building, and *Hamlet* and *Plunder* would be the first shows to rehearse in its huge, brand new rehearsal spaces. Both productions would open at the Old Vic, then move to the Lyttelton Theatre in March 1976 for the unveiling of the South Bank building. I was now spending a great deal of time in the new offices of the casting department, working with Gillian Diamond and Ann Robinson on *Plunder*. The supporting cast was falling into place, and I thought I had at last found a likely D'Arcy Tuck in Dinsdale Landen. He was a nervy, quick-witted actor, with a comedy style that relied a little too heavily on a number of well-honed effects – the double-take, the triple-take, the snorting laugh and the delayed response. However he could be genuinely funny and had played enough clones of D'Arcy Tuck in rep to have a feeling for what was required. I hoped I would be able to encourage him to play D'Arcy with the same simple reality that Ben Travers (who in his ninetieth year was enjoying a final West End success with *The Bed Before Yesterday*) told me Peter O'Toole had brought to the role.

I had yet to cast the other leading male part, Freddy Malone. Then one morning I had a call from Michael Birkett requesting a meeting. 'I've just been talking to Frank Finlay,' he began after I'd taken a seat in his office. 'And he's absolutely crazy about *Plunder*! He longs to play Freddy Malone.' Frank was a fine actor who was already contracted to play the lead in John Osborne's new play, *Watch It Come Down*, in the New Year. He had made his name in Arnold Wesker's Trilogy at the Royal Court, and in the early days of the National had had numerous successes. Most of the roles he'd succeeded in were working class, so it surprised me that he was desperate to play a toff in the revival of a thirties farce. However, I had sufficient faith in his talent to believe that if he was convinced he could do it, so was I.

Much later, after he'd accepted the role, Frank told me that at the time the offer had been made he had not even read the play, let alone had an opinion about it. He undertook the part because he thought I'd particularly asked for him. I wondered if Michael Birkett had been under instructions to ensure that Frank was cross-cast in *Plunder* in addition to his role in the Osborne play, because it saved the National an additional salary. If so, it irritated me to find I had been manipulated in this way. Fortunately Frank had a convincing shot at playing a part for which, on the face of it, he was unsuitable. In a true company this would have been something to celebrate, but there was now no such thing as a National company. The Artistic Director cast his principal roles from the open market, and other directors felt similarly entitled.

I tried to interest Bill Bryden in Pauline Collins for his production of *The Playboy of the Western World*, and she apparently gave a brilliant reading, but Bill exercised his right to go elsewhere. This meant, as it had with *Grand Manoeuvres*, that at the end of the run of *Engaged* the entire cast was 'let go'. Once the new building was fully operational with three theatres opening their doors every night, Olivier's ideal of a National Company might well have proved impossible to sustain. But at the moment we were still a one-theatre operation and would be for some time, and changes were coming about by default rather than through discussion and agreement.

Casting departments are usually social and rather jolly places. Productions begin their lives there when hopes are high, and actors and directors frequently poke their heads round the door for news or encouragement. Because they are always dealing with offers and contracts they are also places where you can learn a great deal about the inner workings of an organisation. Casting and speculative gossip mingle, and I was picking up scraps of information that were as riveting as they were unsettling. *No Man's Land*, after a brief run at the Vic, had just moved to the West End, where it was selling out, and I was told that Peter Hall's take was a full four per cent of the weekly box office – that is to say the amount a commercial management would have paid him once the costs of the production had been recovered. But how was this possible after only forty-odd performances at the Old Vic? I did not oppose West End transfers once the show in question had had a proper run at the National Theatre and had fulfilled its obligations to our audience. Nor did I object to the creative staff benefiting from such transfers, as long as such deals were completely transparent and took account of the fact that those benefiting were already in receipt of a regular salary.

But what was Peter's salary exactly? Everything about his deals at the National Theatre was cloaked in secrecy. The salaries of the heads of other organisations that were backed by public money – British Rail, British Telecom – were a matter of public record, but Peter's contract with the Board was a matter of blanket confidentiality.

There were, however, clues to what he was earning, and one of them was evident in the new salary structure for actors that the two Peters were putting in place. Radical changes were afoot, but they were not something that had ever been broached at an associates' meeting, and the more I came to learn about them the more questionable they seemed. Larry's scheme for paying actors had been meticulously thought through and, though austere, typified his desire to see that actors were treated justly. The top salary was about £60 a week, and the bottom about £25. These sums, however, were augmented by a performance fee which actors received every time they appeared, and which was calculated as a percentage of their basic salary. Thus a star who was giving, say, five performances a week in a variety of parts, could take home a reasonable amount of money, and a young actor playing tiny parts, or perhaps just walking on, but who would probably be employed every night, could likewise augment his earnings. In this way the pay of each actor, whether star or beginner, was directly related to his or her workload.

The Peter Hall plan abandoned performance fees altogether. The salary of the lowest paid would be improved to £35 a week, which left them pretty much where they already were. However, the salaries of the highest paid, that select band of knights, dames and film stars who so frequently augmented Peter's productions, now shot up to an astonishing £500 a week. This applied even if they performed only once in any seven days.

There was a peculiarity about this arrangement. All the actors in this select group were represented by the same agent, Laurie Evans, a brilliant operator with the most prestigious client list in London, who nosed around town in a beige Rolls-Royce. And there was a second peculiarity. It seemed the next tier in the salary structure dropped precipitously to £250 a week. This was for actors like Diana Rigg and Frank Finlay, both of whom were stars in television and therefore meant something at the box office. And both happened not to be represented by Laurie Evans. And a third peculiarity was that Laurie Evans was also Peter Hall's agent, and it was unlikely that he would have negotiated a salary for Peter a great deal less than that of the important people Peter employed. Judged against the gross excesses of today's executive pay, a figure nudging towards £500 a week does not seem an enormous amount even when adjusted for inflation (a multiple of eight), but at that time it was unprecedented. Olivier had been paid some £70 a week; he had of course additional perks – a London flat to stay in when he didn't go home to Brighton, a chauffeur-driven taxi to take him around London, and a generous budget for such things as entertaining. But Peter had inherited a similar range of benefits.

It seemed to me that what Peter was jettisoning – ahead of time in a changing Britain – was Larry's ethic of public service, of doing the work at least partially for its own sake. This is actually at the heart, and always has been, of any theatre attempting to break ground. It applies as much today at the Royal Court, the Donmar or the Almeida as well as at theatres up and down the country, as it did at Olivier's National. Peter was turning the organisation into that entity which would later become much loved by politicians of both parties, the public–private partnership, where the Government puts up the money and the un-supervised executives reward themselves with whatever sums they think fit. Was this what all those people who believed in a National Theatre and who, for almost a century, had been doing uncompromised work for peanuts in theatres up and down the country had been hoping for? It was a little like asset-stripping.

In his *Diaries* Peter carefully charts his drift away from Labour into the arms of Margaret Thatcher. This admiration was not reciprocated. If Mrs Thatcher had little sympathy for publicly subsidised art, she had even less for publicly subsidised art that made people rich, and she had few kind words for Hall. However, both marked their ascent to office with an identical policy – challenging the power of the unions and demonising them. Thatcher took on the miners, Peter the stagehands, and both characterised their battles as dramatic victories for the souls of the causes they served. Peter was prefiguring the type of Englishman Mrs Thatcher did so much to encourage: the new meritocrat, standing clear of lesser men, and unashamed about claiming for himself the reward he considered his due. There is a telling entry in Hall's *Diaries* for 18 April 1976. The press had been questioning the amount paid to conductors. Georg Solti, for example, was earning £3,000 a concert. Peter comments: 'So what's the problem? They are unique men, very rare.'

My concerns about Peter's regime were reaching a point where I knew I had to respond in some way. But how exactly? I could resign, but on what grounds? I was certainly disenchanted with the way he was running the National and had occasionally been shocked by his behaviour, but he had done me no real harm. Indeed, in the first year of his tenure he had offered me marked support. And if I was to resign, would I then blow the whistle? This was the last thing the theatre needed in this crucial lead-up to the unveiling of the South Bank building. I had worked at the National for five years, believed firmly in its importance, and I had no wish to give succour to the sceptics looking on who had a doctrinaire hostility to the very idea of a cultural subsidy and would have been happy to see us fail.

In any case, what exactly was I to whistle-blow about? I had identified trends, tendencies, but no succession of facts to prove a case. Peter had set up the machinery, if he so wished, to make a great deal of money out of the swift transfer of productions to the West End and Broadway, but at the moment the only example of this was *No Man's Land*. Likewise, he had appointed a deputy, Michael Birkett, not himself a director, who could hold the fort and keep usurpers at arms' length if Peter chose to spend long absences working elsewhere. But he hadn't yet done so. These things would happen, and Harold Pinter would one day resign because of the many months when the National was left without effective leadership. John Schlesinger would follow. But this had not happened yet.

I couldn't make up my mind about Peter. Was he simply a self-serving schemer? This was hard to believe, because I still admired the grasp and energy he brought to most aspects of his job. Was he perhaps a narcissist, who could not discriminate between what he wanted for himself and the well-being of the people around him? He was certainly the greediest man I had ever known. Not only did he want seconds, but thirds and fourths. Yet there is a certain innocence about greed. We are born with appetites and what is more natural than to want to feed them? Peter reminded me of the fat boy at the children's party, who, when offered a slice of cake, takes the cake and leaves the slice, and then when repri-manded wails that nobody told him *which* slice.

Quite as culpable in my view were Lord Goodman and the senior members of the Board. They had appointed him, and they should have kept him under control. At the very least they could have insisted that Peter made money for the National as well as for himself. They could have refused him permission when he wanted to take two days off a week hosting *Aquarius* on TV, and later said an emphatic 'no' when he announced that he was taking over the artistic directorship of the Glyndebourne Opera to run on the side. But they had pushed through his candidacy in secret without consulting anyone, and now they were stuck with him. Anything Peter wanted was an unlocked door on which he only had to push. Certain leaders, usually politicians, can promote themselves with such plausibility, that they seem invulnerable to criticism. Like a drop of penicillin in a petri dish, they are surrounded by a barrier that neutralises all attack. For a while – the eight years chronicled in his *Diaries* – this was the case with Peter. But the real loser was himself. By the time he left the National, the prestige and respect he had accumulated at the Royal Shakespeare Company had been dissipated and, at least in the theatrical community, his integrity and his artistic abilities had become matters to be questioned.

Some years after I left the National I directed *Noises Off* in New York for the American producer Roger Stevens. A taciturn, impressive man with the head and bearing of a Roman senator, he had made a fortune in real estate (reputedly he had bought and sold the Empire State Building in a single day) before turning to what really interested him – the work of playwrights and actors. Many successes, including *West Side Story*, would never have seen the lights of Broadway without his intervention. When I knew him he was running the Kennedy Center in Washington on a nominal salary of a dollar a year, while maintaining an office in New York for his Broadway work. He had been one of the producers of the National's production of *Betrayal* when it went to

America, and he told me that the arrangement whereby Peter transferred his National successes to Broadway would not have been countenanced for one moment by the board of an American theatre receiving public money. And indeed it was a very British story. The country's Establishment, though not easy to penetrate in the first place, is inclined to be indulgent to those it has made its own, and Peter moved comfortably among them. Larry's genius put him in a category apart. To the Board he seemed unpredictable, sometimes frightening and even, on occasions, silly. After all, when you came down to it, he was just an actor. They were far more at ease with Peter, at least to begin with – someone who spoke their own language, and shared their healthy respect for the good things of life.

If I was to make my protest, how was I to proceed? About one thing I was certain: I had to speak with only one voice – my own. If I secretly lobbied any of my fellow associates beforehand, or if I looked for support from people outside the organisation, like Jonathan Miller, I could be accused of conspiracy, and my case discredited. To be effective my protest had to be truly disinterested. Should I bring the matter up at an associates' meeting in the hope of sparking off a debate? But I had no confidence in my ability to marshal my arguments and make a just presentation of them in the context of a lot of people talking. There would be counter-arguments, raised voices and possibly a huge row, which would of course blow over with much embarrassment and murmured apologies. We would be right back where we started.

It was impossible to challenge Peter with words that were merely spoken. He was a master at manipulating them, and in any case they left no trace. But for words on paper Peter had a genuine respect because they were immutable. A plan began to occur to me. I would prepare my thoughts and carefully write them down. I would not discuss them with anyone, and their first and only exposure would be at one of our regular associates' meetings. If others had a measure of agreement with me, perhaps the Captain could be prevailed upon to set the ship on a better course. If not, I could resign and Peter could take the theatre in any direction he liked. I would not make further trouble for the National; my responsibilities would be over, but at least I would leave something behind to show that I had once taken them seriously.

However, all this had to go on hold. First I had *Plunder* to direct, followed by something which would galvanise the entire organisation – the countdown to the long-awaited opening of the new building in March 1976, an event over which I had no wish to cast a shadow. I turned my mind to the work in hand.

As a facility the rehearsal space in the new building was as good as you could get, but it was daunting to enter it for the first time. As big as a warehouse and smelling of new concrete, it had as yet no memory of the travails and rewards experienced by other actors at other times. The huge room yawned in your face, and defied you to imagine. On the first day of rehearsals we gathered against one wall, feeling diminished, and I made a halting and rather solemn speech about what was, after all, a comedy. At the back of my mind, and I daresay many others in the organisation, there was the thought that *Plunder* would either add a third to my string of flops or break the cycle, and this was a pressure I had never had to deal with before.

We started work and it soon became apparent that Frank Finlay and Dinsdale Landen were, as actors, very different animals. Frank had come from the Royal Court, was ruminative, thoughtful and eschewed flashy effects, even in a part that rather called for them. Dinsdale, on the other hand, wanted to be brilliant *at once*, had already learnt much of his text and entered a scene assuming a comic expression as if announcing ahead of time that the funny man had arrived. He also had a tendency, so instinctive that I doubt it was conscious, of taking a step upstage whenever he was sharing a scene with another actor.

Working on the first half of the play was rather like attending a funeral where all the mourners have been disinherited. There is nothing quite like the edgy gloom that attends rehearsals of a comedy that has yet to be funny. Ben Travers occasionally dropped into rehearsals, and at ninety had no interest in disguising his thoughts. He liked Frank but deplored Dinsdale. Once we reached the burglary in the bedroom, however, we might have been rehearsing another play. I became confident about what I had to do, and the two leading men at last began working well as a team. Dinsdale executed a very funny bit of business where D'Arcy Tuck, taking an exploratory sniff of the chloroform that the robbers have brought with them to subdue the housekeeper should she wake up, only succeeds in knocking himself out and collapses full-length on the bed beside the woman he has come to rob. For the first time Ben looked pleased and chuckled.

The scene at Scotland Yard that opens Act Three was brilliantly played by both men, and Dinsdale became as outrageously funny as, so far, he had only longed to be. This became the pattern of the show – dull beginning, great ending – which was duly replicated when we opened at the Old Vic in January. During the first interval the audience was decidedly apathetic, and, from the far side of the foyer the words reached me. 'The wrong cast! And the wrong director!' I looked across the space and the speaker, in opinionated conversation with Ned Sherrin, was that same Caryl Brahms whom Jonathan Miller had once so brilliantly conjured up. The second interval was like an extraordinary improvement in the weather, and I was surrounded by happy, and it must be said, surprised faces.

By the time the curtain came down I knew we'd got away with it. Our lighting designer, Lennie Tucker, had installed a spotlight at the side of the upper circle to train on Ben during an ovation, should the occasion merit it. Fortunately it did, and when he rose from his seat in the middle of the stalls and toasted the house with a glass of champagne, the audience went wild. And there was something more personal for me to celebrate; I was off the hook – just.

Plunder was to play at the Vic through January and February, then take its place as one of the productions that would open the Lyttelton Theatre in March. In the intervening weeks it became a much better show. Once the cast accepted that rewards were waiting for them in the second half they relaxed and found other ways of making the expository first act interesting. The playing became more detailed and real, and Frank and Dinsdale now acted together with trust and enjoyment. When Jack Kroll of *Newsweek* came over from New York, he hailed *Plunder* as the real surprise in the repertoire and gave it pride of place in his review of the week's productions.

This success put me in a better position to press on with my protest, because it helped mitigate any charge of bitterness or personal grievance that was likely to be levelled against me. By now I had decided on a way forward. I would compose a paper in which I would identify certain adverse trends in the running of the National. I would not dispute Peter's authority as Artistic Director, but would suggest that he would be better served by the associates if they questioned some of his initiatives. I would be extremely frank, but not disloyal. The paper would be for the associates only and no one else. To this end I would have copies made, one for each of us, which I would first distribute immediately before reading the paper aloud. Afterwards I would invite discussion. If people wanted to take their copy home and think about it they would be free to do so.

I had yet to decide on a date. At that time we were still having our meetings at Peter's Barbican flat, and it seemed awkward, not to say discourteous, to attack a man within the confines of his own home having just accepted a good dinner. However, we had been told that before long the dinners in Peter's flat were to be discontinued and that thereafter the associates would be meeting in the conference room of the new building. The first occasion this would happen would be the Wednesday after the Monday grand opening. This seemed as good a night as any to read my paper. The ship would have been launched. Now was the time to give some thought as to where it was heading.

TWELVE

First, of course, I had to write it. Because I thought confidentiality was of the essence, I neither consulted anyone about its contents nor asked for an opinion after I had arrived at a finished draft. It's perhaps a pity I didn't, because the paper could have done with some editorial help. There was, at best, one misjudged joke. Writing about the paper now – about something else I wrote almost forty years ago – I have re-experienced some of the doubts and misgivings I had then. For instance, was I resentful of Peter because of distant events in our past at Stratford? Would any resentments have even existed if all my productions under him had been as successful as they had under Larry? Was I merely jealous of the sheer scale of the things he was hungry for, and the energy with which he pursued them? But the more I thought about it, then as now, the more the answer became a firm 'No'. Something was going wrong at the National, and it needed pointing out. Over a number of drafts and emendations this is what I came up with:

In this paper I would like to discuss the role of the Associate Directors in the running of the National Theatre. I'm reading it rather than distributing it in advance, because I would like to be wholly responsible for its confidentiality. My contention is that our planning committee has strayed a long way from the role originally intended for it, and further, that because we have never really acknowledged that drift, our usefulness to the organisation not individually but collectively has all but withered away. Our function needs to

275

be defined anew, and the thrust of this paper, which I would like you to keep in mind throughout, is towards some such definition.

But first, why and how do I think this group has lost its way? All National Theatre programmes state: 'The above directors are members of the Planning Committee and under the chairmanship of Peter Hall share in all decision-making, artistic and administrative.'

This indeed was the proposition when each of us was invited by Peter to join him. Together we were to draw up a blueprint of what a National Theatre should be and thereafter to share in its implementation; to make decisions that affected not only what was seen on the stage but the nature of the working community that would eventually be gathered in unprecedented numbers on the South Bank. This was a comprehensive ideal and like all of us I was pleased and flattered to be asked to subscribe to it, even if from the very beginning I had some misgivings about its practicality. My previous experience suggested that the policy of a theatre is dictated less by statements of intent, no matter how complex or considered, than by those day-to-day crises that arrive on someone's desk at eleven in the morning demanding a solution by three that afternoon. The policy of any theatre is most truly the accumulation of these daily decisions – decisions which reveal priorities, create precedents and eventually map out a discernible course.

Alas, it is precisely in this area that no committee can possibly participate. At all our meetings and dinners Peter has been scrupulous about keeping us fully informed, but of necessity much of what he has had to tell us has been after the event. What then has been our function? Firstly, I suppose, to decide which of us shall do what, to divide the artistic cake. Beyond that to read and discuss a great many plays the bulk of which will not be done, and to propose projects for the future most of which will have to be scrapped. This think-tank work is not without its value – we know it to be essential – but it is not policy. In fact if we examine the record we will find that very few practical consequences have derived from our many hours of lofty but generalised discussion about the kind of theatre we want. On the other hand consequences stemming from decisions of which we've had no part have been considerable. And for reasons which sometimes have had to do with tact, with confusion about the limits of our brief, also with the fact that it frequently seemed too late to influence the matter one way or another, those consequences have largely gone unremarked by this committee.

Our effectiveness as a group has been further diminished by our size. It is surely no accident that our most successful dinners have depended less on the composition of those present than on the number of those who stayed away – the smaller the gathering the better the exchange of ideas. With a full complement of associates, opportunities to speak, except for the very determined, come round about every half hour, and in the case of our more taciturn membership once in an evening. We have functioned well from time to time as an Eating Committee, as a Jokes Committee, even as a Personal Complaints Committee, but rarely as a Planning Committee. We simply do not, cannot, and probably should not 'share in all decision-making, artistic and administrative'.

I would like to give some examples of our ineffectiveness. These fall in three categories.

The first category are instances of policy-making decisions bypassing this committee. The second are instances of a policy approved by us in general principle, but overlooked by us in a differing implementation. And the third category are instances of decisions actually opposed by us (albeit in a muted fashion) that still went ahead.

What follows rakes over past history, and past history as it was best understood by myself; that is, those events which most impinged on my own activities. I have to ask you all to take on trust two very important things: that none of what I say springs from personal grievance, and that my goodwill to the National and to Peter is intact. As I proceed you may have reason to doubt both these contentions; I can only repeat that they are true.

ONE: *Instances of policy-making decisions bypassing this committee.*

These mainly concern the planning of the repertoire and I apologise in advance that my first example has already been advanced to some of you. It concerns one of my own productions, *Grand Manoeuvres*. This was a text that had been approved for production by all the then associates with the single exception of Mike Kustow. It opened to a particularly hostile press, and within two days of the first night an irreversible decision had been made to drop it from the repertoire. This may have been the correct decision, but it was a decision in which this committee took no part. Indeed two associate directors had not yet seen the production. It was made in advance of the Sunday papers, and before we could be certain that the notices would affect the box office. Whatever were the reasons supporting it, it was a decision with practical consequences of no small importance. A very large company of actors, many of whom provided continuity with the previous regime, were to be dropped and dispersed. Quite as important, it also carried serious implications of policy. For instance, was it now the case that the bad opinion of the press immediately invalidated the good opinion of the associates? Had, for instance, we given the first performance of *Look Back in Anger* or *The Birthday*

Party, would they, too, have been dropped after the first night?

There are other examples of significant changes in repertoire planning being presented to the associates as accomplished fact; for instance, the decision to drop all Jonathan Miller's projected work for 1975. Before *Figaro* and *The Freeway* Jonathan had three productions planned for the following year, *The Importance, She Would If She Could* and a revival of *Measure for Measure*. Subsequently all three were to be cancelled. This was a decision with considerable repercussions. Not only did it make Jonathan's resignation a foregone conclusion, it appeared to chart for the theatre at large our attitude to failure, and it made for the organisation its most articulate and righteous enemy. Even less drastic repertoire decisions, for example the dropping of *Next of Kin* or *Engaged*, have meant the dispersal of companies of actors in the selection of whom we have spent many hours agreeing. The recent reorganisation of the programme in the Olivier was again a matter about which this committee were informed, but not as a body consulted. My point is not that any of these decisions were necessarily wrong or should not have been taken; only that the associates did not have the least influence on them. Yet they were at the very heart of what we call planning.

TWO: *Instances of policy approved by us in general principle, but overlooked by us in a differing implementation.*

This will involve me talking with some frankness about money, a delicate subject, which, however, our failure to confront represents this committee's worst oversight. My first instance concerns the increased salaries paid to actors. This matter was first raised by Peter at an afternoon planning meeting, and we all murmured our assent to his general contention that actors in the subsidised theatre were underpaid and that this should be corrected. Now this question of a salaries policy could well have been designated an area not the concern of the associates, since in a sense it embraced each of us, but as in all the instances I shall mention our participation in it was by invitation.

In the previous regime the differential between the lowest and the highest salary was very approximately one to three; that is, the highest paid actor received three times the salary of the lowest. This does not take account of performance fees which in fact swung the balance rather more in favour of the leading actors but it does give us a mode of comparison. Since the new increases the differential is in the order of one to ten. While the lowest salary remains exactly where it was in the forties the highest is now £500, and this for perhaps only one or two performances a week. Per performance this is a much higher salary than 10 per cent of the gross of most West End theatres.

It has been argued that the £500 category embraces a very select and atypical group of senior actors, Sir John, Sir Ralph and Dame Peggy, but the recent inclusion of Albert Finney in this group makes nonsense of this proposition. Albert is a talent we enormously admire and for whom we share the highest expectations, but at the time of his engagement was his record of consistent achievement in the theatre or indeed his capacity to draw a house any greater than say Diana Rigg or Alec McCowen, actors who are on £250 per week? In a worldly sense it could be argued that Albert's theatre work prior to the National, *Krapp's Last Tape* at the Court and *Chez Nous* in the West End, put him beneath Diana and Alec in both these respects. One need not begrudge Albert his salary to wonder with concern how long it will be before others demand parity. Frank Finlay's agent in fact did, and was only put off the scent by a judicious lie that £250 was our top. With the recent renewal of his contract Frank, too, is now nudging into the £500 category.

What was it then that Albert had in common with Sir John, Sir Ralph and Dame Peggy? One answer is the same agent, Laurie Evans, who is also Peter's agent. And Peter, too, is in that top category. One is not in any way hinting at conspiracy to say that in PR terms both outside the organisation and within this is surely a bad situation. But there is more to it than the indignity of having the National Theatre of Great Britain apparently held to ransom by an agent. What we have done is jettison a tradition that has not only sustained the idea of a National Theatre over the years but has actually made it possible. From Granville Barker and Devine at the Court, to Lilian Baylis, Guthrie and Olivier at the Vic, not to mention the work at Stratford, some sacrifice of potential earning capacity has long been accepted as the price for doing uncompromised work, even perhaps as a guarantee of seriousness.

This is a very English, puritan, and perhaps philistine tradition, but it had life in it, and until recently was widely understood and accepted by the profession. When John Gielgud joined the National in the sixties it was for a salary of £67, a ludicrous figure, but one which he was prepared to accept, as was every other major actor invited to join. With a recent proposal of Laurie Evans – I gather resisted – that in the new theatre the knights be paid a thousand pounds not a week but a performance, one can see how far we have drifted away from the notion of company and towards the realm of hard-nosed Broadway transaction. We would all agree that increases, particularly to star actors, were in order, but has it been wise to so completely abandon a tradition which not only produced a remarkable theatre in the past, but which with each day's headlines seems more appropriate to the chilly future? I say 'completely abandon';

Stephen Skaptason, perhaps the best cutter of stage costumes alive, still works for less than what the commercial world would pay him. There are others like him, every secretary in the building for instance.

My second instance of a policy which the associates were asked to approve in general principle, but did not consider or discuss in implementation is the matter of West End transfers. At another afternoon meeting Peter proposed that in the case of such transfers the artistic personnel should be entitled to their full commercial reward. Again we assented. So far there has been only one transfer to the West End, *No Man's Land*, so any discussion of the way this policy works out in practice must centre on this single instance. I think we know the background to *No Man's Land*; Harold offered it to the National on the condition that after a certain number of weeks at the Vic it move to the West End. Being himself an associate of this organisation, there was perhaps some conflict of interests here, but I think we would all concede that as the play's author Harold's first loyalty was to its best exposure. As Artistic Director, however, Peter's first loyalty was clearly to the welfare of the National Theatre, and the *No Man's Land* situation was pushing him towards the creation of two far-reaching precedents, both theoretically endorsed by us.

The first was that it was acceptable for a member of this organisation to draw two salaries from it at the same time for the same job of work. The second was that a playwright, or any theatrical figure with sufficient muscle, could make the offer of his services conditional on a West End transfer; in other words use the National and its resources as a try-out situation. This was precisely what Peter O'Toole expected us to do with *Plunder*, and he argued his demand, to my mind unanswerably, on the precedent established by *No Man's Land*. For the good of the theatre I was expected to oppose him, and did so, though how it is possible for me, or Peter, or any one of us, to give detached consideration to the welfare of the organisation when some thousands of pounds of personal income are in the balance, escapes me. In the case of No Man's Land of course I'm not saying the National shouldn't have done it. It was too good a play to reject on the grounds that the deal somewhat compromised our policy. But compromise it, it did. And was it desirable that the man who had to decide about that compromise should be seen to benefit directly from it?

This matter of royalties on top of salary raises innumerable questions. When the National Theatre becomes a commercial management so that powerful figures within the organisation have no choice but to negotiate with themselves the terms of their services for a West End transfer, are we not straying into the area of monopoly? If we decide to exploit a production in a run at the Lyttelton will royalties be paid? And if not why not, since in both cases the presenting management is the National Theatre? If the Olivier is not completed in time and Tamburlaine has to play at the Albery, will this be a royalties situation? And if not, how does this differ from the No Man's Land situation at the Vic when we were waiting on the completion of the Lyttelton? And who decides which play transfers and which doesn't? Even if administered with perfect fairness, the policy is a fruit machine paying out double money to one or two lucky winners, and is essentially divisive. In the past, the work of the National Theatre has been widely exploited both in the West End and abroad, but never before have those participating in the rewards continued on full salary here. Do the associates really believe this to have been a wise departure? There is a bit of paper somewhere in the files that says we do.

THREE: *Instances of opposition to decisions which nevertheless went ahead.*

My first instance concerns the post of Deputy Director. When Peter first suggested the need for such an appointment (and I need hardly say that this was at a time before we knew Michael Birkett as friend and valued colleague, before indeed the question of a candidate had even been raised), the attitude of the associates was to a man sceptical. Peter explained how useful such a producer figure would be to a director involved in a production, but all the directors present said they had managed without such support in the past and were happy so to continue. He also candidly admitted that from his point of view such an appointment would allow him the same freedom to pursue outside work as was at present enjoyed by the associates. What none of us said but most of us thought was that Peter's curtailment of freedom was at least one of the reasons why he was paid his salary and we ours. John Schlesinger, his disinterest established by his film commitments, put into words something else that was in our minds: why create a new highly paid appointment when there was already so much spare capacity among this committee? The matter rested there but was brought up again at two subsequent dinners. One by one we lapsed into silence and a candidate was named. But how could the associates possibly have felt comfortable about such a proposal? By creating a self-sufficient three-man executive it removed them still further from the centre of decision-making. A few months later this was to be graphically demonstrated in programme material when a black line appeared separating the names of Peter Hall, Michael Birkett and Peter Stevens from those of the associates.

My second instance is again one the associates were invited to consider, the *Aquarius* engagement. When Peter consulted us about this our response was markedly unenthusiastic, though a number of things inhibited robust comment – some uncertainty as to whether it was actually our business, and perhaps, too, some admiration, not to say envy, for Peter's appetite for work and reward. Certainly the misgiving which we shared at that meeting was not that Peter would do one job at the expense of another, but that given the magnitude of the move to the new building in PR terms he ran the certain danger of this seeming to be so. But beyond this matter of appearances we neglected to discuss an equally important question – the effect within the organisation of the precedent which would be glaringly established should the Artistic Director take a day and a half off a week to do a second highly-paid job. In the past the accepted practice was for National Theatre staff to forgo salary here when taking on outside work. The rules were bent a little – when an actor did a voiceover for instance, or when a director did a guest production for a meagre fee at somewhere like the Court. But by and large the rule stood, and on it depended such specifics as the exclusivity of our contracts with actors, as well as the many intangibles of commitment throughout the organisation. If these things have been eroded, the associates as they are at present constituted share in the responsibility.

So far this paper may give the impression that I have used the pretext of discussing the role of the planning committee to launch an attack on the Artistic Director. As I hope to show this is not the case. My concern is with us, the associates, and how we can most genuinely be useful to the theatre and its leadership. And I believe the first thing we must do is abandon the pretence of decision-making. If we are to have power we must have a vote, and since this is transparently no way to run a theatre we must surrender power. At the moment this committee is sometimes a rubber stamp,

285

sometimes a way of ensuring that the risk of an ill-advised decision is spread, but hardly ever an effective decision-making body. Let the three-man executive run the organisation with a free hand. By all means let this committee continue as a think-tank. By all means let each one of us accept responsibility for those areas over which the individual has real control – John Bury in the Design Department, Bill Bryden at the Cottesloe, people like myself with our productions, etc. By all means let us continue our meetings and our dinners, to be briefed by Peter on what has been decided and to share with him through discussion the immense problems of running the organisation.

But let us call ourselves what we are, not a Planning Committee, but an Advisory Committee. And let us rename ourselves tonight. Our function is to advise and consent; also from time to time to advise and emphatically dissent. We know the Artistic Director to be a man of unique energy, ability and persuasion. He is best served not only by our loyalty and support but by our watchfulness and scrupulously argued differences. Let the executive be free to initiate a policy of royalties additional to salary, but let us not hesitate to point out that in a time of financial stringency 4 per cent at the Wyndhams was enough to finance a new production. I hope the posture I have suggested, part adviser, part scrutineer, with the power only to insist on dissociation from questionable policy, may, with no loss of friendliness, relish and common purpose, commend itself to the associates as their proper role.

*

So as March approached I, unlike others in the organisation, had two first nights to be nervous about, the Grand Opening on Monday 15 March in the Lyttelton Theatre, and two days later on Wednesday 17th a solo performance of my own in the National

Theatre conference room. Preparations for the rather more important of these two occasions were well under way. Our schedule was as follows. The National's last night at the Old Vic was on 28 February, and we were to celebrate the occasion with an evening honouring Lilian Baylis, whose seasons before the war with her director, Tyrone Guthrie, and stars like Olivier and Laughton, had renewed the momentum for a National Theatre. In the week leading up to this event the various productions that would be on show in the brand new Lyttelton Theatre would start having their technical dress rehearsals. With luck all five productions – Hall's three, *Hamlet, Happy Days* and *John Gabriel Borkman*, Bill Bryden's *Watch It Come Down* and my *Plunder* – would then be ready for our critics' week starting 8 March. These performances in front of the international press would be deemed previews. The Grand Opening would be a week later.

Arrangements for this event had been discussed at one of our larger planning meetings. The first thing we had to decide was: which production would declare the new theatre officially open on Monday 15th? The occasion was to be celebrated by a charming touch. In Shakespeare's day a rocket had been fired from the upper reaches of the Globe Theatre to inform the town that a performance was imminent. (Whether this rocket was the cause of the fire that had later burnt the theatre to the ground is not recorded.) But when Olivier was making plans for the new National, Sir Ralph Richardson had suggested that he mark the first and subsequent performances with one of the Globe's rockets. This ceremony, now referred to as 'Ralph's Rocket', had been saved up for the opening of the new building on the South Bank. After years of delay and innumerable difficulties, the lighting of the touch paper was almost upon us.

I was in no doubt which play should inaugurate the opening of the new building – *Hamlet*. It was the most famous play in the language, and Larry had chosen it to launch the National's first performance at the Old Vic thirteen years before. This made for a nice symmetry and I argued for it strongly. Other people at the meeting seemed to agree, and it was all but decided when John Goodwin, our Head of Press, looking mischievous and amused, remarked, 'You know, Peter, don't you, that Monday the 15th is the Ides of March?' This made some of us laugh, but when I looked across at Peter there wasn't a trace of a smile on his face. He was taking it with utter seriousness. Most theatre people, like sportsmen and others who are obliged to be at their best at a specific moment on a specific day, are superstitious, at least where an opening night is concerned, but I had never heard of anyone identifying with the murdered Julius Caesar. Peter was clearly disconcerted. I might have reassured him that he had little to fear from the Ides of March. The date to avoid would be two days later when he would be seeing the flash of my rubber dagger.

'Hang on a moment,' he murmured, 'maybe we should think about opening with something else.'

'A comedy perhaps,' suggested John Goodwin. 'A comedy might be better anyway because that's the night of the Charity Gala.' There was only one comedy in the repertoire, *Plunder*, and I'd been told that Peter didn't care for the production. Over the next ten minutes the opening night was picked over as if we were examining the entrails of a goat, and the decision that emerged was that *Plunder* would open the new building.

'I know what!' said Peter suddenly. 'Let's not have an opening night at all. Let's have an opening *week*! Let's give all the shows equal importance.' Everyone nodded and said an opening week was an excellent idea. Secretly I couldn't help feeling a certain glee that a show of mine would be first up, and some days later a story appeared in the *Evening Standard* announcing that *Plunder* would indeed mark the official opening of the new building.

Before that, however, there were challenging hurdles to clear. Technical dress rehearsals are usually something of an ordeal, but in a newly erected theatre, where untried stage machinery is constantly breaking down, and not even the handles on the dressing-room doors can be depended on to work, they can become a nightmare. *Plunder*, which at its final performance at the Vic had purred like a well-oiled piece of machinery, fell apart on the Lyttelton stage. One scene change, usually thirty seconds in length, took forty minutes. We got to the end of the play wondering if we would ever be ready for the critics' week beginning on 8 March. *Plunder* would be the first show in the new building in which actors and an audience would meet.

That's what I thought until I discovered that Peter had scheduled a matinee performance of *Happy Days* on the same Monday. This desire to be first was perhaps understandable on the part of an artistic director, but it deprived *Plunder* of a very necessary dress rehearsal before we faced our first audience. I was so concerned that I thought it advisable to address the house and apologise in advance for any technical glitches or delays. As I was waiting in the wings to go in front of the curtain and make a short speech, I sensed a figure behind me. I turned and it was Peter. He said he would prefer it if he was the one to make the announcement, and he slid past me and into the lights. It seemed there could be only one public face of the National Theatre.

In the middle of these weeks of turmoil there had been the farewell to the Old Vic, organised on a Sunday so that theatre people could attend. Without any explanation, Larry had declined to participate, so Albert Finney had stepped in to compère the evening, which he did with magnanimous self-assurance. It was a well-organised and well-written event in which Peggy Ashcroft impersonated Lilian Baylis, the woman to whom the evening was paying tribute, and did so brilliantly. One had become so accustomed to her usual lofty, well-enunciated delivery that it was a complete surprise to see her being so funny and colloquial, sketching in with a sure hand Miss Baylis's cockney accent and physical peculiarities. Peggy was in touch with some memory from her youth and it suggested the possibility of an entirely different career.

Towards the end of the evening Larry was honoured, but in the strangest way. As the audience sat staring at an enormous full-face photograph of him projected on to a screen at the rear of the stage, one of his recorded speeches from *Henry V* was broadcast into the house. Hearing that voice once again but at one remove, a voice which was encoded into the theatrical DNA of every person present, only underlined the fact that the stage itself was quite empty. At the end of the evening, during the applause, Dame Sybil Thorndike, now in her nineties and in a wheelchair, was pushed slowly down one of the theatre aisles so that she could be picked up by a spotlight. She had been Bernard Shaw's first St Joan and throughout her career a champion of the kind of theatre the National was meant to be. She smiled gallantly under the lights and waved a frail hand, but having nowhere to go had to be wheeled slowly backwards, until, still waving, she was swallowed up by the shadow of the overhang of the circle. Nothing could have so poignantly summed up the end of an era.

The critics' week passed without disasters, and although some of the shows had seen better nights, it was deemed a success. We could relax and enjoy our official opening. That Monday I ran into Michael Birkett.

'Well, tonight at last, Ralph's Rocket makes its ascent,' I said, and for a second his expression veiled over. Then he smiled again and said gently, 'No, no, Ralph's Rocket goes off *tomorrow* night. With *Hamlet*. Not tonight. Tonight's a Charity Gala.'

'But I thought the idea was to have an opening *week*!' I said.

'Yes, yes, we are, we are. But the week begins on Tuesday. With *Hamlet*. Tonight's performance is a preview. A charity preview.'

It would have been demeaning (and pointless) to argue, so I nodded and we parted. The following evening, fifteen minutes before the curtain was about to rise on *Hamlet*, I was standing in the foyer when I saw the determined approach of Peter Hall, Peter Stevens and Michael Birkett. They wore the excited, smug expressions of newly appointed prefects striding down the school corridor on the first day of term, and I knew exactly where they were heading. They were off to launch Ralph's Rocket.

Only Michael had caught sight of me among the crowd, and I saw him debate with himself for a moment before his better nature got the better of him and he hailed me. He was a man it was difficult to dislike. 'We're about to light Ralph's Rocket,' he called jubilantly. 'Come along!' So I joined the party and followed them to one of the upper terraces of the building where the rocket was waiting. Sir Ralph himself duly launched it, but because it was not yet dark it didn't amount to much. A bird swerved, but no one on the pavements below looked up, and it would not be long before the rocket would be abandoned as a way of announcing the start of a performance. I no longer cared much either way. I had other things on my mind, not least an unsettling encounter I had had the night before at the Charity Gala.

I had been asked to put on a black tie and make an appearance at the champagne reception. It was an imposing gathering that included Board members and other recognisable establishment figures, and they all appeared to be having a good time, so John Goodwin's hunch that their charitable impulses would be better rewarded by *Plunder* than by three and a half hours of Shakespeare had probably been correct. I spotted a friend among those present, the arts journalist, Gaia Servadio. She was now weaving through the guests and coming towards me with a certain intent. We had met four years before when she interviewed me for the *Evening Standard* at the time of *Long Day's Journey*. With numerous acquaintances in common it was not long before I had become friends with Gaia and her husband, Willie Mostyn Owen, and I was soon a frequent visitor to their house in Chelsea. However, it had been some months since I had seen either of them.

'I thought you might be here tonight,' said Gaia. 'I have a favour to ask of you.'

'What?' I enquired.

'I'm doing a piece on the National for the *Standard*, and it may ruffle a few feathers. I wondered if you'd look it over for factual accuracy?'

If I hadn't been entirely sober a moment before, I was now. My mind went into overdrive. Normally I would have met such a request with a pleasant but firm refusal on the grounds that my position within the organisation made it untenable. But in two days' time I would be reading my paper to the associates! What if the criticisms in my paper and hers in the article overlapped? I would immediately be accused of a leak to the press, and everything I had written would be discredited. In my conversations with Gaia we had often talked about the National, but I had been careful never to reveal anything that I considered confidential; I had never mentioned that I was thinking of writing a paper, nor what the contents of that paper might be. But what if something had slipped out? What if something of mine had now been duplicated in her article? I had to find out, yet I couldn't explain to her why.

'All right,' I said cautiously. 'I'll look it over, but only to check it for factual errors.'

Gaia reached into her bag and produced a long envelope. Like something in a spy film she passed it to me and I put it in my breast pocket, aware, even as I did so, that I might be making a calamitous mistake.

Relief of a sort was waiting for me later when I read her article. Except that we both censured Hall, there was no overlap of any kind, and it had been foolish of me to worry. And no wonder: I had the inside dope, and she didn't. Her piece, however, contained a few errors. For instance, she described Peter as the richest man in show business, which might have been his aspiration but was far from being the case; there were playwrights much richer. I also felt, particularly at this moment in the National's history when the institution needed all the support it could get, that you shouldn't criticise Peter without acknowledging his strengths. As must be evident, I no longer liked Peter much, but I readily acknowledged that he had a genuine, if skewed, dedication to the whole idea of theatre and that there was no more brilliant advocate on its behalf, precisely the man to have in your corner when you wanted your subsidy improved or when a politician tried to interfere in the way your theatre was run. The purpose of my paper was not to unseat Hall but to bring pressure on him to run the place in a more principled way. I rang Gaia and offered her my corrections.

My paper was now ready to be presented to the associates. I'd had a fair copy typed for me by a friend of my wife's who had secretarial skills but no connections with the theatre, not even as a playgoer. I then made ten photocopies, nine for the people who I thought would be present at the meeting, and one for John Schlesinger, who would be in flight to Los Angeles. I then asked my old secretary from Aquinas Street, Sue Higginson, who had risen dramatically in the organisation to become PA to the Artistic Director, and who usually minuted our meetings, to make sure I had a half hour to address the associates on Wednesday night. The more my plan fell into place, the more it seemed to be acquiring a life of its own. It was sweeping me along, and I had an unsettling insight into the mind of the terrorist. He begins with a strongly held conviction. Then he decides to act on that conviction. He lays his plans only to find they have created a momentum independent of the original conviction and it becomes almost impossible to turn back. In the days leading up to the Wednesday meeting I had many of these uncomfortable thoughts.

In his autobiography, Peter Hall asserts that John Schlesinger was present at the reading of the paper and took his side against me, an error which later made its way into John's biography. But it is not correct. Knowing he would be unable to attend because he was off to LA on his latest film, I rang John and asked if I could visit him at his Kensington house the day before the flight.

He was the only person at the National to see the paper in advance of its presentation, and it was an enormous relief being in the presence of someone to whom I could legitimately reveal myself. With John I did what I would do later at the meeting: I read the paper out loud to him. When I looked up he was grinning broadly. 'Good! Very good!' he said. Then he giggled, and whispered 'But I wonder if you should have gone on so much about the money?' This was a very English observation and reminded me of my days as an actor in rep, where it was considered bad form to compare your salary with anyone else in the company. Even then I wondered why, since such restraints could only be to the advantage of the employer. I preferred the more robust American approach which, when you're after the truth, advises 'Follow the money.' There wasn't much time to discuss in any detail the points I raised in the paper, but John left me in no doubt of his endorsement of some of them and his belief in my right to express my mind. He said he regretted not being able to be present, and wished me good luck. I left him feeling heartened and much less neurotic.

The conference room was a large modern space, smelling, like everywhere else in the complex, of new building works, and was dominated by a long table, the top of which was an immensely thick slab of black wood. I chose a seat and placed in front of me my briefcase containing the nine copies of my paper, including one for Paddy Donnell who had not made an appearance. As I pulled in my chair I detected that the table-top wasn't thick at all. It consisted of a sheet of industrial hardboard to the sides of which at right angles were attached strips of wooden siding to provide the appearance of depth. Was this a sign of some sort? But a sign of what? I was as taut as an over-wound spring and was seeing significances everywhere.

The meeting began with a surge of affability. Peter thanked those present for their contribution to the successful opening, and then the usually reticent John Bury paid an emotional and obviously sincere tribute to Peter's leadership. Both men were in each other's debt, Peter because John's austere monumental designs had provided the signature to many of his most lauded productions, and John because for a middle-aged man with a new family of young children to raise his association with such a successful director put to rest a number of practical anxieties. I admired John and it only now occurred to me how much my paper would upset him.

In fact for the first time I began to examine in my furiously active head the practical politics of what I was attempting. I had been so concerned with proceeding ethically that I'd hardly given a thought to the more mundane matter of whether the strategy would succeed. Perhaps the whole thing was no more than an exercise in moral self-regard. John Bury would most certainly not take my side, nor was it right to expect him to. But what about the others? So many of my arguments sprung from a comparison between Hall's regime and Olivier's, yet I'd all but forgotten I was the only associate present to have had the experience of both. John Russell Brown and Mike Kustow were almost certain to be Peter's men. Neither had been in the permanent employ of a theatre before, and they owed their positions entirely to Peter.

There was a newcomer among us, the composer Harrison Birtwistle, but as yet he knew little about the theatre and would be bewildered by the issues I was raising. He, too, would support Peter, if only by default. As for Michael Birkett and Peter Stevens, they had been engaged specifically to be Peter's guard dogs and they would undoubtedly be true to that assignment. This left the associates who were the three actual theatre practitioners, John Schlesinger, now, alas, far away in Los Angeles, Harold Pinter, who I knew I could depend on for a just hearing but who it had been impossible not to implicate in the matter of the transfer of *No Man's Land*, and finally Bill Bryden. He was a gifted young Scotsman, being both playwright and director, inclined to be garrulous, but extremely alert. He was also highly ambitious, and it would be asking a great deal of him to stand alone in my defence. These were the thoughts that were rushing through my head as the time drew near for me to speak. All the people in the room were looking at me, curious and a little mystified. What was this matter so important that I had asked for an uninterrupted half hour to address them? I had reached the point where there could be no turning back. I began talking.

I explained that I had written a paper which I intended to read to them, and described in some detail the care I had taken to maintain its confidentiality. I further explained that I had made copies for everyone present (though for no one else), which I would shortly distribute and which they could take home with them for further consideration at the end of the meeting. My voice sounded higher than usual and I wondered if I looked a little mad. The expressions around me were changing from good-natured perplexity to vague alarm. I opened my briefcase, withdrew the copies of the paper, each with the recipient's name handwritten at the top, and the bundles were pushed across the black table-top, sorted out, then distributed like a parody of gifts at Christmas.

I started to read. My mind was jumping all over the place, and it was as much as I could do to articulate the words, let alone think about what I was saying. From time to time I glanced up from the pages to watch myself being watched. The group were looking at me as they might a man standing high up on a window-ledge on the point of jumping. (How awful! But at the same time how *interesting*!) Only Peter was not looking at me. His face, shiny with sweat, was turned slightly away and he was blinking furiously. I guessed his mind was in the same state of turmoil as my own.

It was not until later, when the *Diaries* were published, that I would understand why he appeared so perturbed. For months now he had been canvassing hard to have his contract renewed.

He had asked for a five-year extension, which he insisted to the Board was the time he needed to see his agenda for the National come to fruition. (And also perhaps the agenda for himself.) This the Board had agreed, but months had passed and they had yet to come up with a contract. Anxious, Hall had then appealed to Max Rayne, who had assured him the contract was on its way. Indeed, at the time I was reading my paper it was only days away from signing. And on top of these crucial negotiations Peter was considering another contract. The first series of the *Aquarius* TV programme had come to an end, and he had been asked to front a second series later in the year. In the *Diaries* he concedes that accepting *Aquarius* in the first place had been a bad idea, but his need for money had left him no choice but to accept the new offer. If word of my paper reached the Board before these contracts were signed, both could be in jeopardy. Peter was right to be alarmed.

That night there was to be another drinks reception during the interval of *John Gabriel Borkman*, similar to the one Gaia Servadio had attended two days before, and this time all the associates had been asked to make an appearance. I finished reading my paper at precisely the hour we were all expected downstairs. So, like an interval at a parallel play, we all rose, holding on to our papers as if they were theatre programmes. We heard Peter's raised voice. 'I would be very uncomfortable if any copies of that paper left this room.' We all looked around wondering where to deposit them. Someone had a briefcase with a lock on it, so the papers were collected, put away out of sight, and the key turned.

In fact the whole evening was beginning to seem like a play. There are occasionally situations in one's life when events become so charged and condensed that you feel you could put them on stage exactly as they have just unfolded. We had participated in an intriguing Act One. If an audience had been watching they would be desperate to return to their seats to find out what happens. Would it turn out to be a comedy or a tragedy? Either way, it was a play of which the Ancient Greeks would have approved because it observed the unities of time and place.

Downstairs at the reception it was as if the paper had never been read. Most of the associates tactfully drifted away from me to mingle with the other guests, and I was left having a pleasant conversation with Bill Bryden. Suddenly a beaming John Russell Brown was at my elbow. 'That was a *wonderful* paper, Michael,' he said in his most enthusiastic tones. 'It's *exactly* the way we should be bringing things up for discussion. I really do commend you. You've shown us the way forward!' This seemed an odd time for royal-baby enthusiasm, but I was grateful for his support, even if he seemed to have missed the insurrectionist thrust of the paper.

We returned to the conference room and took our seats – talkative moments before, now silent. The briefcase was unlocked, and once again the papers made their way around the table. Later on I realised that this was the point I should have left the meeting. I had written the paper. I had then taken full responsibility for it by reading it aloud to my colleagues. It was now up to them to give it their consideration. At a later meeting we could discuss it. Instead I stayed. I suppose I felt I needed to hold my ground and accept some punishment for the views I had expressed as a guarantee of their integrity. Unfortunately, I was not in much of a state to do so, because the reading of the paper had left me utterly exhausted.

The discussion began in an uncertain but civil manner. Until the associates had read the material for themselves and made up their minds about it, it was difficult for anyone to know where to begin. John Russell Brown reiterated the view he had expressed downstairs, that writing such a paper was a splendid idea, and Peter responded with the simplest and most unexpected thing he said during the entire evening: 'But John, not everyone might be able to express themselves in a paper like that.' It was the last thing I had expected him to say, since it certainly didn't apply to him, and I found it almost touching. Then, as unexpectedly as the beginning of a dog-fight, the mood changed. Peter Stevens and Michael Birkett had done some quick thinking about the material during the break and they had some questions ready. Peter intervened with a quick aside to Sue Higginson. 'Sue, I don't think any of this discussion should be minuted.' She put her pad to one side and looked at me evenly, as if the prospect of my comeuppance was something to look forward to. This rejection from someone with whom I'd once taken trust and good humour for granted was distressing, but I didn't blame her. She had become completely in thrall to her new boss.

Peter Stevens and Michael Birkett now took over the meeting, the one on the offensive, with Peter Hall offering support from time to time, while the other skimmed through the paper preparing the next line of attack. The thing I'd most hoped to avoid was happening. We would soon be shouting at each other, making wild claims, and becoming abusive. I tried as hard as I could to stay calm, but I knew this was no longer a discussion; it had become an inquisition, and my guilt was the foregone conclusion. The purpose of the interrogation was to find out its exact extent. Peter and Michael went hunting for errors of fact, and found a couple of small ones, which they trumpeted as discrediting the entire paper. I had said that the decision to drop *Grand Manoeuvres* from the repertoire had been taken before we'd seen the notices in the Sunday papers, but this was incorrect; it was taken on the Monday. However, this did not alter the fact that it involved the dismissal of an entire company of actors, many of whom represented the remaining link with the previous regime, and that it was a decision taken without any reference to the associates. At the very least, I had argued, we should have been consulted.

Eventually we moved on to the subject of the new salary structure, and the £500 paid to select top people. Peter began raising his voice and jabbing the table with his finger. 'And you know who suggested that figure?! *Larry!* Larry suggested £500!'

He was shouting the way boys in a school playground try to win an argument. When some time later I mentioned this to Olivier, he became angry and quite unequivocal. 'That's a lie! When they asked me, I suggested £400. Never 500!'

We had been talking for what seemed hours. I had conceded very little, but by this time I was reeling with exhaustion.

'What I don't understand, Michael,' said Peter, 'is what did you hope to achieve with this paper? *Why* did you write it?' I was now surrounded by people who were all asking me '*Yes, why?*' and I struggled to order my thoughts. The National was running into danger, I said, and the things that now worried me would eventually be raised by people outside the organisation. 'Who are these people?' asked Peter. And I was surrounded by demands of '*Yes, who?*' People in the theatre, I replied, and in the press. Peter Stevens shot back 'What people in the press? How do you know that?' The '*Who?*' now turned to '*What people?*' I felt myself increasingly cornered. The associates were now hunting as a pack.

'Well, I know of one instance . . .' I muttered, and too late realised that I had blundered fatally. Peter Hall, who had been slumped in his chair, was suddenly alert with a look on his face that was almost triumphant. A leak to the press, a second conspirator, this was something he could understand!

'What is this instance?' he asked, and 'Yes, what?' came from all directions. My mind was not only spinning like a top, it was wobbling precariously. Did I have the right to implicate Gaia? And if I did, what use would it be to either of us? And what effect would it have on what I hoped to accomplish? There was a pause before I said weakly, 'I'm not going to name names.' Peter Hall gave an aggressive 'Huh!' as if all was now clear and from Peter Stevens came a snort of derision. The heretic had been broken; now it was only a matter of lighting the faggots. The tide of the meeting seemed to have turned full against me. It was well past midnight; now all anyone wanted was to get up and go home.

'Well, there we are,' said Peter. 'What do we do now?' We sat for a moment in silence, then Mike Kustow, at his most ingratiating, spoke. 'May I make a suggestion?' Peter nodded. 'Why don't those people who want to study Michael's paper further, take it home with them. And those people who don't, give it back to him tonight?' Once again, Peter's eyes lit up with interest. 'That sounds like an excellent idea,' he said. Whereupon Mike pushed his paper delicately towards me. Immediately from across the table Peter Stevens and Michael Birkett pitched theirs. Peter's copy followed, then John Bury's and, after a moment of hesitation, Harold's. Carefully avoiding eye contact, John Russell Brown slid his copy towards me, as did a somewhat baffled Harrison Birtwistle.

Only one paper had not been returned – Bill Bryden's. He was sitting at the other end of the table furthest away from me, and he was showing no signs of moving. I recognised at once that Bill was in an impossible position. If he retained the paper and it was leaked, he would join me as the only other suspect. He had his career at the National to think about, and was presently making plans to stage a season of plays at the Cottesloe with his own company of actors, the only occasion during the Hall regime when the idea of a company would be taken seriously. It was unreasonable of me to expect him to take my side. Even so, less for my sake than for his, I longed for him to hold out. He was young, fervent, and even if he didn't always agree with me, knew perfectly well the sincerity of what I had attempted. No one in the room was looking in his direction, but we were all aware of his lone paper, burning a hole in the black table-top in front of him.

Then something quite weird happened. Spontaneously, the group began to make light conversation. They asked about each other's wives and children, then discussed topics such as what we all planned to do over the forthcoming weekend. In the middle of this chat, and himself participating in it, Bill slowly rose from his seat, ambled along the table and absently put his own paper on top of the pile in front of me as if he was doing no more than laying aside a magazine. I could see that he really didn't have a choice in the matter, but it still struck me that this was the saddest thing that had happened all night.

I set off home with my briefcase as heavy as it had been when I arrived. All the papers had been returned to me. Not one word of our turbulent discussion had been minuted. Something which had happened had now never happened, and a moment in the National's history had been neatly erased. I felt like one of those discredited Soviet politicians whose likeness has been entirely removed from a group photograph. I had to acknowledge not just a defeat, but an utter rout. If Machiavelli had decided to write a book on how *not* to get your way in the world, my case could have furnished him with an entire chapter.

It had been absurd of me to expect a sympathetic hearing from my colleagues. They had no arguments with Peter (though these would follow) and I had essentially asked them to choose between him and me. Not only had this been unsuccessful, it had probably made things worse, because, having been forced to demonstrate their loyalty to Peter, they would now be obliged to turn their eyes away from subsequent behaviour about which they might otherwise have had reservations. Peter was now in a position to do whatever he liked and in the next few years would do just that. I had only one consolation, though it would not be available before some time had passed. I had been right, and the things I had tried to warn against would happen.

And yet I soon grasped that the matter was not quite over, and couldn't be. My paper existed, all nine copies of it, and though I intended to keep my word about its confidentiality, it still represented the thing with which Peter was most uncomfortable – words on paper. He, too, had realised this, and two days later at home I received a call from him. He couldn't have sounded calmer or more reasonable, nor for that matter, when I responded, could I. Would it be possible for him to have his copy back, he asked, because there were a couple of points about which he needed reminding. With matching politeness, I answered that no, I'd offered it to him on Wednesday night; he'd had his chance then, and I wasn't offering him another one. At that moment both of us were thinking the same thing, though from opposite perspectives. In writing the paper had I been guilty of defamation? I hadn't given a thought to the legal ramifications, but he was an intimate of the most famous lawyer in the land. Was I in trouble? Sure enough, according to the *Diaries*, Peter soon visited Arnold Goodman and Max Rayne to give them a comprehensive account of 'this sordid Blakemore business'.

If I wouldn't let him see the paper, Peter then asked if we could at least discuss it. 'Of course,' I said, and we agreed to meet at the theatre at the end of the day.

I came into his office determined to be reasonable. I admitted to a couple of small errors in the paper which, however, were immaterial to the arguments I was making, and apologised if the tone had seemed needlessly hostile. I then offered him my resignation.

He insisted that this was not what he wanted. As a director relating to actors, I've always looked first for something to like in the performance that is being offered to me. By beginning with a compliment, you are offering an assurance of good will, and you can then, if necessary, go on to express a few reservations. There was much I still admired about Peter's powers of application, and I proceeded to pay tribute to him in much the same terms as I had to Gaia Servadio earlier in the week. 'But, Michael,' said Peter. 'In your paper you as good as called me *venal*.' We stared at each other. I didn't think I'd written that, but it was probably what I thought.

'Well, you're an extremely greedy man. You seem to want helpings of everything,' I replied, and then went on to discuss his hunger for money. 'What you may not realise,' he said, 'is that I have eight people to support.'

At that moment I had one of those insights that come at you sideways, and I saw what it must be like to have Peter as a son. I knew he'd acquired a house for his parents, the Suffolk station-master and his wife, and I didn't doubt that in their retirement he was proving a generous and dutiful offspring. What did they make of him, I wondered, this enchanted only child whose climb up the ladder of British life must have left them as bewildered as they were proud. Then I reminded myself of the probable reception an actor would have received if he'd appealed to Peter for a raise on the basis that he, too, had an extended family depending on him.

'What I can't understand, what really puzzles me,' said Peter, 'is what was your *motive* in all this?' I felt a surge of impatience. Was all human behaviour really a matter of stratagems and advancement? Surely there were more impulsive, even foolhardy reasons for the things people did. Maybe I simply got seriously fed up attending meetings where cant and humbug were always prowling around the periphery. Maybe I simply wanted to let Peter know that at least one of his associates saw exactly what he was up to. These were thoughts which I didn't express, but they told me the discussion was going nowhere.

THIRTEEN

The following day, Saturday, there was a special meeting to revisit, with cooler heads, what had transpired on Wednesday night. We met as before in the conference room, which now seemed a quite different place, washed clean of drama by broad daylight and the wide vistas to one side of us of the river and the city. The meeting began with an apology from me and a sincere one. I could see that the manner, if not the matter, of my presentation may have offended the collegiate spirit which should exist in a group such as ours. I had, in a sense, ambushed them and they had reason to feel affronted. The associates gave me a courteous hearing but their stillness and frequently averted gaze told me that I was now outside the pack, padding along to one side. I then went on to explain to them my plans for the immediate future.

Because of the way both *Hamlet* and *Plunder* had been rescheduled, there was no slot available for me to do a production at the National in the immediate future. My next show was meant to be Granville Barker's *The Madras House*, in about a year's time. It was a play I really wanted to do, but in the meantime I needed to find some interesting outside work. Peter Nichols and I were again friends and he had asked me to direct his new play, *Privates on Parade*, but after *The Freeway* he had decided to offer it to the Royal Shakespeare Company. This was awkward but as things stood, no reason for me to decline directing it for him.

For the time being my duties at the National would consist of turning up at meetings and vetting the numerous scripts that arrived each day for consideration. There was one in particular I had yet to read – a play called *The Kingfisher* that had come to us with Peter's recommendation. However, he told the associates that he would be issuing copies to us with the name of the author removed from the title page because he thought it might prejudice our reading of it. I had therefore decided, I told the associates that Saturday afternoon, that I would take a pile of scripts with me to France, and also a copy of my paper. This I would reconsider, less in terms of the past than of the future, and try to remove from it any hint of rancour. On my return I would resubmit it for their consideration. After I'd finished speaking, the meeting soon broke up; it was interrupting those plans for the weekend which had been under discussion when Bill Bryden was considering his options.

Just before Easter I left for Biarritz with the family, hoping for a foretaste of summer – sunny skies and perhaps a swim. But we had more to learn about how fickle the Basque coast could be in the disposal of its favours. The sky stayed a monotonous grey, the ocean was freezing and, while the temperature was not exactly cold, it felt continuously draughty as if, beyond the mountains, a huge door had been left ajar. I worked in the mornings and in the afternoons Shirley, Conrad and I went for long walks beside an inhospitable sea. In the seventies there were few restrictions about the way ships disposed of their rubbish in transit, and out of season the beaches accumulated an endless fringe of toxic litter. We made bonfires of old besmirched driftwood and a huge variety of plastic waste – lengths of garishly coloured rope, dented bottles and dirty drums that had once contained suspicious chemicals. Mesmerised by the flames, we took care when the wind changed to avoid the twisting columns of noxious black smoke that took the pollution up from the beach and fed it into the open sky. During my childhood in Australia the only debris to arrive on our shores from across the Pacific had been the elegant glass floats, still entwined in fragments of fibrous netting, which the Japanese had used in their fishing. The world was changing fast.

I progressed through my pile of scripts, beginning with *The Kingfisher*, the play with the mystery author. It was a well-crafted, elegiac comedy about an upper-class couple living in the country and coming to terms with their advancing years, the kind of classy entertainment on which the West End had relied for years. A far more formidable task than reading plays was the reconsideration of my paper. The trouble was that every time I looked at it, I realised I hadn't changed my mind about a single word. I could slightly modify the tone, but to what purpose? I would read a couple of paragraphs and then, agitated and angry, go striding around the room as if I was in some kind of cage. Sometimes I simply stared out of the open window of the balcony and picked blisters of paint off the exterior sill. It seemed no time ago that the paintwork had been as pristine as a leaf in spring, and already it was beginning to flake.

I'd asked my agent in London, Terry Owen, to keep me closely informed about any developments while I was away, and one morning I received an envelope containing the Gaia Servadio article which had recently appeared in the *Evening Standard*. Even as I was unfolding it, I realised that once again I had blundered badly; to be out of the country the week of its publication must surely have given the impression I had something to hide. I read the article and my heart fell further. It was very different from the typescript I had been asked to check, but even so there were no direct links to my paper. What was identical, however, was Gaia's acknowledgement of Peter Hall's merits. Her words practically duplicated the praise I had showered on Peter just before I left London.

I received two further items of mail from my agent. One was a letter he had received from Peter Stevens stating that the National intended to rationalise the way it paid its associates. Future agreements would be more in line with the existing contracts of Harold Pinter and John Schlesinger. I was immediately on my guard. Because the bulk of their income came from elsewhere, Harold and John were on small retainers. People like Bill Bryden and myself, who were presumed to be working full-time for the theatre unless we had requested unpaid leave to do outside work, were paid a proper salary – some £125 a week. We couldn't possibly survive on a retainer like Harold's. This was a matter that needed urgent clarification as soon as I returned.

The second letter was disturbing in a different but all too familiar way, and I read it with an disbelieving wag of the head. It consisted of the minutes of a meeting I'd been unable to attend at which *The Kingfisher* had come under further discussion. The author of the play was now unmasked – William Douglas-Home, whose hits over many years practically defined Shaftesbury Avenue. His new play, however, would be staged at the National, be directed by Peter Hall and star Sir Ralph Richardson. After a short run in the Cottesloe it would transfer to the West End. Clearly, it would take more than was in my power to persuade Peter to change his ways, though, in the event, this was one of his manoeuvres that didn't come off. The London commercial managers rose in revolt and insisted that the National release the play so that it could be presented, like Douglas-Home's other hits, in the West End. It went on to have a successful run at the Lyric Theatre, produced by John Gale, starring Ralph Richardson and Celia Johnson under the direction of Lindsay Anderson.

I was back at the National by the beginning of May and was soon aware that Peter Hall's narrative explaining the genesis of my paper was now widely accepted: that it had been concocted in cahoots with a journalist who had then leaked it in her newspaper. It is perhaps not surprising that he believed this, but I had given my word to the contrary, and so had Gaia Servadio, with whom in my absence Peter had insisted on a meeting, which she declined, in the hope of vetting her article prior to publication. On reflection surely conspiracy was an improbable surmise. I, after all, had been the person who had signalled the *Evening Standard* article in advance, something I would surely not have done had I been in cahoots with the journalist concerned. One morning in the associates' office I ran into Harold and Bill, and decided to give them a full account of how Gaia came to be involved. Harold gave me a sympathetic hearing, though he clearly thought I'd been rash to the point of foolishness. About Bill I was less sure. He now knew where he stood, firmly in Peter's camp, and in the *Diaries* he is soon reporting this conversation back to Peter who cites it as further evidence of my guilt.

Peter had told me he didn't want me to resign, but it no longer felt that way. One edgy day followed another as I pondered on what I should do. Then one afternoon I had a call from my agent, Terry Owen, telling me that my monthly salary from the National was a week overdue. He was more convinced than I that there was an innocent explanation for this, and was surprised when I asked him to telephone Peter Stevens as a matter of urgency and insist upon an explanation. He rang back later in the day in a far less sanguine state of mind. He'd phoned the National twice, but on both occasions had found no one prepared to answer his questions. A few days later he reported back to me with a horror story. I asked Terry if he could set down what he had just told me in a letter, which I received the following day. Words on paper were now my only defence.

Dear Michael,

You will remember that on Tuesday last week you queried the fact that you had not yet received from us your cheque for the National Theatre for the month of April.

I asked our accounts department to deal with this and was informed by them that although we had invoiced the National Theatre for this amount in the usual way, the money had not been received. I then asked them to telephone Mr Tomm at the National Theatre and see why the cheque had not been sent and Mr Tomm explained that he had received a written instruction from Peter Stevens 'to make no further payments to Michael Blakemore until further notice'.

On Wednesday evening I telephoned Peter Stevens as a matter of urgency to obtain an explanation of his action in stopping payment of your monthly salary cheque without informing either you or me; he was not available and I left an urgent message with his secretary for him to phone me the next day. I received no call the next day either from him or his secretary. I phoned again and was told that he was not available. I then spoke to Mr Tomm who was extremely sympathetic about the situation but said there was nothing he could do, and I asked him to convey my concern about this to Peter Stevens and to get him to call as a matter of urgency.

By Friday afternoon in spite of many telephone calls to the National and further messages left for Peter Stevens' secretary, I still had not been able to contact him.

And so late on Friday I phoned yet again and spoke to Peter Stevens' secretary and asked her to tell Mr Stevens that I did not intend to leave the office without some kind of explanation from him as to why your salary was being stopped, and that I considered the withholding of your contractual salary to be improper and, in fact, illegal. Later that evening she telephoned me with a message from Mr Stevens that he was instructing Mr Tomm to send a cheque for six months' retainer fee in advance. I told her that this was entirely unacceptable because we had not agreed terms for your new contract, and that until we did payments must continue to be made under the existing arrangements.

This morning (Monday, 10 May 1976) I have at last made contact with Peter Stevens and told him that he had no right to withhold payments which are contractually due to you; he has now agreed to pass the necessary instructions to resume payments under the existing agreement.

I have also arranged to see Peter Stevens on Friday to discuss the details of a revision of your existing contract.

Best wishes,

Yours sincerely,

Terence Owen

My resignation had become a foregone conclusion. What had happened to Jonathan was now happening to me. He had had his productions taken away, I was having my salary withdrawn. I wasn't being sacked, nothing so provocative or newsworthy. I was simply being put in a position where it was impossible to stay. I sat down and myself wrote a letter.

Dear Peter,

The waters have now got so muddied with misunderstandings and mistrust that I think the best thing I can do all round is to resign as an Associate Director. If you want me to continue an association with the National on a freelance basis I'm happy to do so, though you may think we have got a little beyond that.

I would, however, like to get the record as straight as possible, so may I make two points:

1. The confidentiality of the paper I read at the associates' meeting on 17 March was, and has remained, absolute.

2. As I have already told you, although I knew in advance of the article on the National Theatre that appeared in the *Evening Standard* on 12 April, I neither encouraged it nor furnished it with the least information. On the contrary, I was disturbed and embarrassed by it, because I knew it would be entirely counter-productive to what I hoped to achieve with my paper from within.

There have been two actions on my part which certainly haven't helped the situation. One was agreeing in principle to do the Nichols play at whatever theatre he chose without first talking it over with you. Then as now no negotiations had been entered into and no date fixed, but in retrospect I can see that my acceptance of the play, even as an understanding between friends, could be interpreted as hostile. Similarly, it was unfortunate that I was out of the country when the *Standard* piece appeared.

For my part I have to register protest and shock that last month the executive gave written instructions to the Accounts Department to stop all moneys to me without the least discussion with my agent, or even notification to either Terry Owen or myself of what had been done. And further, that when my agent learnt of the situation it was six days before anyone would pick up the telephone to discuss the matter despite repeated calls daily on his part. I gather that Peter Stevens has arranged to meet Terry Owen this Friday to discuss the terms of a new contract. I would now suggest the meeting be used to agree the formalities of my resignation.

Finally, though my departure is of some consequence to me, it is a lesser matter than the continued welfare of the National Theatre. So I would like to wish you and the associates purpose and exuberance in the days ahead.

Yours ever,

Michael Blakemore

By a curious coincidence on the day I resigned from the National Larry decided to attend a performance of *Plunder*, which was playing that night in the Lyttelton Theatre. I knew he would be offered a drink in the VIP Room during the two intervals so I thought I would go to greet him in the second interval by which time the strength of the evening would be better established. However, when I arrived he wasn't there; he'd gone to inspect the new Olivier auditorium which was some months away from its official opening. I tracked him down. He was surprisingly cool and I realised that he thought I'd been avoiding him. We made conversation and I expressed a small reservation about the design of the building, to which with cold-eyed sarcasm he replied, 'What shall we do then? Pull the whole thing down? Is that what you want?' I wasn't offended because I knew I'd been misunderstood, and in any case I had a card to play. Just before we were expected to return for the last act of *Plunder* I told him, 'I've just resigned.' Quite literally his jaw dropped. He stared at me for a full three seconds before crooning, 'You wouldn't care to join Joanie and me for a little light supper after the show?'

The three of us went to a restaurant in the Old Brompton Road and I told the Oliviers about my paper and the circumstances of my reading it to the associates. I thought Larry would enjoy the drama of it, but he was a man whom it was very hard to impress. What most exercised him was that my money had been stopped. 'That's a shitty thing to do! Absolutely shitty!' he said, and I thought of him at the very beginning of his career, the son of a penniless clergyman, trying to get by at a time when, if you were broke, you were on your own.

The most remarkable thing about him that evening was that he had entirely recovered his old looks. The pointed nose had gone, and once again he had a face that reminded me of one of the big cats, with watchful unintimidated eyes and a mouth over which his tongue occasionally flicked. During the next decade, as he recovered from one illness only to be struck down by another, his appearance would change back and forth with the same exactitude with which he had once put on and taken off one of his brilliant make-ups.

His career was again miraculously on the upswing. With Joan's brother, David Plowright, he had embarked on a series of television films, in at least two of which he gave performances on a level with his best work, in *Daphne Laureola* and Pinter's *The Collection*. International films would follow, some as good as *Marathon Man*, many as bad as *The Jazz Singer*, but all paying

313

extremely well. He had found his last cause – providing for the security of his family – and he set about it with his usual resolve.

For more than ten years he had given his life to the National, and had ended up with no savings and with his health imperilled. I suspect that in some way he felt he'd been made a fool of, especially now that the ethos he had tried so hard to foster at the National had been abandoned. From now on he would dance to a different tune. In the years to come his capacity for hard work, his resilience, his ability to spring surprises would amaze me as it had always done, but the fact remained that the reputation of his greatest days was being buried, little by little, under a succession of indifferent movies. His television work was more interesting and in the mix there were moments of the true Olivier, his death scene in the excellent adaptation of *Brideshead Revisited* for instance, but there were never quite enough of them.

My letter of resignation received a prompt reply from Peter Hall, who was as intent on laying down his own paper trail as I was. It begins, as had Jonathan's, with 'My dear Michael', and expresses 'sadness' and 'regret' as well as warm assurances of sincerity and good faith. He then goes on to put an exonerating slant on the immediate circumstances that prompted my resignation. I was having none of that, so I sat down and wrote another, longer letter rebutting him point by point. It was hard work and took me most of the day to compose.

Back came a reply of equal length. The 'My' had been dropped, I was now plain 'Dear Michael', and the letter began the only way now available to him. 'I don't think either of us should labour the question of the salary payments, disturbing though that aspect of the matter has been to you. To me it seems that the contractual misunderstanding was truly coincidental and it should not, if we are honest with each other, somehow become the cause of your resignation when we both know it is not . . . I would have thought that your knowledge of how well Peter Stevens is disposed towards you would have prevented your loading the sequence with a significance it honestly doesn't have.'

I now sat at home, waiting for a call from John Goodwin to agree the wording of the press release announcing my resignation. When, after a few days, I'd heard nothing I decided to initiate the call myself before I was buttonholed by a journalist demanding a statement. I told John I had no wish to stir up trouble for the National and he sounded pleased; and that I would be keeping the contents of my paper confidential, whereupon pleasure became delight. By the time I suggested we add to the press release that I would be returning on a freelance basis to direct *The Madras House* he and I were the best of friends. I then asked him that he sketch out something on paper about which we could both agree, and that he send it to me as soon as possible because I wanted to be prepared should one of the papers get wind of the resignation ahead of time. This he promised faithfully to do.

More days passed, then one night after dinner I went to the lavatory and pissed a stream of bright red blood. I was very shaken, but it was too late to visit a doctor so I rang Jonathan for an instant diagnosis. 'It's not a negligible symptom,' he replied carefully. 'You should see a good urologist as soon as you can,' and he gave me the name of a specialist. 'He's a strange old bird but he knows what he's doing.' The following morning the bleeding had stopped but I seemed to be developing a fever so I took myself to bed.

This is where I was, still waiting for mail from John Goodwin, when the telephone rang. It was Sydney Edwards, theatre correspondent for the *Evening Standard*, who had heard that I'd resigned. I told him I'd agreed to a joint statement with the National Theatre, the exact wording of which was still being determined, and suggested that he first speak to John Goodwin. He could ring me back later that morning. When his call came he told me he had made three attempts to reach Goodwin but on each occasion was told he was out of the office. I then asked for a further fifteen minutes to try and reach John myself. All right, Sydney agreed, but only fifteen minutes; he had a deadline to meet.

Much agitated, I then rang John's office but could only speak to his assistant, Vivien Wallace. She told me John had gone to the country and would be away from the office all day. Sydney rang back on the dot and I improvised my way through a statement. He then told me that he'd heard from two independent sources that I'd had major disagreements with Peter Hall and was this true? No, I responded; there were a few differences about policy as there often are but it was an amicable departure and I would be continuing my association with the National on a freelance basis. Sydney seemed satisfied and the conversation ended. Ten minutes later the phone rang again. It was John Goodwin. 'How did it go?' he asked breathlessly.

'Where have you been?' I demanded. 'They told me you'd gone to the country for the day!'

'No, I've been in the office all morning. I just felt it better if the story came straight from you. Without my input. But what did you say?'

I started to fill him in as best I could, but when I came to the bit about having some differences about policy, he exploded. 'But you promised you'd say nothing negative!' he screamed.

'And you promised you'd tell me what to say!' I shouted back, with matching anger. I wondered if there wasn't a kind of madness emerging from the corridors and offices of the National Theatre. Whatever it was, I no longer had any interest in dealing with it.

The Tynans, who had not yet left for America, had heard about my resignation and asked me round to Thurloe Square. We sat in front of the fire while I relived the whole story for them. Later that night I woke up with abdominal pains which came in waves so increasingly severe that I started vomiting. Dawn was breaking when I was taken to Emergency at the Royal Free Hospital where I at last learnt the cause of the bleeding. I had kidney stones. Was it now my turn to be ill? These attacks would recur every couple of months until eventually I was forced to have the stones and one calcified lobe of my left kidney surgically removed. Before the end of the year another seriously uncomfortable condition came out of ambush, a fistula, which led to a further four weeks in hospital having it attended to. During the two years that followed my resignation not only my health but my personal life began to fall apart, due, it must be said, entirely to my own recklessness. Only one thing in my life appeared to be holding up, and that was my work. In the theatre world I still had many friends, a number of whom were in a position to offer me employment, and my calendar was soon full.

I made one last attempt to set the record straight with my fellow associates. I knew they would be receiving a very selective account of why I had departed, so I had copies made of all the relevant correspondence – my agent's letter about the withholding of money, my letter of resignation and the correspondence with Peter that ensued – and sent a bundle to each of the associates. For John Schlesinger, still abroad, I also included his copy of the paper and an account of the way all the other copies had been returned to me. He replied on Paramount Studios stationery with a charming letter that began, 'My dear Michael' (quite okay on this occasion). He thanked me for sending him his copy of the paper and added '*I* see no reason for returning it to you! I must confess I think a lot of what you say is worth careful consideration.'

I also had a letter from Harold, big black writing on both sides of a white page, in which he said 'The whole matter of your resignation has disturbed me,' followed by the suggestion that we meet for a drink. I heard later that at an associates' meeting he demanded answers from Peter to some pointed questions, and made it clear that the answers he received were not satisfactory.

317

That done, all I now wanted was to put the National behind me and get on with the next leg of my career. But this was very difficult to do. Kathleen Tynan and Gaia Servadio, both with wide connections in the world of newspapers, rang me independently of each other with an identical warning: the official line coming out of the National Theatre press office was that I had resigned because I had been caught out in a leak to the press. Knowledge of my paper's existence, if not of its contents, had become widespread and I kept getting calls from reputable journalists asking if they could look at it. One of these was from Max Hastings, writing for the *Standard*, another was from Mervyn Jones of the *New Statesman*, both of whom would go on to write excellent pieces about the National but without my help.

Another enquirer was John Elsom, the theatre critic for the BBC publication *The Listener*. He had been commissioned to complete the history of the National Theatre after its author, Nicholas Tomalin, had been killed reporting the Yom Kippur War. Elsom had been snooping along the corridors of the National Theatre, and he had made some uncomfortable discoveries of his own which he was eager to discuss with me. However, to him and to anyone who asked, I said I was not free to disclose the contents of my paper. On top of all this I kept on receiving through the post the minutes of the ongoing associates' meetings, now proceeding without me. I had no idea why, since I was no longer in the National's employ.

This lingering aftermath became so oppressive that when a chance to escape it for a while came along, I seized it. The Peter Summerton Foundation in Australia invited me to conduct a seminar with a group of aspiring directors in Sydney. They would pay my fare, my accommodation and a small fee, and I would be there for about a month. One morning I was sorting out things for the journey when, among the morning's mail, the latest minutes of an associates' meeting fell through the front door. As usual I began skimming through the contents until I was brought up short by one particular paragraph. This was Item 6, which I read not once but twice. I was disgusted and very angry, and I immediately started scribbling the draft of a letter to Peter Hall.

Dear Peter,

In the copy of *Notes from the Associates' Dinner* for 26 May 1976 circulated to me I have come across the following:

6. RESIGNATION OF MICHAEL BLAKEMORE.

Noted that press report had appeared before date of agreed NT press release and that MB apparently endorsed that there had been policy disagreements . . . PH made quite clear that if any adverse press comments originating from M. Blakemore occurred between now and next year then the offer (of *The Madras House*) would be withdrawn.

May I simplify the situation for you by myself withdrawing the offer of my services for future work with the National Theatre? When I originally suggested to John Goodwin that mention of a freelance production of *The Madras House* be included in the press announcement of my resignation it was intended solely to give credibility to the proposition that my departure from the National was amicable. It was not to safeguard for myself an avenue of employment.

I followed this with a full account of my dealings with John Goodwin over the press release and concluded the draft as follows:

You know as well as I do the reasons for my resignation, in the light of which the statement reported by Sydney Edwards is a great deal milder than it might have been had I been of a mind to make trouble. I have not made public the very questionable circumstances that triggered my departure (i.e., the fact that in breach of contract my salary was stopped)

319

nor the contents of the paper that I read to the associates
a couple of months ago.

You will remember that at your request the many hours
of discussion that followed upon the reading of that paper
remained unminuted. So after five years with the National,
eight productions later, the only record of my departure in
the theatre's annals is one ambiguous paragraph confirming
improper relations with the press. This attack on my probity
is one which I intend to fight.

This was a letter I never sent. What was the point? Peter had
found his strategy for discrediting the paper, and me along with
it, and the truth was of no interest to him. It was time I recognised that I had acquired an enemy; I had become someone to be
neutralised, expunged, written off. He had an organisation and
a press office behind him. I was sitting at home, with a domestic
telephone. However, there was one thing I could still do. I rang
John Elsom and told him I was giving him my paper to do with
it what he wanted. Then I continued packing for Australia.

A few weeks later I found mail from England waiting for me
in my Sydney motel bedroom. It was one of Peter's 'My dear
Michael' letters, discussing the future of *Plunder*. Before long it
would be coming to the end of its run but the business had been
consistently excellent and the National were considering either
extending its stay at the Lyttelton or transferring the show to the
West End. What were my thoughts about this? I replied that
Item 6 on the Minutes of the recent associates' meeting pre-
cluded me from accepting ongoing work at the National, but since
Plunder predated my resignation I was prepared to redirect the
show, preferably in the West End.

Accordingly in due course, and some time after I'd returned to
London, Eddie Kulukundis agreed to mount a transfer, a bold
undertaking given the size of the cast and the show's many scene
changes. A theatre was found, the Savoy, the actors' agents were

telephoned and negotiations proceeded about the terms of the transfer. Suddenly, in mid-discussion, the talks broke down. The National had now decided it needed to keep *Plunder* on the South Bank to prop up the existing repertoire. The assumption was that I would no longer want to be involved, so to redirect it they had assigned my assistant from the original production, Sebastian Graham Jones. However I wasn't having that. I had loyalties to Ben Travers, to such members of the original cast as we were able to retain, and indeed to my own work. I said I would direct it myself.

Each morning I took sandwiches to the rehearsal room and stayed there throughout the day. Then one lunchtime Christopher Morahan, who had now become an associate director, came down to the empty rehearsal room looking for me. He was an old friend whom I had come to know when he was making a series of films for the BBC from original scripts by Peter Nichols – brilliant work from both men. Christopher insisted I join him for lunch in the canteen. Otherwise, except for some actors, I encountered none of the people I had once worked alongside.

So *Plunder* stayed at the National Theatre to complete 147 performances. It never moved to the West End. The next production to do so was Alan Ayckbourn's *Bedroom Farce*, co-directed by Peter Hall.

AFTERWARDS

It would be some ten years before the issues I had raised in my paper would receive official vindication, though by that time it was a little late to start closing the stable door. Peter Hall had long ago galloped off with his royalties and, having depleted them in divorce proceedings, was now taking leaves of absence from the National Theatre of up to five months to make up the new short-fall. In 1986, following an investigation by the *Sunday Times* Insight Team into the subsidised theatre headlined 'Laughing All the Way to the Bank', the Arts Council appointed an accountant, Sir Richard Cork, to chair a committee examining exactly the things which had concerned me, even down to the matter 'of agents who negotiate for transfer receipts on behalf of artistic directors against their own theatres'. The committee proposed sensible guidelines for the subsidised theatres, which of course should have been in place from the beginning. Peter Hall's formid-able strengths would then have been put more squarely at the service of the organisation that employed him, bringing benefits to both the National Theatre and his own reputation.

According to the *Sunday Times* the report recommended: first, with regard to money earned from transfers, that the theatres should receive at least 50 per cent of whatever the individuals in the creative team, other than the playwright, collectively earned; and second, with regard to leaves of absence, directors should be expected to remain at their posts for at least forty weeks in any one year.

In August 1976, when I returned from Australia after the seminar, these reforms seemed impossibly distant. In any case

I was now embarking on a freelance career and was doing my best to put the National behind me. I had *Separate Tables* to ready for production and there were two shows under discussion for the following year, *Privates on Parade* with Denis Quilley for Trevor Nunn at the RSC and *Candida* with Deborah Kerr for Eddie Kulukundis in the West End. Before I started rehearsals on the Rattigan play in September, there was just time to take myself off to France and stare at the waves for three weeks. *Separate Tables* proved an extremely taxing assignment, not artistically but for reasons of health. During my wander around the world I had been slowly developing an anal abscess, and anyone who has experienced this condition will need no instruction about the derivation of the expression 'a pain in the arse'. It is excruciating. For the entire third week of rehearsal I was in hospital having it dealt with, a procedure which relieved the pain but left me with a further operation to look forward to some months later. We opened on tour in Billingham, and since it was uncomfortable both to sit and to stand, I conducted the technical rehearsals from a recliner stretched out in one of the theatre aisles. The company, splendidly led by John Mills, rallied around their ailing director and, working against the clock but oddly exhilarated, we somehow reached the point where we were ready for the opening performance on the Saturday night.

The following morning, lying flat in bed and no longer obliged to get out of it, I opened the *Sunday Times* to confront a half-page article by Stephen Fay entitled 'Tamburlaine the Greedy?' Reading on, it was soon evident that the bias of the piece was very much directed towards the question mark. It described a campaign against Peter Hall 'characterised by bitchery, exaggeration, and even misinformation which would gladden the heart of the most cynical CIA man'. I, together with Ken Tynan, Jonathan Miller and Joan Plowright, were identified as the principal conspirators, embittered because Olivier's crown had been torn from our clutches. There was a police line-up of photographs of all of us, and I learnt that I had left the National with 'ever ascending degrees of acrimony'. One anonymous source, interviewed by Stephen Fay and referred to only as a 'veteran', told him of 'an incredibly spiteful and envious campaign'.

Even if such a campaign existed it was surely clear from my recent itinerary that I couldn't have played a very effective part in it. Had Fay bothered to consult me I would freely have confessed to following with relish certain hard-hitting articles about the National by Max Hastings in the *Evening Standard*. I would also have pleaded guilty to gobbling up any scraps of unkind gossip about Peter Hall that came my way. This is human behaviour. But to assert that I was a principal figure in a planned campaign against him was ridiculous. If there was a campaign of any sort it was more likely to be emanating, via the National Theatre's Press Office, from Peter Hall himself.

In the *Diaries* this way of responding to his enemies, through a sympathetic journalist, adheres to a pattern. His tactic when faced with criticism was to sidestep the charge and instead attack the good faith of whoever was making it. Thus the signatories of the letter to *The Times* – Richard Eyre, Lindsay Anderson, Joan Littlewood, etc. – who questioned the National's growing monopoly of resources are characterised along with his other enemies as 'public moralists and private shits'. When the journalist Terry Coleman asks about 'the old Miller–Blakemore accusations', Hall writes, 'I just blew and called them a couple of bastards'. Elsewhere in the *Diaries*, he draws a parallel between his critics and the loathsome characters in Ben Jonson's *Volpone*, a play which he is just about to rehearse. 'Malice,' he insists, 'masquerading as moral virtue.' Such a strategy is extremely effective. The target is forced to neglect his case for the moment and rush to the defence of his own character, and the smear is invariably more vivid and memorable than the accuracy or otherwise of the issue that has been raised.

Stephen Fay's piece made me angry all over again, and getting angry again made me even angrier. I wrote to him demanding equal time. He replied courteously and when I returned to London we made a date to have afternoon tea at his club, the Garrick. From the steely affability with which he greeted me I knew he believed what he had written and wasn't going to change his mind. We sat beneath one of the club's lofty moulded ceilings, with a pot of tea between us, as I struggled to find some way to put my case.

'You say I participated in an extremely spiteful and envious campaign, but your source for this is someone you only describe as "a veteran". Who is he?'

'Ah, that is something I'm not at liberty to say,' he replied with impregnable good nature.

'You mean I'm accused of something and I'm not allowed to know the name of my accuser?'

'All I can say is that it came from a very distinguished source – very distinguished *indeed*.'

I felt completely at a loss. Without knowing who made the charge, how could I properly address it? From the *Diaries* it is just possible that the very distinguished source was Peter Hall himself. Just a few days before the article appears he reports 'having a very interesting couple of hours with Stephen Fay . . . He asked me to speak frankly. As I trust him, I did.' When the piece appears that Sunday Peter is pleased to find it 'balanced and clear'.

I left the Garrick feeling vulnerable in a new sort of way, because what I had picked up from Stephen Fay, apart from my inability to make my case, was that there was now a public perception about me taking hold that hadn't been there before. I was becoming – what? That Australian troublemaker perhaps? At any rate some sort of outsider, something I had never before felt during my time in England. I had seen the same sort of thing happen to Ken Tynan as he was eased to the periphery of English life, and I didn't much like it.

In the theatre world itself, among people who had known me in other and better contexts, I felt as secure as I ever had. My relations with the West End managements were excellent – people like Michael White, Eddie Kulukundis and Duncan Weldon, with whom I had already worked – and over the coming years they would offer me more shows to direct than I had time for. However, among certain journalists, whose trade is to mould opinion, in the course of which they have no choice but to take sides, and among the sort of people who sit on the boards of theatres, I would have an uneasy relationship for a long time to come. Even twenty years later when the National Theatre published a short history of its first thirty-four years, I would still have to read that I was 'the disappointed Crown Prince of the Olivier years' who had to resign 'after an abortive press scandal worked up by his friends'. The Hall version of events had become history.

In this sort of climate making a clear distinction between a legitimate concern that one is being misjudged and what is probably no more than a neurotic reflex becomes very difficult. An example might be my departure in 1980 from the newly reconstructed Lyric Hammersmith theatre. I had been invited by its Artistic Director, Bill Thomley, to join him for a six-month season with the title 'Resident Director'. I would be staging four productions one after another, a formidable workload but no more demanding than I'd already experienced at the Glasgow Citizens Theatre. Rehearsals had barely started on the first play, Michael Frayn's *Make and Break*, when Bill Thomley became seriously ill and had to give up his position. I was now responsible for an entire season of plays but with an indeterminate status in the organisation.

However, one by one the productions reached the stage with greater or lesser degrees of success and by the final show, *The Wild Duck*, I was beginning to feel quite proud of what we'd achieved. No new theatre could have hoped for a better start. I decided to throw my hat into the ring when the Theatre Board convened to decide on Bill Thomley's official successor. I was in a Sydney motel trying to set up a small film and the sun had only just risen when I was woken by a telephone call from the Chairman of the Board informing me I wouldn't be getting the job. He was apologetic but not inclined to explain why, and when he hung up I was left blinking in the horizontal shafts of sunlight slicing through a gap in the curtains with only my surmises for company. There was a woman from the BBC on the Board who from the start had treated Bill Thomley's departure as some sort of inexplicable coup – could it have been her? There was also an accountant employed by the National – maybe it was him? But there was no way of knowing what part, if any, Chinese whispers had played in such a decision. First I was dismayed, then deeply depressed. But a few days later I didn't care one way or another. I had arrived at the somewhat arrogant conclusion that it was their loss, not mine, and, like Coriolanus, turned my back on the lot of them, on boards and committees and the politics of large organisations. Again like Coriolanus, I told myself 'There is a world elsewhere'. And fortunately this proved to be the case.

A year or so later I was revenged for this rejection – a revenge of the most interesting kind. Michael Codron was about to produce a new comedy, *Noises Off*, which he'd asked me to direct, and we were discussing somewhere to try it out before coming to the West End. He suggested a couple of venues before saying, 'I suppose going back to the Lyric Hammersmith is out of the question for you?'

'Not at all,' I said. I didn't have to think about it. I had no animus against Peter James, the candidate chosen over me, but more than that, the stage was ideally suited to facilitate a smooth and inexpensive transfer. So that's where *Noises Off* was given its first performance. It then went on to the Savoy Theatre where it ran for four years and made so much money for the Lyric Hammersmith that at one point it rescued the theatre from acute financial embarrassment.

In due course this same play would take me to Broadway and to a wealth of new possibilities and friendships, and it would be there, in that American welcome, that I could finally put behind me the bad dream that the National Theatre had become. Later on I would return to the big concrete building on the South Bank and stage productions for all three of the National's subsequent artistic directors – Richard Eyre, Trevor Nunn and Nick Hytner – and, I think they would all agree, without a single cross word between us.

However, before then there would be one formidable hurdle to clear, the publication in 1983 of the Peter Hall *Diaries*. By this time Peter's career had gone from a bad patch to a spectacularly good one, at the centre of which was his justly admired production of *Amadeus*. The National was now fully up and running and deemed a success, and Hall's enemies were scattered and in disarray. By the end of the *Diaries* he is clearly riding high. Even his domestic life, to which he had made brief references throughout the volume, has undergone a startling change for the better after he meets the opera singer Maria Ewing. A few pages from the end of the volume he tells the reader that he is 'deeply in love' and that he and Maria Ewing will be making a life together in the New Year. The last entry in the book describes an *Evening Standard* award ceremony in which he is given a special award for his twenty-five years of service to the theatre. And so the curtain falls on a standing ovation.

Peter Hall was far too intelligent a man to risk blatant fibbing, but there are other ways of not quite telling the truth, notably what you decide to omit. An example of the discreet redactions in the *Diaries*, and one close to home, was the way Peter deals with my resignation. Its immediate cause goes unreported – the withholding of my salary. He merely records the arrival of my letter of resignation and his response to it: 'I can't say I'm surprised.' There is no mention of the indignation expressed in that letter, nor of the lengthy correspondence that followed which was to keep both of us extremely busy during the rest of that week. Instead the impression is given of someone loping, friendless and rejected, along the corridors of the theatre until, tormented by remorse, he takes a length of rope and, Judas-like, hangs himself.

In the summer of 1983 I was again in Biarritz for a few weeks quite unaware that the Peter Hall *Diaries* were about to be launched upon the world, and that soon his version of events would be the only one available. One morning I went to the letterbox and found that someone had sent me a parcel. It was a proof copy of the *Diaries*. There was no letter enclosed, and since the proofs had no index I decided the only thing to do was read it through from the beginning – which I did over two extremely distressing days.

Why, I wondered, had I been selected to see it in advance? Was someone worried that I might be provoked into taking legal action? The book, in my opinion, certainly misrepresented events and probably gave me grounds for defamation. However, I was aware how dangerous the English justice system was when it came to libel, and I had a temperamental horror of going to law, even had I the funds to do so.

The things I disliked about the book were not exclusively to do with me. I was exasperated by Peter's artistic epiphanies, which he experienced in advance of any forthcoming production, and which he always managed to find time for in the midst of his high-powered schedule. There was one in particular that I could hardly believe. Reflecting on *Hamlet*, he decides that Claudius is 'in a sense the most honest person in the play'. This is his judgement on a character whose first words are a murderous public lie. It occurred to me that if I was casting *Hamlet*, Peter would make a very plausible Claudius. This in turn led me to wondering what sort of a diary Claudius himself would have kept had he managed to find the time. I sat down at once and inscribed on the top of a page 'The Claudius Diaries'. I then started to write, and was soon laughing out loud at my own jokes. Without being identified as such, Larry slipped effortlessly into the part of the murdered King, I modestly assumed the mantle of Hamlet, Ralph Richardson, at that time a Peter loyalist, was Polonius, and the Town Crier, to whom I had Claudius leak numerous exclusives, was a local London rag. Writing this parody was one way I could answer back and when I finished it my mood was much improved.

I was in New York with Michael Frayn rehearsing *Noises Off* at the time the *Diaries* were to be published and reviewed in London to enormous hoo-hah. The *Sunday Times*, I'd learnt in advance, intended to serialise them, so I sent a copy of my 'Claudius Diaries' to their Sunday rival, the *Observer*, who agreed to publish them concurrently, and gave them pride of place on their editorial page, with a photograph of Peter, looking shifty and wearing a lop-sided crown. With the passing of the years the piece has lost a good deal of its comic point, since the reader needs to be familiar not just with the Shakespeare play, but with the content and style of the Hall *Diaries*. But it can still make me smile.

In New York Michael Frayn and I were visited by his beautiful teenage daughter Rebecca, and after work the three of us would first find a restaurant, eat well, and then set out on quests to locate the site of the old jazz clubs that had once symbolised the exuberance and liberty of American life for many young Englishmen of Michael's generation on their first visit to Manhattan. Towards midnight, when the British papers, fresh from their flight across the Atlantic, would be delivered to the newsvendor on 42nd Street, we would rush uptown again to check that my piece had appeared in the *Observer* or to peruse other journals for reviews or opinions. Michael's particular gift for humorously empathising with both the highs and lows of a friend's career was much employed that week in both capacities, as an excoriating review of the *Diaries* in one paper was followed by a rapturous one in another.

*

A month or two later *Noises Off* opened in America to a wonderful reception, and it was all behind me. Earlier that same year, in May, Harold Pinter had quietly resigned from the National, where he had just directed Giraudoux's *The Trojan War Will Not Take Place*. He had been working at a theatre where there was no one in charge. A 'ghost ship' was the way Alan Ayckbourn described the South Bank building when he was there directing *Way Upstream*. Peter was constantly absent – in New York, at Glyndebourne, and in Bayreuth, where he spent almost five months staging *The Ring*. Harold had intended to make his departure as low-keyed as possible but three months later he had clearly changed his mind when he gave a full-page interview to Michael Owen of the *Evening Standard* headed 'Pinter: My Split with Hall'.

He now spelt out why he had resigned. He 'did not approve of the way the theatre was being run'. However, his reasons for deciding to go public were much more personal and related to the publication of the *Diaries*. 'Within the book there are certain entries I found referring to my private life in 1975 over which I was never consulted and my permission was never asked.' He was referring to the revelations about his affair with Antonia Fraser and the break-up of his marriage to Vivien Merchant, which is first broached in the entry for the 23 March: 'Harold is in love with Antonia Fraser . . . The romance began some six weeks ago. Since when it has raged passionately.' The couple's ongoing story now becomes one of the threads in the narrative.

There was another reason, undisclosed to the *Standard*, why Pinter was so enraged. He had not been the only person at the National who had found solace outside an unsteady marriage. Peter Hall, too, was in the midst of a serious affair, and indeed it was the similarity of their situations that drew the two friends closer together. Peter had even gone so far as to share a second home with his new partner, a development which was to have its complications from the moment he met Maria Ewing. There is absolutely no reason why Peter should have been obliged to disclose any of this in his *Diaries* if he didn't want to. However, Pinter considered it unforgivable that he had not exercised a similar restraint over the details of a close friend's private life.

Suddenly Harold and I were on the same side. He and Antonia rang me in New York when the 'Claudius Diaries' were published to offer me gleeful congratulations. 'Every target a bullseye!' said Harold. However, except at social events to which we were both invited, we didn't see a great deal of each other. As he did with many of his friends, he sometimes sent me one of his poems, and when I telephoned to thank him (which he expected) I would usually encounter a stern message on the answering machine, not a word longer than it needed to be. On one occasion the machine was malfunctioning and all I heard was the one phrase repeated over and over again: '*I'm not in! . . . I'm not in! . . . I'm not in!*' It might have been one of his shorter plays.

Increasingly he seemed to me to be at some sort of crossroads. He was withdrawing from writing full-length plays, and instead was pitching much of his energy into political activism. It is not many successful, well-off men who, after fifty, passionately commit themselves to radical causes. Harold seemed determined never to come to comfortable terms with a comfortable life. Instead he went seeking causes and, if it had to be so, the unpopularity that came with them. Perhaps it was his way of confronting the problem of success, trying to live a proper life behind the simplistic facade of a reputation. Whatever it was, I found it admirable.

One evening I went to have a drink with him at the workroom he maintained off a side street behind his house in Camden Square. I was about to stage *Sweet Bird of Youth* in America, which Harold had already directed at the Haymarket and with the same formidable leading actress, Lauren Bacall, and I thought he might have some advice for me. He uncorked one bottle of white wine and then another, as we discussed this and other matters over a couple of hours. As I got up to go Harold said, 'Michael, there's just one thing I'd like to say . . .' I saw him marshal his expression into something appropriately grave. There was a Pinter pause. 'I would like to apologise for returning your paper to you that night at the associates' meeting.' He didn't enlarge on this. He had said precisely what he wanted to say, but I was touched and amused that he had made this effort to settle his ethical accounts. It had been generous, perhaps a shade pompous and something not really required of him, certainly by me, but I felt gladdened that he had done so and – my mood already improved by the best part of a bottle of wine – I set out to search for a taxi.

It was easy to stay in touch with Larry, partly because one way or another he was always in the news, and partly because the Oliviers were so generous with their hospitality. Every year they gave lavish Christmas parties at which many of the actors who had been part of the National Theatre company would once again come together. Seeing them all there under the same roof you realised what ripples Larry's National had sent around the world, in the same way that Tyrone Guthrie's time at the Old Vic before the war had seen the flowering of many of the great talents of the earlier generation – Olivier himself, Richardson, Guinness, Laughton, Michael Redgrave and many more. After the Oliviers bought their country place in Sussex, the Malthouse, they regularly invited National Theatre alumni to spend time with them, and on Sundays the house had the Shakespearean dimension of a Court in Exile. I wasn't much good at being a courtier so I didn't participate in these events but I often spoke to Larry on the phone or saw him on my own.

One occasion was when I visited him in hospital after yet another of his medical calamities. The radiation which he had received years before for cancer of the prostate (and about which there was now some doubt as to whether it had been correctly diagnosed) had left him with some inert tissue floating about in his abdomen and this, now wrapped around his urethra, was strangling a kidney. He was taken to hospital in great pain and had to have the kidney removed. A few years previously I'd had a similar operation for kidney stones, but at a much younger age, and I had a sharp idea of what he must have been through.

I was trying to decide on a suitable present to take with me to hospital (of course, a half-bottle of champagne, his favourite tipple!) when the telephone rang. It was Harold Pinter, who was still much exercised by Peter's long absences from his post at the National. He was thinking about going public with a joint letter to *The Times* and, since I knew him best, asked if I could prevail on Larry to be a signatory. I told Harold I would be seeing him in two days' time, and if it seemed appropriate would broach the matter.

I duly arrived at the hospital with my half-bottle and was shown into a private room which might have been a liquor store running a special on champagne. On every available surface there were bottles of all shapes and sizes from modest halves like mine to vintage magnums, and the space glittered with gold-foil tops. They had flooded in from all over the place, from New York, from Hollywood, and I realised as never before that I was in the presence of Serious Fame. These were tokens of obeisance to someone whom the world thought of as one of a kind. And the world was probably right.

To the patient this tribute of champagne couldn't have mattered less, though he thanked me for adding to the collection. He was making a good recovery but was still in some pain, and he asked me to help him reach a more comfortable position on his pillows. We clung to each other as he eased himself, little by little, up the bed and came to rest. We began to talk and I debated whether it was appropriate to mention the letter. Finally I decided just to pass on what Harold had said to me on the telephone and scrupulously avoid anything that resembled persuasion.

He heard me out, thought for a moment, then gently shook his head. 'No, I can't do that,' he said. He didn't have to explain himself. His rueful smile spoke for him. Of course Peter Hall had been his usurper; of course he had taken the National in directions that Larry deplored. But Peter was only a single director among what would eventually become a line of many. In the meantime there was only one institution, one National Theatre, which Larry had helped bring into being and which might prove his lasting memorial. What was the point of redressing a temporary wrong? It would be like spraying graffiti on his own monument. I understood him completely, and had never admired him more. I reported back to Harold and after due consideration the idea of writing to *The Times* was dropped.

On another occasion I had visited Larry at the Malthouse, where increasingly he was spending most of his time. Joan instructed me about train times and told me I would be met by Larry's New Zealand nurse who would drive me back to the house. She was very young and very Antipodean, and as we talked during the journey it became clear that she had only the vaguest idea who her illustrious patient was. She'd never seen him on stage or at the movies, and to her he was simply another frail elderly gentleman needing attention. Larry was waiting for me when I entered the large living room, and he rose to greet me with his right arm in a sling. He'd had a fall in the garden and badly sprained his wrist. He seemed a little nervous, and had that faint air of apology old people sometimes display when they are anxious that a failing memory and their withdrawal from the world will make them poor company.

'Hello, old friend,' he said stretching out his good hand, and I was momentarily surprised by the intimacy of his welcome. Then I thought about it, and realised that that was exactly what we were, old friends, going back a quarter of a century. The New Zealand nurse hovered for a moment and then withdrew. 'She's a compatriot of yours,' Larry said to me in an aside. 'Sweet girl. Very helpful. Can't remember her name.'

He led me to the dining table to one side of the room and I noticed it was set for two.

'Joanie wanted this to be just you and I,' he said. 'She's resting upstairs. Got a show tonight. *The Shrew* at Chichester.' I wondered if my visit might be providing his much younger wife with a welcome respite. Lunch was provided by two rather smart, assured young women, the sort who manage to find an interesting temporary job while their lives wait upon a proper outcome. We ate steamed salmon, new potatoes and peas. 'Funny, when I was a boy salmon was considered the rarest delicacy. Now people eat it all the time,' he said. The New Zealand nurse popped back to see that everything was going as it should be.

When the conversation was becoming a little perfunctory, I decided to talk about the time when we had once shared a stage as actors, if in rather different capacities. I recalled his two great successes as Titus Andronicus and Coriolanus, and reminded him of how he had played the mighty speech 'I am the sea', when Titus likens himself to the raging ocean and his mutilated daughter to the weeping heavens. It had been the most exciting sound I had ever heard resonate around a theatre. Larry was beginning to enjoy himself, and, confusing the two plays, gave a vigorous reading of Coriolanus' line 'You common cry of curs'. He then giggled like a cheeky boy. Mischief had always played a part in his acting, that determination to ambush an audience, to pick it up by the scruff of the neck, look it in the face and shake it. The New Zealand nurse had crept back in again and was listening intently. Larry looked at her and she blushed and slipped away. 'She's a compatriot of yours,' he confided in me once again. 'Can't remember her name. But very sweet.'

I steered the conversation to his famous death in *Coriolanus*, when, mortally wounded, he had hurled himself from a ten-foot height at his mortal enemy, Aufidius, only to be caught by the ankles at the last moment so that he dangled upside down like the dead Mussolini. The sudden intake of breath this elicited from a thousand-odd people I have only seen replicated on one other occasion. This was when Barry Humphries had a planted member of the audience, sitting in a box to one side of the circle, reach out to catch a gladiolus thrown to him from the stage, only to lose his balance and topple forward over the side. He hung there in a concealed safety harness, apparently clinging on desperately with one hand while the entire house gasped. I'm not sure the great actor and the great comedian didn't both regard their audiences in much the same way, as a kind of prey to be stalked. And that afternoon, numbered among the prey, was certainly his New Zealand nurse. She was watching us with her mouth ajar. I was pretty sure that from now on she would have a rather different view of her patient.

After lunch Larry took me for a walk in the garden to show me the various works he had undertaken and the line of protective lime trees he had planted marking a border of the property. He told me that in two days' time he would be flying to Vienna to do a couple of days on a film. This seemed extremely rash. I doubted if he could lift an overnight bag. When the time came for me to catch my train, Joan appeared and offered to drive me to the station. In the car I expressed my concern about the forthcoming trip, but she didn't seem too worried. 'It's what he wants,' she said, and I realised she was probably right. Work was what his life had always been about – hard, challenging work, not fading away in a house in the country.

I began to visualise how the trip to Vienna would turn out. On the morning of the shoot Larry would be made up and buttoned into his costume with his injured wrist tucked away out of sight. He would be taken to the set where everyone was waiting for him, and he would begin to get nervous. Someone would say 'Action!', the adrenaline would kick in, and with a heave of the chest he would say his first line and Something would happen.

Not like it used to happen, but Something, enough to propel him towards the next offer of work.

Some time later I made another visit to the Malthouse. I was about to depart for New York for a period of three or four months and I felt a need, and perhaps the obligation, to see him once more before I set off. After all, he was now eighty-two, and there had been little respite in the bouts of wretched health that had buffeted him for the best part of twenty years. This time I found him on a sofa in a small sun room, propped up with cushions. It was warm so I asked if I could take off my coat. 'That's a lovely jacket,' he said, studying the garment closely. He had always been keenly interested in appearances, in what people wore. He would notice a new tie that you might be wearing, or a change in the style of your glasses. My jacket was not new but it was well cut, a light tweed in big soft-coloured checks, and in the forties or fifties it would have been considered smart. I could see he rather coveted it.

The New Zealand nurse was nowhere to be seen but the assured young women were still in attendance, or two very like them, and they provided lunch. As before we had steamed salmon, new potatoes and peas, which we ate off a low table. And as before I guided the conversation back to the past, first to *Titus* and *Coriolanus*, then further back to the Old Vic tour of Australia just after the war when the spell of his Richard III had lured me and a number of other young Australians across the oceans and into this life of bountiful exile. I don't think Larry ever thought of the two of us as being particularly close – we regarded each other across a gulf of generational and national difference – but sometimes, like today, he would *pretend* that we were, and this was enough to be going along with. For my part I would always be in his debt and for reasons which he could only guess at.

Shortly after lunch the two young women returned to take him away for his rest, and it was only when they got him to his

338

feet that I realised how frail he had become. The cortisone which he had been taking in such large quantities, and for so long, appeared to have softened the vertebrae in his spine and his head had now sunk deep between his shoulders. Just to move, he needed a helper on either side, and as they turned and eased him, all pain and infirmity, towards the open door, his outline evoked for a moment a pale ghost of his most famous part: 'Deform'd, unfinish'd, sent before my time / Into this breathing world, scarce half made up.' Then the three of them went through the doorway, turned abruptly right, and that was the last I saw of this great Englishman.

As for Peter Hall, after he left the National he continued to hurtle down the motorway of his formidable career, usually with a full load of passengers aboard, one studying the road map, another occasionally taking the wheel, another unwrapping the sandwiches, all assuming they were there for the journey. Occasionally one of them would find himself sitting stunned and abrased on the hard shoulder, and staring in disbelief as a carload of people vanished over the hill. One such was John Bury, who had been dropped from the production of *The Ring* at Bayreuth, which the two men had been planning for years.

What Peter had in common with Larry was a driven, almost heroic capacity for work, and the qualities I had deplored in him at the National I rather came to admire in his later career. Like all of us who work freelance he used his hits to bury the memory of his flops and to set up his next string of engagements. I enjoyed a number of his many productions, among which were his *Merchant of Venice* with Dustin Hoffman and his international success with Oscar Wilde's *An Ideal Husband*. He was cleverer than the producers he worked for, and devised contracts that ensured that he, if not they, was never out of pocket whether his shows succeeded or failed. When any one producer could no longer afford him he would move on and find another.

He was constantly flying back and forth across the Atlantic, pursuing more opportunities than a single director could possibly accommodate. This provoked my New York agent, Robby Lantz, who had also briefly represented Peter, to invent a conundrum. 'Why,' Robby would enquire in his permanently amused Berliner accent, 'is Concorde a *disaster* for Anglo-American theatre?' 'Why?' you would dutifully ask him, and he would answer, 'Because it reduces the preparation time of Peter Hall's productions from eight hours to three!'

Later, Peter was to bring his career elegantly full circle by lending his name to the new Rose Theatre at Kingston upon Thames, and to an annual season of plays at the Theatre Royal, Bath. Working on his own behalf he was an impresario of inextinguishable flair, and good actors, gifted designers and numerous assistants of one sort or another would all be caught up for a time in the spell of his momentum. Theatre is partly about creating occasions of Glorious Fuss that the public will be eager to talk about and will jostle to see, and Peter was at the centre of a lifetime of them.

However, it is one thing to bang the drum on your own behalf, quite another to rewrite history in order to promote yourself and your achievements above others. When the *Diaries of Kenneth Tynan* were posthumously published, *The Times*, whether by invitation or because they were asked, gave the book to Peter Hall to review. His notice is not a good one – no surprise given that Ken's *Diaries* flatly contradict a number of his own assertions. On the first page of the Peter Hall *Diaries* he is addressing Olivier and states, 'There is one person I said categorically I could not work with – Kenneth Tynan.' He later reiterates this unambiguous position to the Board, and asks their permission to tell Tynan himself. He concludes this entry with: 'I believe the only rule is to be as truthful as possible. People never thank you for softening the blow by lying.' The confrontation duly took place two days later: 'A fascinating meeting with Ken Tynan. Before I could deliver my blow he told me he was thinking, after ten years at the National, the time has come to move on. I wonder who warned him?'

This is Ken's account of the meeting. 'He pays extravagant and sincere tribute to my part in creating the NT and adds (he is too much of the diplomat to imply "but") that he hopes I don't envisage that I'm to be thrown out.' Eight months later, according to Ken, Peter is still in a reassuring mood. 'As far as I'm concerned you won't leave a minute earlier than you want to. No bull-shitting.' There follows Ken's unforgiving description of the man addressing him: 'This quiet genial predator who wants me out of his tank . . . Behind that strange round face, boyishly puckering, ruefully grinning, is a more voluptuous love of power than any I have known except possibly that of Lord Goodman.'

A few weeks later, but unrecorded by Peter in his own *Diaries*, the two men are now dining together at L'Etoile – 'an affable occasion' during which the discussion turns to the best use of the Lyttelton Theatre. Hall suggests a season of plays built around a particular theme, and asks Ken if he would like to take charge of one. A week later they are again discussing the National's future and Peter 'invites me to plan a season of artificial comedy for the Lyttelton'. The following September Ken receives a letter from Peter saying that the Lyttelton seasons would not be happening for some time and that the soonest he could hope to involve Ken would be the end of 1975 or early 1976.

What is one to make of all this? Peter Hall was nothing if not an astute assessor of the reputations and talents of others, usually in that order. When he acknowledged Ken's contribution to the success of the National Theatre he doubtless meant it. He was also aware that Tynan's reputation at that time was at its lowest. He had fallen from fashion, had earned the enmity of the Board, and had become someone it would do no harm to characterise as an embittered and unprincipled enemy, which is how first Ken, then Jonathan Miller, and then I are portrayed in the *Diaries*. However, Peter was alive to Ken's gifts, and by not entirely shutting the door on him he was protecting himself against the day when Tynan's star would rise again. Unfortunately Ken was far too ill for this ever to happen.

In his *Times* review of Ken's *Diaries*, Peter begins 'This is a depressing book . . . Ken quotes words I never said, in situations where I wasn't present. Well, one can't sack someone and expect generous notices . . .' Towards the end of his review he discusses the National under Larry and he makes the following assertion: 'By the time I arrived there, the atmosphere was like the last days of Stalin, with a sick and anxious Olivier; a naturally protective Joan Plowright; Michael Blakemore and Jonathan Miller as two bitter lieutenants who obviously thought they had been passed over; and Ken busily stirring the pot.' This is a statement false in every particular. Larry was in good health and enjoying the crowning triumph of his career; Joan had only one thing from which to protect her husband – Peter; I was on the crest of a wave with two huge hits at a theatre which was enjoying the best box office in its ten-year history; and Jonathan Miller couldn't have been an 'embittered lieutenant' because he wasn't actually on the staff, and wouldn't be until Peter offered him permanent employment as an associate.

As for Ken, though fighting for his survival, he was having the satisfaction of seeing three plays he had championed, *Long Day's Journey*, *Jumpers* and *The Front Page*, reach the stage to acclaim. What is not said in Hall's version of events. because the implication is obvious, is how fortunate the National was to have Peter standing by to ride to the rescue. During the last year of Larry's reign, his theatre was a rewarding place to work and a happy one, and the reference to 'the last days of Stalin' is a disgrace, particularly since the first days of Stalin were just around the corner. Equally deplorable is his dismissal in his *Diaries* of the work and character of Tyrone Guthrie, because these two men, Olivier and

Guthrie, more than any others, put in place what would be possible for the actors and directors that were to follow. And that included Peter just as it included me.

Authentic memory – that precipitate of facts suspended in a volatile element of feeling – must always be a little different for each of us, but it remains important for anyone who works in the theatre. Stage performance is so transient that all we have left of the work we most believed in are these traces of honest recall. A passionate witness like Kenneth Tynan can help hold these fragments in place. Of equal importance is another memory we cannot share: that crucial encounter with the talent of the generation that preceded us, experienced perhaps in a cheap seat far from the stage, or close up against a screen in some dusty provincial cinema, that may actually have changed our lives.

This encounter, all the more fervent for being private, is one that later in our careers we will sometimes regret as an infection we had the misfortune to contract, but at other, better times see as a kind of apostolic succession, going back to Garrick and to Shakespeare, and perhaps much further back to Aeschylus and beyond, to the first storyteller who ever stood in front of a random group of people, tamed them into becoming an audience, and then, little by little, began to induce in them something akin to awe, so that they forgot their personal concerns and collectively began to see the world around them and their own place in it in a new and unexpected way. Every good performance, every good production is simply another link in that long chain, of which we are part and on which we are dependent, because it connects us to belief. In theatre literature the Peter Hall *Diaries* will always remain a formidable achievement but perhaps the time has come to shelve them not under History but under Public Relations.

When Kathleen Tynan was writing her biography of Ken she wanted to check on the details of his National contract, so she approached the NT Assistant Board Secretary, Yolande Bird, only to be told that, alas, this was no longer possible. 'Word had come down from above' – Yolande's exact words as reported by Kathleen – that files relating to the National's time at the Old Vic were to be 'collected in black plastic bags, taken away and burnt'. Apparently there was no longer sufficient space to store them.

This is not the calamity it sounds, because both Larry and Ken were determined archivists of their own careers, and their voluminous papers are safe and available. Also the National Theatre's own archive has a box for each production staged at the Old Vic, containing such items as newspaper cuttings, photographs and contact sheets as well as a collection of posters of the various shows. Some things have certainly been lost – Ken's contract for one, though Kathleen was already aware of some of its details. During his ten years at the National Ken earned on average £46 per week, and at his own insistence he went off-salary whenever he accepted outside work. Also lost is my own file of correspondence which I was foolish enough to leave behind, including letters dealing with my productions, such as those I received from Eugene O'Neill's daughter Oona Chaplin and from Charles MacArthur's widow Helen Hayes extolling *The Front Page*.

Who exactly it was who sent 'word down from above' there is no way of knowing, but it's certainly true that the National under Olivier has not received its fair share of attention in the intervening years. Much has been written about the great actor himself, far less about the sort of theatre he tried to bring into being. It's one of the reasons for the existence of this book which I have tried to write from the point of view of the person I was forty years ago.

However, age mollifies, and increasingly I look back on the battles with Peter with almost as much amusement as anger. Over the last couple of decades we have often run into each other, increasingly at memorial services, a few of them remembering people who have figured in these pages. And it is worth reminding the reader that in my story the stage blood has come out of a bottle, which with a little soap and water will soon wash away. No one has been put up against a wall and shot (though there may have been one or two mock executions). No one has been left rotting in prison for twenty years for something they never did. Or sent to the Gulag. In the wider world of politics and money things happen every day which reduce any charge Peter Hall or I might lay against each other to the merest misdemeanour. But then in the arts things are meant to be different; there is no point to them otherwise.

When Peter and I have met we have invariably been courteous to each other. He came to the London first night of my musical, *City of Angels*, complimented me generously afterwards and introduced me to his fourth wife, Nicki, who I'm told has done much to reconcile the numerous members of the extended Hall clan. I made a journey to Bath to see his production of *The Browning Version*, and I was able to tell him afterwards how much I enjoyed it. 'A perfectly constructed play,' he said with a certain intimate soft smile, more like a wrinkle of the nose, the persuasive charm of which came back to me in a rush. In fact at all our meetings I have encountered some slight surprising thing that tells me I haven't been carrying around in my mind the entire man. And perhaps never will.

ILLUSTRATIONS

THE NATIONAL HEALTH
All photos: © Reg Wilson/Rex Features,
except bottom right: Doug Jeffrey
© Victoria and Albert Museum, London

LONG DAY'S JOURNEY INTO NIGHT
Photos: © Zoë Dominic

THE FRONT PAGE
Photos: © Sophie Baker

MACBETH
Photos: © Zoë Dominic

THE CHERRY ORCHARD
Photos: © Sophie Baker

In rehearsal
Photos: © Zoë Dominic

INDEX

Also by Michael Blakemore

ARGUMENTS WITH ENGLAND

In the days when Australians called England 'home', Michael Blakemore, an eager young man en route to RADA, made the long sea voyage to 1950s London to find himself in a distinctly foreign country . . . And so began his struggle to come to terms with the realities of a less than perfect Promised Land.

Candid observations about life and art, from his shock on witnessing the poverty in the North to his sense of excitement on reading the works of Proust and Webster, sit beside colourful escapades at drama school and recollections of working with characters such as John Osborne and Tyrone Guthrie. Blakemore recalls life as an actor before his directorial success with *A Day in the Death of Joe Egg* propelled him to the National Theatre and the start of a glittering career.

'Anyone who has read Michael Blakemore's classic novel *Next Season* knows he is one of the best writers we have about how life onstage may feed into life off. His beautiful memoir *Arguments with England* is perhaps better still – a pitch-perfect account of dreaming youth, driven, frustrated and eventually deepened by a realistic love of the theatre.'   David Hare

'Honest, perceptive, and explosively funny.'
                          Selina Hastings, *Sunday Telegraph* Books of the Year

'Some of the most exhilarating writing about theatre ever committed to paper.'   Simon Callow, *Guardian*